THE MEMORY
of the
CHRISTIAN PEOPLE

THEOLOGY AND LIBERATION SERIES

Eduardo Hoornaert

THE MEMORY
of the
CHRISTIAN PEOPLE

Translated from the Portuguese by
Robert R. Barr

ORBIS BOOKS

Maryknoll, New York 10545

The Catholic Foreign Mission Society of America (Maryknoll) recruits and trains people for overseas missionary service. Through Orbis Books, Maryknoll aims to foster the international dialogue that is essential to mission. The books published, however, reflect the opinions of their authors and are not meant to represent the official position of the society.

This book is a translation of *A Memória do Povo Cristão* © Editora Vozes Ltda, Petrópolis, Brazil

First published in this translation in the United States of America by Orbis Books, Maryknoll, NY 10545; published in Great Britain by Burns & Oates/Search Press Ltd, Wellwood, North Farm Road, Tunbridge Wells, Kent TN2 3DR

ORBIS/ISBN 0-88344-574-3
0-88344-573-5 (pbk.)

Theology and Liberation Series

In the years since its emergence in Latin America, liberation theology has challenged the church to a renewal of faith lived in solidarity with the poor and oppressed. The effects of this theology have spread throughout the world, inspiring in many Christians a deeper life of faith and commitment, but for others arousing fears and concerns.

Its proponents have insisted that liberation theology is not a subtopic of theology but really a new way of doing theology. The Theology and Liberation Series is an effort to test that claim by addressing the full spectrum of Christian faith from the perspective of the poor.

Thus, volumes in the Series are devoted to such topics as God, Christ, the church, revelation, Mary, the sacraments, and so forth. But the Series will also explore topics seldom addressed by traditional theology, though vital to Christian life — aspects of politics, culture, the role of women, the status of ethnic minorities. All these are examined in the light of faith lived in a context of oppression and liberation.

The work of over one hundred theologians, pastoral agents, and social scientists from Latin America, and supported by some one hundred and forty bishops, the Theology and Liberation Series is the most ambitious and creative theological project in the history of the Americas.

Addressed to the universal church, these volumes will be essential reading for all those interested in the challenge of faith in the modern world. They will be especially welcomed by all who are committed to the cause of the poor, by those engaged in the struggle for a new society, by all those seeking to establish a more solid link between faith and politics, prayer and action.

Contents

vii

PART TWO
THE MISSION

PART THREE
THE BASE CHURCH COMMUNITY

Preface

The objective of this work is to collect and to present to non-specialists certain elements of the history of the church in the first three centuries ordinarily found scattered throughout scholarly writings intended for the specialist. The bibliography at the end of the volume lists my primary and secondary sources.

The main thrust of this investigation is limited to the first three Christian centuries. So I owe the reader an explanation for the occasional excursions into later history. When I examine certain later historical figures or movements (especially in chapter 7, "Mission Cycles of the First Two Centuries," dealing with figures such as St. Ephrem the Syrian or movements such as the Ethiopian missionary cycle), the reason for these "excursions" is that these persons and movements shed some light on our current situation in Latin America. The excursus on mysticism in chapter 15, "A New Relationship between Women and Men," has the same purpose.

I have relied rather extensively on certain easily accessible New Testament texts, to the relative neglect of patristic sources such as Justin, Irenaeus, Tertullian, Clement, Origen, Hippolytus, or Cyprian. The works of the Fathers are not always readily available, while the great majority of readers are likely to have access to basic New Testament texts, research, and commentary. For patristic sources, I have relied more extensively on brief documents produced by the early communities than on the more ample treatises, as it seems to me that the former present a clearer picture of the life of the communities. I present these documents in chapter 10, "Some Documents from the Base Communities."

Finally, it seems to me that, if they are to understand the history of the church of the first three centuries, Christians of today really need to make an effort to "know less." That is, they should try to learn to prescind from the imposing ecclesiastical system so familiar to us today. This system has developed only subsequently, by way of superimposition on the Christian tradition of the early centuries. Primitive Christianity was not hegemonic. It lived a hidden life in the capillaries of society, where it was propagated by the daily witness of friends and neighbors. It lived and grew by personal contact, in the pluriformity of concrete, everyday living.

There is actually a surprising parallel between the current experience of the base communities and the life of the first Christian communities. The pastoral ministers of today's base communities who so enthusiastically exclaim, "Why, this is the way the first Christians lived!" are far from mistaken. The following pages have been prepared, most painstakingly, in the hope of etching this historical memory still more profoundly into the minds and hearts of the Christian people of Latin America.

THE MEMORY
of the
CHRISTIAN PEOPLE

INTRODUCTION

CHRISTIANITY AND MEMORY: CHURCH HISTORY AND THE MEMORY OF THE CHRISTIAN PEOPLE

CHAPTER I

Christianity and Memory

JUDAISM AND CHRISTIANITY AS "MEMORY RELIGIONS"

Judaism and Christianity are "memory religions." Unlike other religions, they are based primarily on a fund of historical data engraved on the memory of the faithful throughout the course of their history. The English historian Herbert Butterfield, in his posthumous *The Origins of History*, has demonstrated the contrast between the historical consciousness of the Jewish people and that of other peoples.[1] Jewish popular consciousness was rooted in the conviction that Yahweh had personally delivered the people of Israel from Egyptian domination. This notion fills the Old Testament from beginning to end. It was the Exodus event that enabled the Jews to fashion a collective memory unrivaled by any other people, and Israel based its religion on this memory. For the Israelites, history was not cyclical — based on an eternal return of things and times — but linear; it was irreversible, and it had a finality. All creation had ever tended toward its apocalyptic end and would ever continue to do so. The Jews were the first people in the history of humanity to conceive of history as goal-orientated. The Judaic conception sharply contrasted with Greek thought in this respect. The latter was essentially anti-historical, based as it was on the "eternal return of identical situations." For the Greeks

3

there was nothing truly new under the sun: *nihil novi sub sole.*
Greek philosophy emphasized the eternal and immutable. The
Stoics held that the entire universe was periodically destroyed in
a vast conflagration, so that all things must ever begin again
from nothing. When the Greeks, such as Herodotus or
Thucydides, took any interest in history, it was to draw political
lessons. Thus we may qualify Greek historiography as "pragmatic." It failed to reach to the core of human existence. It had
no religious dimension.

Christianity has inherited Judaism's "memorial" character.
But it has centered its memory on the incarnation, life, passion,
death, and resurrection of Jesus Christ, liberator of his people
not from Egypt merely, like Moses, but from domination in all
its forms. Unlike the Judaism of its origin, Christianity locates
the center of history in Christ. Jews continue to look for the
Messiah. Christians strive to actualize, in time itself, the Reign
of God inaugurated by Jesus. Christians' historical vision is
dominated by three great moments: the creation, the Jesus
event, and the parousia. The Christian regard is fixed on Christ.
For Christians, then, hope is bound up with memory. The
vehicle of Christian hope is Christian memory. Without it
Christian hope simply would not be. Hence the fundamental
Christian religious need to "remember." We see it in Christian
doctrine, whose content, when all is said and done, is the
memory of sacred events. We see it in the Christian liturgy,
which is commemoration: the liturgical year commemorates the
Jesus event through time, from Advent to Pentecost, including
Christmas, Lent, Easter, and the Ascension. The liturgical day —
in every Eucharist — commemorates the words of the grand
memorial: "Do this in memory of me" (Luke 22:19). The
calendar of the saints functions no differently, recalling the
memory of the saints, who were the imitators of Christ in the
diversified practice of the various times and places in which they
lived. The calendars, the martyrologies, the *libri memoriales* of
the Middle Ages, the canonical hours, and so on, are all
commemoration, memorial, memory.

Christians well knew that their religion stood or fell with the
veracity of their memory. Small wonder, then, that they so
promptly sought to replace their purely oral memorials with

written documentation. This evolution found a witness as early as the end of the second century in Irenaeus of Lyon. It was the key importance of memory, once more, that inspired Christians with their reverence for the "ancients," those persons of memory par excellence who had been so useful to the Christian community in bygone times and continued to be so in a later age. A veneration for the ancients steeps the whole course of the Middle Ages, to disappear only with modern times and the self-sufficiency of modern science. After all, the alphabet itself "was invented to preserve the memory of things," medievals remind us, and of course "a pupil ought to record everything in the memory." For St. Anselm, the three "dignities of the soul" are intelligence, will, and memory. The great scholastic St. Thomas Aquinas attributed a key role to memory in the study of theology, developing sophisticated mnemonic methods to assist its function. And so forth and so on. Medieval Christianity was altogether conscious of the crucial role of memory for its religion and religiousness.

But the Christian concern for memory is ultimately rooted in the rabbinical traditions as preserved down through the ages by the synagogue. The rabbis stimulated the memory of their people with lapidary sayings, parables, meaningful facts, examples, proverbs, and comparisons. The religious system based on the proliferation of the synagogue throughout a vast diaspora presented advantages over a centralized system that had been so dependent on Jerusalem, with its archives and its scribes, where the danger lurked that the "gifts of memory" might become "gifts of oblivion." The compromises of the masters of the temple with the gift of power in society could all too easily compromise the faithful transmission of a dangerous, potentially subversive memory like that of a deliverance from slavery and from the oppression of a mighty foreign power. The temple priests so easily remembered one thing and forgot another! The synagogues were relatively free of this type of "memory manipulation" and shakily managed to preserve the message down through time, perfecting numerous techniques of memorizing and communicating.

Jesus made remarkable use of such rabbinical resources in his communication with his apostles and with the people. Jesus wielded a trenchant discourse that went straight for the marrow of things. He made use of parables. His responses to questions or challenges could be thunderbolts. His lapidary expressions stuck in his hearers' minds (and this is why we have them today). He reacted vigorously to the stereotyped attitudes of the religious authorities of his time and place, as evinced for example in their silence when it came to women, Samaritans, centurions, prostitutes, foreigners—or the *'am ha 'arets*, the "people of the earth" or land in general, the poor and the marginalized. Jesus ringingly declares that these persons exist. They are "around." We live in their midst. What Jesus recalled to people's minds was precisely what had been lost to social memory as manipulated by the temple. His perceptiveness here is mind-boggling and still unique. Certain Christians, we see, have succeeded in imitating him in some respects while completely failing to do so in others.

Those Christians who have most convincingly succeeded in emulating Jesus' practice in their own time and place have felt the need to perserve a certain memory. The most winning and most important of the medieval saints, Francis of Assisi, ordered that it be inscribed in his testament as his dying wish that his brothers and sisters might, "in token and memorial of my blessing and my testament, love one another always."[2]

But Christians' living experience has convincingly shown that the memory of the Jesus event cannot be transmitted in all peace and tranquility. The Christian memory has survived only by dint of an arduous struggle. Second-century Christian literature is pervaded by a language of harshness and odium. What is the reason for this vehemence? Manifestly, an anxiety for the preservation of the Christian memory in the face of confusion created by the proliferation of divergent traditions. We can trace this development from Papias of Hierapolis (A.D. 130)[3] through Hegesippus (154–66),[4] Justin in the latter half of the century,[5] to Irenaeus of Lyon at its close.[6] Up until the time of Papias, Christians preferred oral tradition. No written tradition had yet been "canonized." Papias claimed to be a disciple of the apostle John and a colleague of Polycarp of Smyrna, and what he received from his masters and compiled was not a cohesive doctrine but a series of "sayings" or *logia*. Then Hegesippus evinced a new concern. In the face of so many stray traditions, he suddenly appealed to a codified apostolic tradition. Justin, too, testified to the anxiety of Christians that their memory be a truthful one and relied on the memorials "redacted by the Apostles and their successors" (*Dialogue*, 103). These "memorials," Justin informs us, together with the writings of the prophets (which for him constitute holy scripture), were read and recalled in the communities in their Sunday services (*Apol.*, I, 67). These apostolic memorials received the name of Gospels. Thus far, then, we have an evolution in the direction of the development of written texts, but without prejudice to oral tradition.

The evolution was completed with Irenaeus, who was the exclusive partisan of a written tradition. It was mainly the challenge of the Marcionite writings that constrained Christians to draw up a canon of writings that would be universally accepted and could be used as a secure point of reference. As we see, Irenaeus was dealing with the Christian memorial or memory from a position analogous to our own today. The point of reference is the canon of books of the New Testament, which is based on the recollections of the apostles—in other words, on the apostolic tradition. We then have need to see how that tradition is preserved unaltered, which I shall examine when dealing with the base communities.

The apostolic tradition, codified and consigned to writing, long coexisted with traditions developed by great heretical leaders like Marcion of Sinope or Montanus of Phrygia. It was only after its establishment as the imperial church that Christianity moved to eradicate the numerous "heresies" it had been forced to tolerate. The *damnatio memoriae*, the damnation or consignment to oblivion of the heretics and their thinking, was so thoroughgoing that not a single page of the works of Marcion, regarded as the father of heretics, is extant today. Later the Alexandrian priest Arius (260–337), founder of Arianism, fell victim to the same *damnatio memoriae*. A medieval engraving represents Arius, flanked by Judas and Lucifer, being trampled under foot by Christ the judge and swallowed by the dragon of hell. Judas tumbles into hell still holding the staff or crook of an apostle. The condemnation is cosmic, irreversible, and everlasting. The violent reaction to the early Christian "heresies" on the part of other Christians has irreparably damaged our understanding of Christian origins.

We should note the peculiar character of the Christian memory throughout the course of history. So frequently that memory was and is that of the defeated and humbled, the marginalized and the condemned, and therefore is not recorded in a "history" composed in the hegemonic historiographical tradition of the great cultures, by way of discourses, monuments, archives, documents, iconography, and architecture. On the contrary, the Christian memory of the humble is transmitted from generation to generation as a popular culture, an oral tradition, a cultural resistance. Hence this Christian memory survives primarily in communities. We see this on all sides. An intimate relationship obtains between Christian memory and base community. St. Paul's classic concept — "God's word is not chained" — presupposes the availability to Christians of institutional tools that can guarantee this freedom of the word of God in the face of the pressure of the powers of this world. It is the basic responsibility of Christian practice to secure sociological models of church that will protect the freedom of the word of God. Christians cannot allow themselves to remain indifferent to the question of church models, as they have received a commission to preserve and actualize the memory of Jesus, the Apostles, the prophets, and the whole history of God's covenant with human beings. This is the guiding concern of Christian practice down through the centuries. When all is said and done, St. Anthony's "desert," Joachim of Flora's "spiritual church," St. Francis of Assisi's "evangelical life," Meister Eckhart's "apologia for Martha" (against a misunderstanding of the meaning of Mary's "better portion"), Luther's "Christian liberty" — to cite but a few of the high moments in this timeless quest — all have one purpose: the revival and *aggiornamento* of a memory everlastingly imperiled by the forces of the systems that govern the world.

Part and parcel of this tradition of struggle for an authentic Christian memory are the current practices of the base communities scattered through Latin America, and it is with these practices in mind that we have undertaken the present study. In the beautiful expression of French historian Henri Marrou, a historian is a "missionary despatched to the past to strike a hyphen between past and present." Church history will always have its role to perform in the mission of reanimating the memory of the Christian communities. Christian memory is by no means a purely individual memory ("my faith, my salvation"). It is a collective memory as well. It is the memory of a people. But just as the individual memory is not a mere mechanism but a living thing, and thus the object of the study of psychologists, biologists, and so on, so too the collective memory is a thing alive, defining the consciousness of a social group. The historian must be able to perceive this and be in a position to respond to the living questions posed by the Christian people. But the Christian people involved in the community experience are presently asking whether Christians met together to solve their problems "in the beginning, too," and whether they lived on the hope animating the Christian communities of today. There is an appeal, then, arising from the communities, and the mission of the Christian historian is to respond to this call. What J. Le Goff asserts of the historian generally is valid for the Christian historian in particular: "The historian's task is to transform memory into science."

CHURCH HISTORY: A SCIENCE AT THE SERVICE OF THE PEOPLE

The science of church history is at the service of the memory of the Christian people. It is at the service of this memory not only in the sense that it gathers their recollections but also in the sense that it transforms their memory into a coherent, intelligible discourse, based on objective documents. The people have the right to history in the full sense of the word, and not only to intermittent, partial episodes. They must be enabled to discover the causes and reasons for events. A church history at the service of the people is not the place for new legends, new apologetics, new triumphalisms, or refurbished populisms. The Christian people of the communities deserve to know the whole truth. They deserve to know not only the uplifting, encouraging things about Christianity but the struggles and the sins of Christianity as well. They must know of the mistaken alliances struck by historical Christianity for the sake of interests that have not always been evangelical. At the same time, a church history at the service of the collective memory of the Christian people must know how to avoid the pitfalls of a totalitarian historicism provoked by the deviations of an excessively dogmatic and mechanistic Marxist interpretation of history: everything must now start again from nothing, we are told; church tradition contains nothing good or constructive; the church has always been on the wrong side, and the clergy have never had any purpose but to tame and control the people. Generalizations of this sort are scarcely likely to assist the Christian people in the reconstruction of their memory. Ultimately these criticisms proceed only from an anti-intellectualism that would abolish any and every effort to penetrate the complex affairs that are the stuff of history.

What we are endeavoring to say about Christian memory finds a striking compendium in words Simone Weil wrote in 1943 concerning the importance of "roots":

> The need to "strike root" may be the human soul's most important and least understood need. At all events it is certainly one of the most difficult to define. Human beings have their roots in their real, active, and natural participation in the existence of a collectivity that cherishes certain treasures from the past and certain expectations of the future. This participation is a natural one. It is the automatic product of one's place, birth, trade or profession, and surroundings. All human beings have need of multiple "roots." They must receive practically the totality of their moral, intellectual, and spiritual life through the intermediary of the milieus of which they are a natural part. . . .[7]

The base communities are instruments of this popular "radication," or "striking root." They provide the soil for the Christian root onto whose stock will be grafted the practices of liberation.

CHAPTER II

Eusebius of Caesarea and Church History

THE *ECCLESIASTICAL HISTORY*

Any attempt to develop a historiographical discourse calculated to lay a scientific foundation for the "memory" of the Christian people will have to deal with a lengthy tradition going back to an ecclesiastical writer of the fourth century known as Eusebius of Caesarea (263–339).[1] Bishop of Caesarea in Palestine at a time when enormous changes were taking place in and around the church, Eusebius wrote an *Ecclesiastical History* in ten "books." His approach to the writing of history strongly contrasted with that of earlier ecclesiastical writers with regard to fidelity to church documents. Eusebius was scrupulously faithful to his sources, especially those of "Asia" (Asia Minor, today's Turkey), Syria, and Egypt. His predecessors had freely mingled history with legend, narrative with exhortation. A product of the illustrious school founded by Origen (185–253) in Caesarea in Palestine, Eusebius enjoyed a wide reputation for erudition. In fact, he was admired by Constantine himself, who selected him to pronounce the official discourse commemorating the emperor's thirty years on the throne and glorifying the magnificence of the new city of Constantinople. The school of Caesarea had a library estimated at thirty thousand volumes, which Adolf von Harnack, the great scholar of the Hellenization of Christianity,

called the "mother of the medieval library." The school with its
library constituted the most important house of intellectual
formation of the third- and fourth-century church, and
Eusebius' authority was acknowledged throughout Christianity.
Eusebius of Caesarea stands as the symbol of the definitive shift
from oral tradition in the preservation of the Christian memory
to a more secure, more easily identifiable written tradition.

The first seven of the ten books of the *Ecclesiastical History*
describe events antedating the great persecution of Diocletian,
which began in 284. The year 284 had become so deeply etched
into the memory of Christians that they made it the first year of
their calendar. (The computation of time from the birth of Jesus
appeared only in the ninth century.) Eusebius' first three books
deal with Jesus, the Apostles, and the sub-apostolic age. Books
4 through 7 furnish us mainly with four lists: the bishops of the
great churches (Jerusalem, Rome, Antioch, Alexandria); the
great heresies; the major ecclesiastical writers; and the persecutions inflicted on Christians by both Jews and gentiles. Books 8
and 9 treat of "persecution in our day," telling the story of
persecutions whose memory in the minds of his contemporaries
was still green. Book 10 recounts the "victory" under
Constantine and the history of the martyrs of Palestine, subjoining a life of Constantine.

Even this simple overview demonstrates that the focal point
of Eusebius' work is the dichotomy between persecution and
victory, oppression and freedom, orthodoxy and heresy. Surely
we must admit that historical Christianity's image of the "age of
persecution" and the succeeding *Christiana tempora* has dwelt
all but exclusively on the same antitheses? We shall return to this
crucial point. But first we must cite Eusebius' towering merit as
a Christian historiographer. That he stands head and shoulders
above all his predecessors is simply beyond question. He is the
first church historian to assign any real importance to the actual
structures of history and its "long duration." He abandons the
customary Greek historiographical ascription of responsibility
for the course of events to "destiny" or "fate" (*fatum*). It is not
fatum, not "destiny," but the rationality of Providence, the
Divine Reason, that rules world events and governs history.
Eusebius is heir to a Christian humanism sensitive enough to

heed those the world despises, the little, the helpless. (See the remarkable page on the Christian martyr Blandina in *Ecclesiastical History*, book 5, chapter 1, paragraph 17.) In point of historiographical technique, he is the first Christian historian to cite his sources faithfully and credit them correctly. His work evinces patience, scruple, and an excellent organization of material. In several areas, we owe our knowledge of the first three Christian centuries entirely to Eusebius. He is our only source for "rabbinical Christianity," for example—the celebrated "church of the circumcision."[2] Again, only from Eusebius (*Hist. Eccl.* II, 14, 6) do we know anything of, for example, Hegisippus, St. Peter's contemporary in Rome.[3] Eusebius is only our source for Montanism.[4] He is our only source for the "Easter controversy," the late second-century dispute over the proper date on which to celebrate the Lord's resurrection each year; indeed he has made the documentation of this affair, so important in the eyes of later ecclesiologists, the object of an exhaustive investigation.[5]

I am far from suggesting that Eusebius has no thesis to propound—no "axe to grind." On the contrary, his ideology is evident in the stark dichotomy he draws between Christianity's victory under Constantine and its afflictions under earlier emperors. Eusebius' portrayal of the persecutions is a highly symbolic one, modeled on the ten plagues of Egypt. As Egypt languished under the ten scourges of the Book of Exodus, so the church has suffered ten persecutions. Constantine is a liberator, a kind of new Moses. Of course, the *Ecclesiastical History* represents only a particular view of the church, one characterized by a passionate enthusiasm for Constantine as its "leader."[6] Doubtless Eusebius' view is that of a particular segment of the Christian leadership of the era, one that entertained great enthusiasm for the new political relationships arising under Constantine, and one that would have readily "understood" Eusebius' projection of these relationships on to a divine plane. For, indeed, Eusebius' theology, altogether novel for the time, can only be characterized as an "imperial theology," a theology of empire. It is difficult to imagine, however, that all strata of Christianity could have shared his view of the church. Withal, the fact remains that, through his historiographical effort,

Eusebius founded a new Christian literary genre, one which sees
no problem in equating Christian memory with an "apostolic
succession" in the sense of a simple succession of bishops in local
churches.

Eusebius manifests an evident concern to establish for each
local church a list of bishops going back to the apostolic age. For
Jerusalem he lists fifteen bishops, a number regarded by
Daniélou as excessive.[7] For Rome he details an intricate
hierarchical framework (*Hist. Eccl.*, VI, 43, 44).[8] Thus he
simplifies a very complex history. Another example: In the
beginning of book 3 Eusebius states that, after the fall of
Jerusalem, the whole inhabited world (*hē oikoumenē*) was
partitioned into zones of influence, each presided over by an
apostle. Thomas took the Parthians; John, Asia Minor; Peter,
Pontus and Rome; Andrew, Scythia. Eusebius' image of the
evolution of the church presupposes the model of a local
territorial church, which ill corresponds to the experience of the
initial communities, as we shall see in this book.

Eusebius opens his *Ecclesiastical History* with an outline of
his project:

> As I have undertaken to make a written list of the
> succession of the holy apostles, along with a rehearsal of
> the times since that of our Savior and down to the present
> day, cataloguing: the names of the glorious governors and
> presidents of that church in its most illustrious sees; the
> many who have preached the word of God in every
> generation by word or in writing; the many who, in their
> respective eras, seduced by a desire for novelty, have fallen
> into the gravest errors, appointing themselves the founders
> of a false science and, like ravenous wolves, impiously
> decimating the flock of Christ; the numberless calamities
> visited upon the whole nation of the Jews the moment they
> had committed their crime against our Savior, and in
> chastisement therefor; how and when the divine word has
> been combated by the gentiles, and the many who have
> endured the combat of fire and torture by reason thereof;
> and furthermore the martyrs of our own time, and how the
> aid of our Savior has shown itself propitious and kindly in

their regard — I shall begin nowhere but with the Incarnation of our Saviour and Lord Jesus, the Christ of God. [*Hist. Eccl.,* I, 1, 1][9]

Eusebius' project departs altogether from what a history of the church at the service of the memory of the Christian people ought to be. He departs from ancient Israel's historiographical motif, replacing it with a dynastic one. He abandons the tradition of the Law, the prophets, and the liberation of the lowly and marginalized, and replaces it with the tools of recollection precisely of an imperial church that sees in the emperor the successor of Moses and David, an individual chosen by God to prepare the way of the Lord and to liberate his people. For Eusebius the enemies are the Montanists, the Donatists, and the followers of Novatian, or the Jews or the "gentiles" (the "nations"), and not the structures of the empire, not the power of the rich who exploit the peasantry through heavy tribute and the urban slave population through forced labor. The church is identified with one of its parts, merely: its organizers. We hear nothing of the "organized" (except in the martyrdom accounts). Eusebius' book was to prove an excellent text for a course intended to prepare future organizers of church structure. But it is a complete failure as an ecclesial exercise in "striking root." It is useless as a tool for the recollection of the covenant God has struck with us in Abraham and transmitted to us through Moses, the prophets, Jesus, the Apostles, and the saints. The memory of the hopes and struggles of a Christian people striving to resolve urgent problems of survival, health, or basic human rights finds no room in the *Ecclesiastical History* of Eusebius of Caesarea. Nor does that author seek, at every moment, regardless of time or place or subject or situation, to allow the course of things and life to be illumined by the light of the memory of the Exodus, the flight from Pharaoh's Egypt, and the entry into the Land of Promise, as divine Providence begins to shatter the mournful concatenation of domination and humiliation that is the history of humanity.

The reason for the success of Eusebius' project in the long tradition of church history as an ecclesiastical discipline is not to be sought in the originality or depth of his thought. On the contrary, his imperial theology is altogether a dubious one, from the viewpoint of even the most elementary concepts of biblical theology. Eusebius' project prevailed simply because it confirmed in writing, and with a thesis, a practical route that an influential sector of church leadership—one that would eventually come to be hegemonic—had begun to travel: the path of an alliance between the ecclesiastical estate and political society. This new model of church, based on an alliance of church and state, finds in Eusebius' *History* a theoretical confirmation of its practice. More than once in the history of the church, the theoretical, but a posteriori, confirmation of a church practice has occasioned the ossification of that practice for long ages to come.

EUSEBIUS' SUCCESSORS

We may define the state of the question as follows: One method of approaching church history aims specifically at the preservation of the memory of the institutions that Christianity has generated in the course of its historical experience. Another method emphasizes the memory of Christianity's manifold prophetical practices.[10] These two approaches constitute antitheses in the dialectical development of the reality we call the Christian historical memory. On the one side we have the Eusebian tradition, on the other the "prophetic" tradition. The Eusebian tradition can only be triumphalistic or apologetic. It will be triumphalistic when the institution prospers, apologetic when it feels threatened. Eusebius' successors appeared as early as the fourth to the sixth centuries, in authors like Socrates of Constantinople, Sozomenos of Constantinople, Theodoret of Cyr, Evagrius the Scholastic, Epiphanius of Salamina, and Isidore of Seville. In the Middle Ages only the chroniclers of the Christian empire pursued church history properly so-called. The major interest of medieval "church history" was limited to a chronicle of the Christianized peoples, the "history" of the episcopal sees, the monasteries and their "chronicles" or "annals," the saints and their "lives." It becomes difficult, then, to trace a Eusebian tradition in the Middle Ages.

The resurgence of an interest in historiography properly so-called, however, in the modern age was accompanied by a resurrection of the Eusebian tradition in its apologetic aspect. At the close of the sixteenth century, Caesar Baronius (d. 1607) attempted to rebut Protestant historical studies purporting to establish that Protestantism, not Catholicism, was the authentic successor to primitive Christianity. Baronius published twelve volumes under the title of *Ecclesiastical Annals*. The *Annals*, which constitute apologetic in its purest form, exerted a predominant influence on church history as a seminary discipline for the training of future clergy all the way to the end of the nineteenth century. Baronius' gigantic undertaking spawned other works, as well, of equally imposing dimensions. Thus we have the historiographical epics of Rohrbacher, which appeared between 1842 and 1849 in twenty-nine volumes, Hergenröther, appearing between 1911 and 1917 in four volumes, and even Fliche-Martin, begun in 1936 and projected for twenty-four volumes.

In the aftermath of Vatican II, however, two works of church history appeared that attempted to transcend the Catholic-Protestant controversy: the ten-volume German series *Handbuch der Kirchengeschichte* ("Handbook of Church History") under the general editorship of Hubert Jedin; and *Nouvelle histoire de l'Eglise* ("New History of the Church") under the direction of Professors Rogier (The Netherlands), Aubert (Belgium), and Knowles (England). In the *Handbuch*, Jedin criticizes the self-concept of the church as a "perfect society" and thus lays the groundwork for a scientific examination of the institution. Jedin attacks the notion of the continuous progress in the history of the church, admitting the existence of periods of decadence in the course of this history, always in the best tradition of Vatican II.[11] The church is *reformata reformanda* ("reformed and to be reformed," the subject of a continual process of reformation), says Jedin. It is an *ecclesia semper reformanda*, a church ever in need of reform.

A reading of church history via the theme of reform, however, fails to articulate with sufficient clarity the relationship between the reform of the institution as such (the celebrated *reformatio in capite* — reform at the "cupola," the pinnacle of the

church edifice) and that reform whose vehicle and agent is a
movement on the "floor" of the church, at the foundation, the
base, as for example in the heresies. What historical forces give
rise to movements of church reform? What social *loci* condition
both decadence and reform, and what relationship obtains
between these *loci* and society as a whole? The *Handbuch* fails
to include this kind of investigation.

In the *Nouvelle histoire*, the period under consideration in
these pages falls to the authorship of Jean Daniélou, the
renowned specialist in the first Christian centuries. We sense
precious little sympathy in Daniélou's pages for what he calls
"eschatological" or "idealistic"[12] Christianity, as expressed in
Montanism, for example, or in figures like Tertullian,
Hippolytus, or even Origen.[13] Daniélou contrasts this "idealistic" Christianity with the model he refers to as "realistic"—that
of an alliance with the political powers of the age, or at least of
a relative "peace" with these powers. Daniélou's preference is
rather for figures like Clement of Alexandria, with his easy
urbanity in the milieus of the Alexandrine bourgeoisie and his
open door for the rich to enter the church without major
difficulties of conscience. The great church debate of the third
century, then, can be summed up, according to Daniélou, as a
"conflict between intellectuals impassioned with an ideal church
and pastors aware of the conditions of the real church."[14] The
church Daniélou styles "ideal" or "idealistic" is none other than
the prophetic church committed to the message of liberation and
thereby in conflict with the powers of this world.

To sum up this brief account of the ideology guiding Jedin
and Daniélou: each of these two writers stands in some manner
in the line of what we might call, at least broadly speaking, the
"Eusebian tradition." Neither questions a model of church that
had broken with the primitive ecclesial model and gained the
ascendancy only in the fourth century of the Christian era.

REDEFINING CHURCH HISTORY

My own historiographical intent differs from the Eusebian on
three cardinal points. First, I differ from the Eusebian approach
in my view of the historical encounter of Christianity with

Hellenism, of which Eusebius was an outstanding interpreter. The Eusebian tradition ascribes an altogether special and positive value to this encounter. Hellenism, we hear, endowed Christianity with a rational, balanced, humanistic character still maintained in the church today. Hellenism is seen, then, as a permanent acquisition. But—without impugning the intrinsic values of Hellenism—I should like to call attention to the manner of the encounter of Hellenism with Christianity. Historians have created the image of an intellectual, theoretical, almost planned meeting of the two great currents. Antecedently to any theoretical meeting, however, a practical one had occurred. The gospel had co-existed with Hellenism on the level of daily, living experience—at the base, at the foundation of the Christian edifice, in the communities—for centuries. The theologians who Hellenized Christianity were only systematizing a phenomenon of daily, and problem-ridden, Christian practice. How could the purity of the faith be maintained when it was forced to coexist with the Greek mythologies? How could the Christian miracle be distinguished from magic? In what sense might Christianity be styled a "philosophy"?

Christianity has, in the course of its history, encountered problems issuing from a variety of situations apart from Hellenization. For more than four hundred years now, for example, Christianity has encountered the animisms of America, Africa, and Asia. This encounter is experienced in day-to-day Christian pastoral practice, and it creates innumerable problems. How may one be a Christian in an African or Afro culture, in Brazil, for example? The entire Chinese Rites question was a matter of practical difficulties in a new historical encounter. But Christian intellectuals and theologians give this fact short shrift, and the ponderous tomes of Christian theological dictionaries are all but unconcerned with it.[15] I ask only one thing: room to carry out reflection without being straitjacketed by the rigid framework of church history in the Eusebian tradition. Perhaps I may then be able to provide Christian theologians the wherewithal to review the relationship between Christianity and the popular religions.

A second element of discrepancy between my historiographic approach and that of the Eusebian tradition bears on the place of erudition and learning in Christianity. The "monumental" character with which church history is traditionally invested simultaneously impresses and repels. Historians frequently manage to conceal their methodological shortcomings under the cloak of erudition. They drown the poor student in a flood of facts, interlocking data, and series of events, and thereby create the illusion of objectivity. But they forget—or they cause the reader to forget—that the authors of these histories cannot but be the prisoners of their own categories when it comes to an analysis of the data of the past. The major defect in Eusebius' method lies in his implicit premise that history is the pure and simple recall of the past, and this shortcoming has been handed down from generation to generation ever since. Seventeen hundred years later we still subject the data of the past to the interpretative grid of today's experience. For example we ask whether the primitive church was episcopal, whether it was hierarchical. We ask whether the Roman pontiff was accorded a primacy in the primitive church. We ask whether Jesus "instituted" the seven sacraments. In asking questions like these we are allowing our view of today's reality to manipulate the documents of the past. We make dead documents—after all, "historiography is concerned with the dead"—say things they never meant to say. We seek to resurrect experiences that do not correspond to our experience today. We tumble into this pitfall because we are so determined to corroborate something in our own experience, and we view the past through the grid of this will to corroboration. Thus we nurture the illusion that we are entirely receptive to the data of the past, wholly devoted to scientific research. But we "know too much." Our memory is conditioned by social influences of which we are unaware. Maurice Halbwachs, in a study no longer of recent vintage but basic for our present considerations, deals with this phenomenon—the influence exerted by society on our way of "reading" the past.[16] The words of Anatole France are wise indeed: "To feel the spirit of an age that no longer exists . . . the difficulty is not so much in what one must know, as in what one must no longer know."[17]

Faced with the impossibility of recovering the Christian past "as it really was" ("*wie es eigentlich gewesen ist,*" the celebrated expression of Leopold von Ranke, father of historicism), I shall aim for a more modest goal. I shall attempt merely to set forth certain material that seems to correspond to questions that have arisen along the course of the Christian pilgrimage of today's communities. My main concern is with the present experience of base communities in Latin America, and thus with the newly emerging model of church. There is a social interest, and not merely an individual one, in recalling certain aspects and motifs of the ancient church. After all, these are the very motifs that sustain our hope today. We wish to retain our bonds with the great tradition of hope that steeps the whole of church history. We must not abandon the Christian memory to the unrelenting threat of its manipulation.

I find an excellent encapsulation of my own thinking in the penetrating words of Walter Benjamin in one of his "theses on the history of philosophy":

> The historical articulation of the past does not require a knowledge of that past "as it really was." It requires the recovery of a memory—one that flashes like a warning light in a moment of danger. . . . Tradition must seek to escape the danger of the conformism that threatens to swallow it up in every age. The Messiah comes not only as savior, but as vanquisher of the antichrist. The gift of fanning the spark of hope is the prize of that historiography alone that is doggedly mindful that not even the dead are safe if the enemy should prevail. And that enemy has never lost.

A third and last point of divergency between my approach and that of Eusebius of Caesarea and his successors concerns the question of power. I do not believe it possible to study the history of the church without touching on the question of power. We must ask the question Leonardo Boff asks in his *Church: Charism, and Power*: "Has the Church as an institution passed the test of power?"[18] I concur with the Christian philosopher Reinhold Schneider: power is the perquisite of no creature. It is only lent to creatures by God. "The use of power signifies a particular, mysterious connection with God. It requires its subject to be available to grace."[19] Eusebius of Caesarea, in my

view, failed to make a truly Christian reading of the relationships of power when he saw in the Roman Empire an exhaustive
model for church organization and in the emperor the executor
of the divine plan on a level with a Moses or a David. I do not
think that the Roman emperor can rightly be regarded as a kind
of super-bishop, legitimately coordinating the internal work of
the church. I am tempted to endorse the penetrating words of
English historian Lord Acton: "All power corrupts. Absolute
power corrupts absolutely." Acton's observation betokens a
passion I share with him. I believe in the possibility of "redefin-
ing the figure of the bishop in a poor, religious popular milieu,"
as Cardinal Aloísio Lorscheider has phrased it.[20] And I would
say the same thing of other church offices. The redefinition will
be the outgrowth of our community experience. Why should
shared power, at the service of the lowly, and exercised in
community, be regarded as utopian in an a-historical sense?

CHAPTER III

Toward a Christian Geography of History

History without geography is crippled, limping along with purely temporal descriptions of spatio temporal occurrences. We must deal with time and space in tandem if we hope to have any comprehension of the past that will be of utility along the pathways of the present. Why bother to speak of Jerusalem, Antioch, Alexandria, Rome, or Carthage at all without knowing where they were and how they related to one another? Not that this will place us in immediate reach of the sweet illusion of an objective, non-ideological geography. But neither need we adopt Yves Lacoste's provocative *mot* (pedagogically justifiable though it may have been for him to formulate it) — "Geography is good mainly for making war" — in order to recognize a sober fact.[1] Inescapably, since the triumph of modern cartography especially, with its "disorientation" of geography in favor of a "north-ification," the ideology of "center and periphery," so typical of capitalism, has prevailed in geographical studies, to the point where even Christianity's maps — of the Holy Land, of the expansion of Christianity, of the journeys of St. Paul, and so on — have been "north-ified." These too place North at the top!

No sooner had the modern world system later called capitalism appeared and begun to spread than the cartographers who composed the first "atlases," or systematic collections of maps, began to implement two changes in their symbolic image of the world. They placed North at the top of their maps, South at the bottom, and Europe (or the North) at the center of the world. We see this as early as Ortelius' *Theatrum Orbis Terrarum* ("Theater of the Inhabited World," Antwerp, 1574), Mercator's *Atlas, sive Cosmographicae Meditationes de Fabrica Mundi et Fabricati Figura,* ("Atlas, or Cosmographic Meditations on the Fabric and Contours of the World," Duisberg, 1595), and especially Blaeu's *Theatrum Orbis Terrae sive Atlas Novus* ("Theater of the Globe of the Earth, or New Atlas," Amsterdam, 1635).[2] Ortelius displays an entire new "architecture" of earth, as it had been created in minds and hearts by the modern world system of the North. In the center of his map of the world he represents Europe, with her scepter and imperial globe; on the left an Oriental princess: the Asia of spices; in the foreground, a destitute negress: the Africa of slaves; on the right a lewd, naked woman holding a man's severed head: cannibalistic, sensual, ignorant, indigenous America; on the right margin a woman's bodiless head: Oceania, or *Terra Incognita*. These new maps are addressed to a new audience, one that consisted no longer of medieval pilgrims but of merchants, bankers, and sea captains toiling in the service of a world system whose expansion had become principally maritime. The imagination of these "navigators" and "discoverers" populated the margins of their world with every imaginable kind of monster and marvel.[3] We may assert without fear of contradiction that the situation is the same today: the peoples on the margins of the system are depicted simultaneously as monsters and as marvels. But this is not a point on which I propose to tarry here. I wish only to indicate that the surface of the globe we inhabit, precisely because it is the surface of a globe, has neither center nor periphery; and to suggest that the more normal and historical way of mapping our globe would be to have the viewer face the rising sun in the East. An "oriented" map of the Mediterranean would have the rivers Tigris and Euphrates at the top, the immense African desert on the viewer's right, and Asia Minor, Greece, Italy, and Spain to the left. Of course, the viewer would surely be inclined to grasp the map and rotate it to the right in order to make it "legible"! But we must make an effort to "de-north-ify" and re-orient at least the mental image that we have of the world, especially in Latin America. Otherwise we shall only continue to entertain an ideological view of our birthplace as "inferior" (below) and "peripheral" (on the margin). In the name of its message of a communion of sisters and brothers, Christianity ought to criticize the "disoriented" image of the world that responds to the narrow, selfish interests of prevailing relationships among persons and peoples.

There is a map, dating from the eighth century that, to my way of thinking, is more "Christian" than those of our cartography today. It was created in the north of Spain in 776 by a certain "Beatus," and it ruled the Christian geographical imagination for at least three centuries (that is, at least until the moment of the official endorsement of the pilgrimage movement by Pope Urban II at the Council of Clermont on November 27, 1095, the date of the official inauguration of the age of the Crusades).[4] The reasons why Beatus' map strikes me as more "Christian" than those of later times are several. First, no city is "central" for Beatus, not even Jerusalem or Rome. His world is a collegial world, divided among the twelve Apostles for governance and guidance. Paradise is in the East and is historicized, not spiritualized. No region of the world – not Europe, not Asia, and not Africa – towers over the others. The accent is on communion and communication among Christian peoples by way of seas and rivers. Christian maps since the twelfth century have been "centered" – either around Jerusalem (in the age of the Crusades) or around Rome (after the Gregorian reform at the end of the eleventh century), or again around Santiago de Compostela in Spain in the era of the *Reconquista*. Why? Because maps were now being produced for pilgrims, Crusaders, or "Romers" (*romeri, Roemer,* etc. – pilgrims to Rome). Beatus' map knows nothing of these centralizations and marginalizations, preferring to follow the ancient church tradition of collegiality. Christians lived together in "colleges." The word *collegium* had a popular meaning in the early church, denoting a popular mutual-aid association under the protection of the laws of the Roman Empire.[5] Beatus distributes the patronage of the Apostles in such wise that each of the various "colleges" covering the face of the world is represented as abiding under the patronage of one of the Apostles (or a pair):

1. India has St. Thomas, whose feast is celebrated on December 21.
2. The rivers Tigris and Euphrates have St. John, December 27.
3. Antioch, St. Bartholomew, August 24.
4. Jerusalem, St. Matthias, February 24 or 25.
5. Alexandria, St. James the Younger, May 11.
6. Constantinople, St. Matthew, May 21.
7. Greece, St. Andrew, November 30.
8. The Coptic Nile, Saints Simon and Jude, October 28.
9. Rome, Saints Peter and Paul, June 29.
10. Gaul, St. Philip, May 11.
11. Galicia (Spain), St. James the Elder, July 25.

We may add the name of St. Barnabas, who worked with St. Paul in Greece and whose feast is celebrated on June 11.

Rome, in the understanding of Christians of the time, was no more "apostolic" a city than any other great metropolitan center. Nor was apostolicity conceptualized in today's terms. All cities were apostolic, and each of them became the center of a "holy land" from the moment of the universalization of grace and of the reign of Jesus Christ.[6]

Another "Christian" quality of Beatus' map is to be found in its "orientation"—not only in its physical orientation (the rising sun is at the top of the map), but also, and especially, in a theological one. The world is on a journey, and the journey is eastward—toward that Rising Sun who is Christ, toward Paradise, the utopia watered by the four biblical rivers. A passage in the Book of Genesis had occasioned the association of Paradise with the Nile, and thereby with Ethiopia, land of the Nile headwaters. Beatus' map, however, followed another tradition, which placed Paradise in the Middle East. Thus both constitutive elements of Christian hope—whose object is "already" but "not yet"—are historicized. Christian eschatology is not projected into an anti-historical, purely spiritual "heaven."[7] The scene of the unfolding of the Christian life, then, is a journey or pilgrimage. Another important feature of Beatus' map consists in its rivers. These include not only the biblical rivers, such as the Tigris, the Euphrates, and the Jordan, but also the rivers that had provided the thoroughfares along which Christianity penetrated the various continents: the Nile, extending into Ethiopia above the sixth cataract, and enjoying the patronage of a particular apostle, St. Simon the Zealot; the Danube, by which the missionary Saints Cyril and Methodius of Constantinople had reached the lands of the Slavs; the Rhone, represented on the map anonymously, with its cities of Marseilles, Arles, and Lyon, the route to Gaul. Even the Mediterranean Sea looks more like a huge river, a kind of main street connecting all the cities, regions, and continents. Finally there is the mysterious, unexplored ocean, with the mythical Antipodes lying far off in the direction of the setting sun.

This map can teach us an elementary lesson in the importance of a human geography for history. The great Christian cities, as it happens, are either seaports or confluence cities. Christianity was not predominantly rural, then, as the people of Israel had been.[8] It sprang up among a suburban population of merchants and artisans. All indications are that the primitive Jerusalem community was still rural. "They sold their holdings and fields . . ." (Acts 2:45). Barnabas sold his farmland and gave the proceeds to the Apostles (Acts 4:36–7). And of course there is the case of Ananias and Sapphira (Acts 5:1–11). But this situation changed rapidly, whether as a result of the work of Paul, at least in the West, or as a consequence of the fall of Jersualem in the year 70, or—and this is the more likely hypothesis—simply in function of the makeup of a Roman world founded on slavery in the cities and on tribute in the countryside. In other words the Roman economy of commerce, crafts, and slave labor was supported by an agrarian economy based on tribute in the form of farm labor, which was procured by way of the census. The census was the formal act by which the people of the land became, in practice, a Roman colony. The Christians of the first centuries, therefore, lived under either a slave regime or a tributary one, as the case might be.

PART ONE

THE MARGINALIZED

CHAPTER IV

The First Christian Self-Awareness

THE EXPERIENCE OF MARGINALIZATION

The New Testament provides us with fairly clear data concerning the consciousness that the first Christians had of themselves and their position in society. We need only read the First Letter of Peter, which describes the actual situation of Christianity in the years 73–92, the period of transition between the apostolic age and post-apostolic times. The letter comes from "Babylon," an eloquent synonym for the city of Rome, and is sent to five churches or communities "scattered [*diasporas*] outside their native land" (1:1): Pontus, Galatia, Cappadocia, Asia, and Bithynia. The atmosphere in these communities is one of depression and discouragement. The purpose of the letter is to teach Christians the art of taking advantage of this "parochial" time of theirs, the time of their "sojourn in a strange land" (1:17), to live lives that will set a good example for those who do not know God (2:12). The communities to whom the letter is addressed are isolated little cells of Christians living within a vast civil society and deprived of any support on the part of the authorities or any friendship with the high and mighty. Peter tells these Christians that in these circumstances it is practice, not preaching, that really matters (3:2). *Paroikia* (1:17) is life without citizenship, the life of persons cast adrift far from their native land and deprived of any civil rights, as J. H. Elliott has emphasized in a recent study.[1] A number of social factors tacitly condition the text of the First Letter of Peter. The Roman Empire was the scene of a mighty migration. The landless, invading barbarians and foreigners without citizenship were on the move. Not having any legitimate status in the eyes of the public administration, and hence deprived of legal protection, these groups were all automatically relegated to a condition of marginalization. The word *paroikos*, denoting a foreigner without citizenship, has the same meaning here as in Ephesians 2:19. The Christian communities had been formed in an effort to make up for this lack, which was both a social and a spiritual one. Their socio-political marginalization was a double deprivation.

Thus the Christian communities acquired the implicit character of an organized social protest, a line of defense against the social atomization that posed such a threat to these landless folk who had to live without rights, without a particular trade, and without protection. The community offered them a "house," God's house (contrast 2:11, 18). To those without a home, God offers God's home (2:5; 4:17). From the viewpoint of society and the system these "foreigners without citizenship" were "household slaves" subject to their "masters" (*despotai*, 2:18). The means of bearing with this humiliating life consisted in humility, patience, and obedience, certainly, since there was no other option. But there was another means as well: the cultivation of virtues that would gradually build "God's house" (4:10), which is constructed through service in communion with one's brothers and sisters—the "charism" (4:10) of serving others. In their marginalization by society Christians constitute the "first habitation of God" and are the "stewards" (*oikonomoi*, 4:10) of these houses of God, which are the communities scattered in the midst of a "world" that does not accept them. The word "house," the key word in this letter, suggests family, cosiness, the community of one's siblings. The "others"—those outside the family—fail to understand the great novelty of the experiment being conducted in the Christian "houses." Christians have to bear with this incomprehension and not allow themselves to be defeated by the temptation to discouragement. "Lead us not into temptation." For Christians of the first generation, the temptation to discouragement and to flee the mission was the greatest temptation of all.

The First Letter of Peter, like so many of the other writings of the New Testament, has been explained away and spiritualized by most of the commentators. St. Peter, we hear, was encouraging the hope of a "heaven" that would come for the slaves and the marginalized after the completion of the course of this earthly life. I have no quarrel with the spiritual dimension of the letter. But it scarcely exhausts the thrust of Peter's message. There is a powerful social message here, as is evident from his use of sociological terms like *diaspora, paroikia, paroikos,* and others. The document has a spiritual and a social meaning at the same time, and bears on the legal situation of foreigners without the right to citizenship in the Roman Empire of the first two centuries of the Christian Era. The situation changed in the third century with the extension of citizenship to foreign, non-Italian peoples. But for the moment, deprived of any civil rights, Christians were embarking on an entirely new experience. Rejected by society, they began to construct, in tiny groups, a new kind of community, based on the memory of the Exodus, the prophets, Jesus, and the dynamism of their eschatological hope.

Observed from without, these communities appeared closed, isolated, and secret, and this gave rise to suspicions and hasty judgments. But within, in their own life, the communities were experiencing a "new land and a new sky, where justice abides" (2 Pet. 3:13), a new Exodus: "Our dwelling is in heaven" (Phil. 3:20), they knew. "Seek the things that are above, not the things that are of earth" (Col. 3:1–2), St. Paul exhorts them: "We have here no lasting city, but we strive for the future one" (Heb. 13:14). The familiar cultural model was expressed in the dichotomy between "heaven and earth." But the meaning of the dichotomy was new and typically Christian: the "exodic" character of the community was an essential note of this new meaning, and it stamped the whole Christian movement with a sense of dynamism (in the dichotomy of slavery and liberation). The static "heaven and earth" of the Greco-Roman world had gone by the board.[2]

We could draw up a lengthy catalogue of the symbols of marginality employed by the first Christians to express their experience. Certain modern anthropologists have discerned a kind of "standardization" in the symbols of marginality and hope prevailing in socially dominated groups. Various cultures are seen to employ the same kinds of symbols to express their situations of marginality and the hope they entertain for better times. A study has been carried out on the marginality symbols used in the redaction of the Gospels, which are the fruit of the living experience of the first Christian communities. Taken together, these symbols make a powerful impression.[3] In the evangelists' accounts, Jesus is not born in a "house," but in a stable, and among beasts, as he is on a journey. His birth is witnessed by the marginalized: shepherds and itinerant Oriental magi. When he is brought to the temple, only two marginalized persons — on the point of death — grasp the importance of his coming life. Unlike his contemporaries he does not marry. He enrolls in none of the theological schools of Judaism. He prefers the company of fishers and other folk of humble social standing. His first public appearance is in the company of another individual who lives on the margin of Judaism, John the Baptizer. His concern is for the popular masses, the *'am ha 'arets* rejected by the dominant society.[4] He is not fond of the rich. He is tempted by power, but he resists. In the "beatitudes," those who live on the margin of society are called "blest." He replaces the law of reciprocity (*Lex Talionis*, "eye for eye, tooth for tooth . . ." is society's law) with the law of charity (". . . turn the other cheek"). The master becomes a domestic slave and washes his disciples' feet. His journeys in the area of Jerusalem are only on the "margins" of the city. Neither the Upper Room, nor Calvary, nor Lazarus' house, nor the Garden of Gethsemane are within the holy city with its mighty temple. And when he finally does enter Jerusalem, he rides an ass and not some royal mount. The words inscribed on the head of his cross proclaim his royalty, but his real crown is a crown of thorns. Jesus' resurrection overthrows the laws of death, and the first to see him after the resurrection are not men, but women. Jesus proclaims an inversion of the most radical character: "The first shall be last, and the last first," he says. These symbols of the inversion of the "normal," of what is accepted by the norms of society, are to be found on every page of the gospel narratives. What is important is that it is precisely these elements of marginality that strike the emotions of persons touched by the word of the gospel and establish the popular acceptance of their message. This would suggest very strongly that, generally at least, human beings identify with some form of marginality. Marginality would seem to constitute part and parcel of the general human experience. At any rate, it is upon this experience that the Christian project is articulated, and it reveals the hidden dynamisms of the human spirit.

Another consideration along these same lines is the sociological character of Galilee, especially as contrasted with Jerusalem.[5] Here once more we have an impressive set of symbols of marginalization. Jerusalem is a power center, and it practices an internal colonialism with respect to Galilee. A good many Galilean peasants have a better life under foreign domination than under the hegemony of Judea and Jerusalem. Even Jesus is a Galilean in Judea, as we read in Mark—a marginalized individual living in the midst of the dominant society. Mark 16:6–7 is pregnant with the implications of this, and we may reread the text as follows: "Do you really want to know Jesus? Then leave Jerusalem. Not even Jesus lives where he was laid to rest. The tomb is empty. He heads a group that would like to take you to Galilee." The Christian experience is to be had in Galilee, then, on the periphery of the system.[6]

The same atmosphere of marginality pervades Christian burial, which adopts the symbolism of the dominant culture but gives it a different meaning. In a certain Christian burial place in Rome we find: the laurel wreath, Roman symbol of victory; a reference to the "gods of the underworld" (*D M, dis manibus*); an anchor, another familiar symbol in the Roman Empire; an image of fishes, used on amulets worn for good luck, but here receiving an altogether new meaning, since the letters of the Greek word for "fish," *ichthus*, form the protogram of "Jesus Christ, God's Son, Savior" (*Iesous Christos Theou Huios Soter*). "Fish of the living" was a kind of code name for Jesus Christ among the members of this marginalized community. Other thematic representations include the Good Shepherd (clothed in

Roman fashion and clean-shaven), a fisher (God selecting the Christians from among the multitudes), boats, anchors, fishes, lamps. Christian burial symbols became more explicit with the multiplication of the communities and eventually included typical biblical scenes like those of Susanna and the elders, Daniel in the lions' den, Jonah in the belly of the whale, the raising of Lazarus, the healing of the paralytic, and the Hebrew children in the fiery furnace. It is as if Christian imagination would ever voice the same refrain: "As you saved Jonah, or Susanna, or Daniel, or Lazarus, and so on, save your people now." Uppermost in the Christian mind was salvation from an intolerable situation of oppression and domination.[7]

LITERATURE ON CHRISTIAN MARGINALIZATION

The Christian sense of marginality fully corresponded to reality, as we may verify in certain writers of the period and their blunt language. Suetonius speaks of Christians as "Jews constantly restless, goaded on by a certain 'Chrestos.'" Tacitus refers to Christianity as an "execrable superstition." Pliny the Younger calls it an "absurd, extravagant superstition characterized by a complete innocence of behavior." Lucian of Samosata (125–85) is more aggressive: Christians have abandoned the gods of Greece, he says, "for a crucified sophist who introduced these new mysteries and managed to persuade his adepts to worship him alone," and Christians are rumored to worship the head of an ass and devour infants in their rites of initiation. "That criminal complicity is the guarantee of their silence," Lucian says.[8] The strongest extant anti-Christian text, however, is Celsus' *True Discourse* (*Ho Alethes Logos*), redacted in the year 170. Almost the whole of this discourse is preserved in the *Kata Kelson* ("Against Celsus") of Origen (185–254). According to Celsus Jesus was a "carpenter by trade, and was crucified" (73).[9] He was a "vagabond and a derelict, who coursed the countryside with ten or eleven followers from the dregs of the people, sailors and tax-collectors. This desperado gained his precarious living in shameful wise" (11). Jesus was the child of "peasants" (7) or a "carpenter" (22), "irascible, quick to curse and threaten" (30).

He "spoke against the rich" (70). He was a "seducer of the people, a charlatan" (75), "imbued with prejudices against the wealthy" (75), "short of stature, ugly and ignoble" (84), a "personage who ended his ignominious life with an ignominious death" (93). Mary, according to Celsus, was a "peasant woman, a carpenter's wife, who had had relations with a soldier" (7; cf. 22, 62), a "woman without a destiny, without royal birth, and without fame, even among her neighbors" (8), a "woman who lived by manual work" (7). For their part, Christians were "a bunch of simple folk, coarse and morally depraved, as one might expect in a charlatan's clientele" (6). They were "ignorant, narrow-minded, uncultured simpletons, mean, ignoble spirits, slaves, poor women, and children" (37), "weavers, cobblers — extremely ignorant, uneducated folk who recounted wonders to children and women of no better judgment than they" (37), people who lived "in cobblers' tents or fishermen's huts" (37). After all, Christians were the descendants of Jews, those "fugitive slaves from Egypt who have never done anything of note and have never been particularly numerous or esteemed" (45), themselves "shoemakers, stonemasons, and metal-workers" (73), a "vulgar, dirty folk" (108).

We find the Christians, then, according to Celsus' coarse, aggressive description, in the narrow streets where craftsmen lived, in the great seaports of the Roman Empire — Antioch, Alexandria, Rome, and Carthage, to name only the principal ones.

Celsus emphasizes Christians' marginality:

> There appeared a new race, sprung from nowhere, without citizenship or traditions, hostile to all religious and civil institutions, fugitives from justice, universally infamous but glorying in their common execration. I refer to the Christians. [1]

In Celsus' opinion, Christians did everything in reverse. "To them," he says, "wisdom is an evil and foolishness a good" (4). They preferred "ignorance to culture, slavery to a respectable social position" (37). Once more we see symbols of marginality. According to Celsus Christians are "enemies of the rich" (70), "sectaries, preferring to form little groups of their own, and isolate themselves from society at large" (99), adversaries of culture (37), and unwilling to do "what everyone else does" (102)—offer sacrifice to the tutelary gods. As for the Christian neglect to toady to the authorities, "What ever could be wrong," Celsus asks, "with attempting to secure the benevolence of those who have received their power from God—especially kings and the other powers of this earth?" (113). Or again: "What objection could there be to cultivating the mind?" (37). And Celsus goes on the attack:

> Christians' antipathy toward temples, statues, and altars is as the mark and sign of their secret, mysterious unity. And their refusal to participate in public ceremonies rests on the same mistaken concept of God. [102]

Here is a description of a radical counterculture. We have a total inversion of values. For Celsus, Christians—whose virtues he admires, and whose strength in unity he does not fail to perceive—have no understanding of the great peril threatening the Roman world—"that the world is on the point of being overwhelmed by the most savage and coarse barbarians" (117). So why not collaborate with the Roman state? Celsus concludes his *Discourse* with an appeal to Christians to abandon their marginality and collaborate with the organized forces of the empire in order to put up a resistance to barbarism:

> Support the Emperor, help him in his defense of right and justice, fight for him if need be. Be at his side as he leads his armies into battle. Flee civic duty and military service no longer. Take part in public functions, for the well-being of the laws and piety. [117]

Celsus is a typical late second-century philosopher—sincere in his wish to construct society and disoriented by the life led by Christians, who obviously were not collaborating with the state. His text is shot through and through with expressions of exasperation with a Christian religion that valued its marginality, expressed itself in terms of the poor, of women, and of children (37), looked down on the wise, including great philosophers like Plato, and sought to destabilize public institutions.

ECONOMIC AND POLITICAL ROOTS OF MARGINALIZATION

Christian marginalization did not result solely because the Christian communities based themselves on Jesus' life and message. Its roots go deeper and are to be sought in the economic and political evolution of the Roman Empire together with the peculiar situation of Judaism in the Greco-Roman world. Jews, as we know, were especially marginalized by the Roman administration owing to their hostility to worship of the emperor, which to them was the most contemptible sacrilege. It was their experience of marginalization, dating from the days of the Babylonian Captivity, that led Jews to create a social support system that went by the name of "synagogue," as we shall see in the chapter on the base community. But Christians were frequently confused with Jews by the less experienced of the imperial functionaries. At the same time, antipathy reigned between Jews and Christians, as the New Testament attests in a number of places. We see the conflict between practicing Jews and the "party of Christ" at Antioch in 43–9, the trouble in Thessalonica and Corinth in 51, and the confusion at Ephesus in 57. As for the long episodes of conflict between Jews and the empire, likewise to be examined below, Christians were between the frying pan and the fire.

Further, there were elements contributing to the marginalization of Christians in the economic and political evolution of the empire. The Roman system itself began to generate a mass of marginalized with the establishment, in Italy in particular, of great landed estates. Small landholders, for whom the soil was everything, were gradually expelled. They migrated to Rome, to crowd the "islands" there (*insulae*, poor neighborhoods, "slums"). As the Christian Era opened, Rome was being transformed into a gigantic city with an estimated population of over a million. The same thing occurred in Alexandria, at the mouth of the Nile. Various efforts in the direction of agrarian reform failed, and the authorities finally settled on a paternalistic solution known as "bread and circuses" (*panis et circenses*) and providing for the free distribution of wheat, olive oil, salt, wine, and clothing. But lest he exhaust the state treasury, the Emperor Augustus limited the number of beneficiaries of this distribution to 200,000. This restriction remained in force until the reign of Diocletian. Practically, then, the number of Roman "citizens" in any meaningful sense of the term was restricted to the same limit, and the *Populus Romanus* was born. The measures had been adopted for political ends. Only men received the distributions. Women and children were excluded. With Trajan, some boys and girls also received them, but in a proportion of 264 boys to 36 girls, according to a study done on one city of Italy.[10] In a word, the "Roman people" included only a minority of those living in the large cities of the empire. Other persons were not regarded as having any political value. They were without either civil rights or any voice in public affairs and were designated in Roman law as the "lowly" (*humiliores*), in contradistinction to the "honorable" (*honestiores*). They were slaves, freedmen and their families, dancers, singers, prostitutes, women, and children. It was among these that the Christians were to be found.

CHAPTER V

The Theology of the Marginalized as "Chosen"

JESUS AND THE MARGINALIZED

Instead of simply acquiescing in the "inferiority complex" their social marginalization might be expected to have bred in them, Christians saw the latter as part of a divine plan of sovereign importance. And they began to develop a theology of the divine election of and predilection for the marginalized. Here we have the birth of the great theology of earliest Christian times.

The theology of the election of the marginalized was deeply rooted in the practice of Jesus. That practice had been regarded as an aberration by his co-religionists, predicated as it was on the premise of God's election of and predilection for persons and groups that "good Jews" all relegated to marginalization: not only sinners, but foreigners, the Samaritan woman, the Syro-Phoenician woman, and the Roman centurion. The attitude of Jesus toward these and other marginalized persons and groups occasioned a deep disgust on the part of numerous pious members of established society, observers of the Law who were convinced of their religious superiority as members of the chosen people. The head-waggers were sure that they had been set apart from all persons of "impure lips," as the latter had been rejected by the God of the Mosaic covenant. But Jesus had explicitly defended his practice, and his parables cut to the quick. Thus we

have the parable of the good Samaritan, or of the hired hands
sent to work in the vineyard (the parable of the workers hired at
the eleventh hour, Matt. 20:1–16). Jesus' insistence on God's
predilection for the "last" was categorical. Nor was this favor-
itism owing merely to his Father's mercy. No, it was rooted in
the urgency of the building of the Reign of God. The pagans
would be first and the Jews last. Thus we have a complete
inversion of the prevailing scale of values. François Houtart, in
language adapted to his young audiences at the Brussels Free
University, presents the person and practice of Jesus as follows:

> The prophet Jesus of Nazareth arose in the midst of the
> scribes and Pharisees. True, he criticized them theoret-
> ically. But he also maintained the basic elements of their
> ideological production. In fact he was frequently confused
> with them. But his opposition to the priestly and lay
> nobility (the lay nobility being the great bourgeoisie), to
> the lower clergy, and to the petite bourgeoisie of the scribes
> or Pharisees entailed the displacement of his locus of
> ideological production from the temple or synagogue to
> the highways and byways of Palestine. He spent the greater
> part of his life as an itinerant preacher, then, in fertile,
> contradictory Galilee, where Zealotism and messianic
> movements were on the wax in reaction to the exploitation
> of the rural masses by the theocratic state and Roman
> troops alike.
>
> Jesus' "class of origin" had been the petite bourgeoisie of
> the crafts. But he did not address his practice primarily to
> this social category. On the contrary, his social base was
> made up of the masses who had been marginalized by the
> production process, along with an illiterate peasantry. In
> other words, his social base consisted of the most ex-
> ploited—the social classes lumped together under the name
> of *'am ha 'arets.* Jesus relied precisely on the social base
> that his adversaries—the Sadducees, the Herodians, the
> Pharisees, and the scribes—disdained. It was on these same
> masses that the Zealot movement, as well as the Pharisaic
> movement, relied, despite the contempt in which they were
> held by the latter.[1]

I quote this long passage because it identifies so precisely both who Jesus was in the society of his time and who the marginalized were. It was his option for this segment of society — those who were the object of the greatest contempt — that led to his exclamation:

> "Father, Lord of heaven and earth, to you I offer praise; for what you have hidden from the learned and the clever you have revealed to the merest children. Father, it is true. You have graciously willed it so." [Matt. 11:25–26]

That exclamation, and the practice that constituted its basis, had profound repercussions on the like of St. Paul, St. Irenaeus, St. Justin, and Tertullian, as we shall see below. John the Evangelist, in his meditation on these attitudes, which contrasted so sharply with the common mentality of society, concluded many years after: "To his own [to Israel] he came, yet his own did not accept him" (John 1:11); "his own" treated him as marginalized and rejected in his own turn. And yet "while the law was given through Moses, this enduring love came through Jesus Christ" (John 1:17).

ST. PAUL AND THE MARGINALIZED

Among the Apostles it was St. Paul who had the deepest understanding of this practice on Jesus' part. We need only read the First Letter to the Corinthians. Not that it was particularly easy to understand the election of the marginalized as a law of the divine economy in the construction of the Reign. St. Paul himself sought, in vain, to preach "worldly wisdom" to the Areopagites of Athens. He then became convinced that he must alter his discourse and preach the cross.

> Christ did not send me to baptize, but to preach the gospel — not with worldly "wisdom," however, lest the cross of Christ be rendered void of its meaning!
> The message of the cross is complete absurdity to those who are headed for ruin, but to us who are experiencing salvation it is the power of God. Scripture says, "I will

destroy the wisdom of the wise, and thwart the cleverness
of the clever." Where is the wise man to be found? Where
the scribe? Where is the master of worldly argument? [1
Cor. 1:17–20]

This understanding led St. Paul's apostolate once and for all
to the despised and socially marginalized, such as the Christians
of Corinth.

Not many of you are wise, as men account wisdom; not
many are influential; and surely not many are well-born.
God chose those whom the world considers absurd to
shame the wise; he singled out the weak of this world to
shame the strong. He chose the world's lowborn and
despised, those who count for nothing, to reduce to
nothing those who were something; so that mankind can
do no boasting before God. [1 Cor. 1:26–29]

St. Paul's insistence on the word "choose" in this passage is the
articulation of a theology of the election of those who count for
nothing in the eyes of the world.

Concretely, that theology applied to the uncircumcised and
those of "unclean lips"—those despised and depreciated by
faithful observers of the Mosaic Law. This raised a difficulty
with which St. Paul, in loyalty to his calling, had to deal—the
greatest problem in the history of the early church. Can the
uncircumcised become Christians without submitting to the
Jewish rite of circumcision? In this question are contained, in
germ, all of the great questions of later church history, the
numerous problems raised by a predilection for the
marginalized:

On the conjugal level, a predilection for women in a world of
male dominance.

On the educational level, a predilection for children in an
adult world.

On the level of production, a predilection for the workers in
an employers' world.

On the level of health and hygiene, a predilection for the sick
in a world of the healthy.

On the level of race, a predilection for blacks in a world of whites.

On the level of the land, a predilection for Amerindians in a world invaded by whites.

On the level of international policy, a predilection for the periphery in a world dominated by the center.

The problem that arose with the Jewish rite of circumcision is not a mere transient, picturesque episode in the beginning of the history of the church, a thing of the past. To our very day it is a problem bound up with the veracity of the Christian memory in the following of Jesus' practice on behalf of the *'am ha 'arets*—the "abandoned masses" (cf. Mark 3:20; Luke 5:1; Acts 7:9), those who live without organization, without a past or a future, without an awareness of their identity, without cultural roots, without historical memory—in order to fashion them into a people (*'am gadesh*, a holy people), a people of unity, of the memory of the Exodus, of hope, faith, and charity.

St. Paul, who so confidently claims the title of "apostle," neither belonged to the original Jerusalem community nor had received the laying on of hands of the "pillars of the church," the Apostles of Jerusalem. In fact, Paul had been a persecutor of Christians. He represents a phenomenon of extraordinary importance for the entire history of the church. We may well ask ourselves how compatible such a figure would be with the church of today! But let us return to the question of circumcision. Let us see what was at stake. We have two accounts. One is from St. Luke, in Acts. Exegetes today admit that Luke's is a conciliatory account, calculated to appease. The other version is from one of St. Paul's own letters, the New Testament letter addressed to the Christian communities of Galatia in Asia Minor. This account is much more lively and realistic, openly referring to "dissension and controversy" that had been stirred up by "certain individuals" who had come from Jerusalem to Antioch to tell converts they could not be saved without circumcision. The reaction of the Antiochene community was to send Paul and his colleague Barnabas to Jerusalem to consult the "apostles and elders." This decision was not made without fear and trepidation, and St. Paul would later beg the Christians of Rome: "Join me in the struggle by your prayers to God on my behalf. Pray that I may

be kept safe from the unbelievers in Judea . . ." (Rom.
15:30–31).

St. Paul's trip to Jerusalem sometime around the year 49 —
sixteen years after Jesus' crucifixion — would come to be called
the "Council of Jerusalem" (or even, by Hefele, the "first
ecumenical council," which is surely saying too much).[2] The
importance for the entire history of the church of this meeting
among the Apostles cannot be exaggerated. What was at stake
was the Christian memory itself, founded on God's election of
the poor, the divine preference for the marginalized. The reality
underlying the circumcision dilemma was a stormy reality of
disturbance and turmoil. We may even assert that Christianity
was born into a world of intense perturbation in the mind of
Christians who naturally could only perceive the church as a
"church of the circumcision" — the faithful following of a codified Mosaic tradition comporting the institutional network of
synagogues served by rabbis, the Jewish system of winning
converts known as proselytism, faithful compliance with the
prescriptions of the Torah or sacred books, the "sign" of the
cross and circumcision on the occasion of the birth of a male
child, with baptism only later, the traditional funeral rites, and
the Feast of Passover celebrated on the fourteenth day of the
month of Nisan. All of this appeared perfectly normal to the
first Christians, who were Jews by culture and Christians by
choice.

But Jesus' practice, commemorated in the communities,
disturbed this religious schema, as we have already seen. And St.
Paul was the first to perceive all the ramifications. The Christian
must forever preserve the historical value of this Paul of Tarsus,
this "apostle sent not by men or by any man, but by Jesus Christ
and God his Father" (Gal. 1:1), this "charismatic" in the
original, most authentic sense of the word. St. Paul sternly
reprimands the Galatians who seek to return to the Mosaic Law,
proclaiming that Christianity is freedom and not the observance
of a "law" — but freedom for a communion of brothers and
sisters and the building of the Reign. Paul does not hesitate to
criticize Peter's position. Peter had begun to ignore the *entente*
of the year 49. First he had gone to Antioch and begun to treat

uncircumcised Christians as equals, even taking his meals with them. But emissaries had come from Jerusalem, sent by James, and Peter then "drew back to avoid trouble with those who were circumcised" (Gal. 2:12). Whereupon everyone began to follow Peter's example, even Barnabas. Paul reflects:

> As soon as I observed that they were not being straight-forward about the truth of the gospel, I had this to say to Cephas in the presence of all: "If you who are a Jew are living according to Gentile ways rather than Jewish, by what logic do you force the Gentiles to adopt Jewish ways?" [Gal. 2:14]

Paul writes this with passion and with lucid perception of the truth of the gospel. He has intuited that an inalienable element of the gospel is at stake, and that what the Council of Jerusalem of the year 49 has dealt with is the most important question in the history of humanity—how to regard one's neighbor, how to treat the "other."

How is one to behave toward these "last" so dear to Jesus, those who count for naught in society's eyes? The picture of the Council of Jerusalem in the year 49 is the picture of an *entente*, a diplomatic accord, a phenomenon of the balance of forces like the accords entered into by politicians. After all, the Antiochene communities did have some weight, and one had to pacify them. Thus it was necessary to arrive at a common denominator. Paul did not see things in this way. For him it was a basic, rock-bottom matter, a confrontation between what he regarded as "Christian freedom" and the following of the Jewish Law. It was a matter of knowing whether Christianity would be happy with being just another Jewish sect or whether it was inaugurating something altogether new, an unheard-of practice based on the practice of Jesus. Paul senses the rivalry among the Apostles and defends himself: "It has been a point of honor with me never to preach in places where Christ's name was already known, for I did not want to build on a foundation laid by another . . ." (Rom. 15:20). And so Paul gradually moved away from what his colleagues preached, and he felt his isolation bitterly. Here he was withdrawing from the "Law" of the ancients and moving into the unfamiliar world of the "nations" (Lat., *gentes*; Gk., *ethne*: "peoples, pagans").

Later on, in the third century, Christian imagination would picture Saints Peter and Paul working in tandem. But this image is scarcely authentic. It is a collage, composed much later, when the victory of the Pauline approach was virtually assured. We even have a representation, dating from this time, of Peter and Paul as the latter-day founders of Rome, replacing Romulus and Remus.[3] Interestingly enough, this image does not yet contain certain iconographic elements that were to emerge with the papal revolution of the eleventh century under Gregory VII, when Paul began to be represented with a sword and Peter with a key. The universal Paul (holding the imperial sword that had universalized Christianity and thus symbolizing the "world" or "orb of the lands," *orbis terrarum*) and the apostolic Peter (symbolizing—by the power of the keys—the church perpetuated in time) were the mighty symbols of medieval Christendom, and our third-century image is without them. Another significant detail to be observed in the more ancient representation, however, is the "elitization" of the Christian imagination, which now showed Peter and Paul not as a fisher and a tentmaker, respectively, but as Roman senators, wearing the toga and installed in the dignity of their "authority."

New Testament scholars have perceived the mutual incompatibility of the concerns of Peter and Paul. Daniélou writes:

> Paul is thinking of Christians of pagan origin, and feels it essential to deliver Christianity from its Jewish ties. Peter, for his part, fears a defection on the part of the Jewish Christians, who, under pressure of Jewish nationalism, were in danger of returning to Judaism. He wants to keep them, insisting that it is possible to be loyal to the Christian faith and the Jewish law at the same time.[4]

The contrast is significant. Paul has no hesitation in taking a leap in the dark, in faith and the discipleship of Jesus, and considers the "last" to be indeed the "first." Scorned minorities are to be defended. In modern terms, he has the attitude of a liberation theologian. Peter, on the other hand, acts out of fear, with a regard to tradition and security. He fails to intuit anything new in Paul's predilection for an insignificant number of converts from paganism (insignificant for the moment — later the ratio would be reversed) over the great Jewish-Christian majorities and their problems. Peter is Galilean enough to perceive that, having managed to cut the ties that bound the new Christian movement to the popular masses of Galilee, the authorities may manage the same thing in Judea, where, "for fear of the Jews," Christianity maintained a precarious existence by presenting itself as a mere extension of rabbinical Judaism.[5] Paul? Peter would rather have James. James, according to Eusebius of Caesarea, "drank neither wine nor other strong drink, never shaved, and passed his life in the temple praying on behalf of the people" (*Hist. Eccl.*, II, 23, 4), like a pious rabbi of the time, a follower of the Law. Paul, who had abandoned the tradition James had seen as the guarantor of the new move-ment's survival, only inspired Peter with insecurity.

History has shown Peter's fear to have been baseless. The young seedling of Christianity was far more hardy than he supposed. The Christian movement was violently expelled from Israel, first by the civil war of 66–70 and then by the destruction of Jerusalem and the temple in 70, followed by successive reprisals on the part of the Roman system against the Jewish liberation movements, including the reprisal of A.D. 130 which stamped out an insurrection in Jerusalem to the tune of a half-million dead.[6] Paradoxically, while the first Christians were entirely innocent of these events, the latter occasioned the survival of the Pauline project and its later consolidation as "pagan Christianity," a Christianity based on the conversion of non-Jewish peoples. Jorge Pixley writes: "It was an ambitious project — that of constituting a historical subject for the Reign of God where for the moment there was only despair and disorganization."[7] But this was precisely what Paul had in mind, and he managed to further his project by forming a number of base communities, as we shall see in the next chapter.

Given the importance for the history of the church of the

Council of Jerusalem, I should be inclined to date that history from the year 49, the year of this first great discussion of the Christian memory and its veracity.

Before concluding this rough sketch of the theology of the election of the marginalized in Paul, we must indicate a consequence of Paul's practice that would eventually occasion so many developments that he could not have foreseen. Through turning to the pagans, who were ignorant of the treasure of traditional Judaism, St. Paul had to present the Christian message in a new way. Now he could no longer appeal to the fulfillment of Jewish prophecies but was forced to use the motifs of popular religion. In Lystra, for example, when the people surprised Barnabas and Paul by taking them for Jupiter and Mercury (Acts 14:12), Paul improvises a discourse. God, he says, "sends down rain and rich harvests; your spirits he fills with food and delight" (Acts 14:17). Here the God of Abraham, Isaac, and Jacob must give place to the God who commands the rain and the harvest in due season. Paul shifts his emphasis from prophetic themes and the legacy of Judaism to elements of popular religion as found in the most diversified of cultures. The first eleven chapters of the Book of Genesis, which recount the antecedents of the call of Abraham, acquire a new currency in the presence of this new reality that has forced itself on Paul and his fellow Christians. Noah replaces Abraham, to borrow Daniélou's characterization of St. Paul's change of language.[8] This new practice was to have enormous consequences one day, and not only in the bureaucratization of popular religion at the hands of an organizing (and profiting) elite. It was also responsible for the emergence of Christian hope in a Christianized popular religion.

THE MARGINALIZED IN THE THEOLOGY OF JUSTIN, IRENAEUS, AND TERTULLIAN

Paul was succeeded by three Christian authors in particular who defend the theology of the election of the marginalized. They are the most important Christian writers of the years before the appearance of the school of Alexandria: Justin (d. *ca.* 165),[9]

Irenaeus of Lyon (close of the second century),[10] and Tertullian (d. after 220).[11] Despite their very different circumstances, this trio of theologians has one thing in common. They all defend the faith of the simple and the poor against the assaults of the powerful and "intelligent." They are champions of the faith of the "nameless" (Justin), "the unlearned" (Irenaeus), the "simple" (Tertullian).

Justin

It is still a pleasure to read Justin today. Martyred in Rome around A.D. 165, Justin was actually a philosopher of Greek culture, born in Palestine and later moving to Asia Minor. His most important work, the *Dialogue with Trypho the Jew*, is a long, desultory conversation between Justin and a Jew who does not (yet) believe in Christ.[12] It is the first book-length work in Christian literature, and its subject is the everlasting problem of our quest for truth and the art of the good life. The quest can be endless, we know. It can absorb one's whole life, as it did that of St. Anthony, father of monasticism, St. Augustine, St. Francis of Assisi, and Dante Alighieri. It is a quest that has produced immortal works such as Cervantes' *Don Quixote*, and inspired legends like the Wandering Jew or (in another direction) St. Christopher.

Despite its editorial shortcomings, Justin's *Dialogue* can only be called great literature. What we are most taken with in Justin, however, is what we might call his pilgrim mentality—his constant eagerness to move on. His life from beginning to end is the life of an itinerant philosopher, first in Palestine, next in Asia Minor where a (real? imaginary?—we shall never know) "elder" reveals to him the tremendous new phenomenon of Christianity, then in Rome where he gathers a circle of disciples, and finally on the hard, one-way road to martyrdom.

Philosophers were in high public favor in Justin's time, and they crowded roads and town squares offering lessons in wisdom and virtue. They wore the philosopher's toga and had won from the Roman system the rights of citizenship (which must have been an important factor in their survival, as we may easily surmise from what we have seen above). People respected and heeded them. Let us not, then, imagine Justin as a philosopher in the academic tradition, aloof from the common people. The philosophers of the first two Christian centuries were itinerant sages who gathered together groups of the curious or interested and attempted to respond to their questions, to make disciples of them, or simply to live in the "philosophic manner" by practicing the virtues of a pure life that would eschew pleasure and devote itself to reflection. Such were the Pythagoreans (who practiced healing of the sick, as we shall see below), the Stoics, the Epicureans, the Platonists, and especially the Cynics (whom the people loved precisely for their "cynical" behavior — they were as indifferent as young pups when it came to social customs and mores). The reputation of the philosophers had spread to the imperial court itself, where various of the Caesars, and notably Marcus Aurelius, doggedly pursued the philosophical ideal. Side by side with both the popular culture and the dominant culture of the system, the philosophic culture was one of the three normal ways of thinking and acting in the first age of Christianity. It constituted a genuine counterculture, however, and its devotees were the many who were rankled by the common explanation of things. Small wonder, then, if we find a philosopher among the first illustrious converts to Christianity.

Philosophy in those days, or at least the sort of philosophy we have just described, teetered precariously between two fundamentally opposed ways of thinking and living. On the one side was reason. On the other, mysticism. On the one side was the cosmological explanation of things; on the other, popular piety. There was the ideal of tranquillity, of personal freedom from fear and anxiety (the celebrated *apatheia*). But there was also social involvement — popular medicine, counsel, solving the problems of daily living.

Justin was immersed in this dialectic. He had successively espoused the "Stoic, Aristotelian, Peripatetic, theoretical, Pythagorean, and Platonic" philosophies, and all had left him unsatisfied.[13] Now he longed to be alone, and he traveled to a lonely locale in the vicinity of the city of Ephesus with the intent of slaking his thirst for solitude. He moved "from the center of the margin," then, from the social world to the "desert," from security in the midst of the great philosophers to a precarious existence amidst the marginalized and despised. And this became his great passage. For, "once I had reached the vicinity of the place where I should finally be alone," he recounts, "an elder, of dignified mien, calm and imposing, fell in a little way behind me."[14] Justin and this anonymous "elder," this symbol of marginality, were soon absorbed in earnest conversation. Their discussion concerned the inconsistency of the discourses of the great philosophers, and the contrasting veracity of a certain new way of life based on what the elder called the "true philosophy." And the elder expounded to Justin the Christian life. Justin's text is as follows:

> There existed, before all of these who call themselves philosophers, certain happy, righteous persons whom God loved. They spoke as they were moved by the Holy Spirit, and foretold events that since have come about. We call them prophets. They have been the only persons to contemplate the truth and proclaim it to human beings. No one frightened them, no one confused them. They were never overcome by ambition. They uttered only what they had heard and seen when filled with the Holy Spirit. Their writings have been preserved to this day. . . .[15]

They were, of course, the evangelists. And these "prophets" had demonstrated the truth of their discourse not by an appeal to argument, but by "wonders," as Justin reports. We shall comment on this later.

On the strength of a new understanding gained from a stranger who had subsequently disappeared from his route, Justin changed the nature of his quest for truth and virtue. Now he sought them no longer in discourse and reasoning, but in practice and life. He began to share the daily life of simple Christians, and behold, he perceived the precious "truth" he sought in the everyday affairs of the communities—in the testimony of a life of chastity, love of enemies, readiness to die for the faith (if need be), and imitation of the practice of Jesus. The communion, the common life Justin had begun to practice—surely symbolized in the personage of the venerable ancient who had converted him to Christianity—leads him to exclaim, enthusiastically, that Christianity is the "only true and profitable philosophy" (*Dial.*, VIII, 1). Christianity's symbol par excellence is the cross, he says—that supreme sign of marginalization. The cross signifies not only physical elimination in death but the moral annihilation of infamy. Justin declares to the Jews: "Never among your people was any called a king whose hands and feet had been pierced, who had died in this mystery—I refer to the crucifixion—but Jesus alone."[16] In Justin the cross acquires a cosmological dimension, as Dom Fernando Antonio Figueiredo asserts in his doctoral dissertation on Justin. "Justin's symbol is the cross, which, 'as proclaimed by the prophets of yore' (*Apol.*, I, 55, 2), is the supreme sign of power and authority."[17] It is an irresistibly attractive symbol, one that St. John the Evangelist had already thematized, and the motif par excellence of the theology of God's predilection for the oppressed victims of marginalization and their election on the universal level of salvation. The cross as a symbol of marginality has lost a great deal of its force with us today. We speak of it so casually. In the first Christian centuries, however, it still retained its full impact as an instrument of torture, social rejection, abomination, and ultimately, insanity or "foolishness" (1 Cor. 1:18).

In an effort to demonstrate the genuinely new truth he had found, Justin began to "search the scriptures," and there, in the prophecies concerning the cross, in the prefigurations of the cross in the serpent in the wilderness, in Moses' prayer "with arms outstretched," and especially in Psalm 22, on which he comments verse by verse, he found that wisdom is on the margin, not in the center—on the cross, not in vain discourses.[18]

Justin pursued the logic of marginality to its ultimate consequences. He suffered martyrdom. We may read, in the incontestably authentic judicial proceedings or "acts" of his martyrdom, the words of his courageous expostulation to the Roman prefect. "No one," declaims our philosopher, "believed in Socrates, for Socrates did not die to confirm what he had taught. Through Christ, however, practitioners of the crafts, indeed persons altogether unschooled, have held the fear of death in contempt."[19] And in response to the question addressed to him by the presiding judge, "To what science do you devote yourself?" Justin answered plainly and forthrightly, "I have studied the sciences in succession. I have finally embraced the true teaching of the Christians."[20] He might as well have been signing his own death warrant.

Without entering into any polemics, surely we may permit ourselves an observation. Justin is frequently presented in a rather questionable light. Daniélou, for example, sees him rather as an erudite academician, as if he had been a philosopher of the kind that appear in history with the Alexandrine school (Clement, Origen). "Justin represents a new type of Christian," writes Daniélou. "Here we have a Greek philosopher who, after his conversion to Christianity, continues to pursue his lines of thought and his lifestyle."[21] Reading between the lines here, one discerns a commonly-held thesis bearing on the celebrated encounter of Christianity with Hellenism. But if one starts from the standpoint of the people, it is important to underscore what might be called the popular cast of Justin and his conversion.

Justin was converted to marginality. From within this marginality he began to reflect on the experience of the life he led in common with Christians. I cannot agree with the assertion that "the whole finality [of Justin's work] is expressed in the basic notion that the Christians represent true piety and that their teaching is in agreement with that of the best of the Greeks — Socrates, Heraclitus, Plato."[22] Such an assertion can only be made, in my view, from a mistaken point of departure. Justin's intent was not to justify Christianity to the philosophical thinking of the time. His concern was to bear witness to his flabbergasting discovery that wisdom comes from the cross, from the conversion of the philosopher to the viewpoint and problems of the poor, from openness to the prophets and especially to the crucified Prophet who has scandalized the world. There is no question of engaging in a discussion on the level of "thought." Justin's intent was precisely to shift the entire question to the level of practice and a living faith.

Irenaeus of Lyon

The second great Christian author to allow himself to be seduced by the theology of marginality was Irenaeus of Lyon, who flourished in the latter part of the second century. A captivating figure, deeply devoted to the church, Irenaeus preferred conciliation to combat, unification to condemnation. He deserves his name: *Eirēnaios,* from *eirenē,* "peace." A Byzantine icon represents Irenaeus receiving a revelation from heaven clad in the stylized toga that became the *haute couture* of the empire only in the third and fourth centuries, the style of clothing that has evolved into the liturgical vestments of the Roman Rite (pallium, stole, chasuble, and alb). In the first and second centuries, however, the toga was still the modest outer garment of the ordinary person. (Or at least of the ordinary citizen. Laborers had practically to disrobe to work, as there was no such thing as a "shirt," and a tunic would have slipped off.) Certain iconographic elements of the same representation betoken a profound identification with popular religion. We see the divine hand emanating from the sun, a cross (symbolizing a non-cyclical, goal-directed movement), and a crown (symbolizing holiness) — each found in some form in the Byzantine liturgy today. Likewise in evidence, however, is the elitization of the Christian imagination. Irenaeus was not actually a member of the social elite of his time. With the appearance of the various Christendoms, however, among which the Byzantine was particularly grand and grandiose, Christians began to project faith realities into a world of the elite.

Born in Asia Minor, a disciple of Polycarp of Smyrna, Irenaeus had probably been sent to the Rhone Valley, in today's France, to be of assistance to the Greek communities scattered along that river from Marseilles to Arles to Vienne to Lyon. A goodly number of Greek colonies had been established in the region by the latter part of the second century. Their inhabitants supported themselves with metallurgy, ceramics, and a textile industry. Lyon, the commercial center of the industrial complex, had reached an estimated population of 200,000 inhabitants — quite a large number for the time.[23] Thus we find Irenaeus in the midst of a Greek world that had been transplanted to Gaul, first as a presbyter in one of the communities of Lyon and later as a bishop. In 177 he was dispatched to Rome to plead with the presbyters and doctors of the Roman communities and the bishop of Rome for a more conciliatory approach to

Montanism, a movement of impassioned prophecy and rigorous ethics that had originated in Asia Minor and proclaimed the imminent return of the Lord Jesus. In 189–90 he traveled to Rome once more, this time on the occasion of a dispute over the date of Easter, which in some communities, notably that of Ephesus, was celebrated on the fourteenth day of the month of Nisan (and thus in conformity with the Jewish tradition for the date of Passover), but in others on the following Sunday. Irenaeus functioned as the spokesperson of the churches of Gaul during this period, and for us today his writings form the oldest historical source of information on the Christian communities of Gaul.

What moved Irenaeus to write? What problem impelled him to take this decision? Irenaeus, let us remember, was a minister of the church. First he had been a presbyter. Now he was a bishop. He was well acquainted, then, with the contempt in which such ministers were held in certain Christian milieus, where they were regarded as far too ignorant and simple to guide the learned, cultivated members of the community along the pathways of the Christian life.

> Those who abandon the preaching of the church accuse the holy presbyters of ignorance. They fail to notice that it is of far more worth to be a simple but religious person than a subtle, but blasphemous and impudent, philosopher. [*Adv. Haer.*, V, 2, 20][24]

An erudite, learned Christianity was gradually making its appearance in the communities, and it marginalized a popular, grassroots kind of learning that treasured "Jesus' tradition handed down by way of the apostles and presbyters." Erudite Christianity was exceedingly hostile to Irenaeus' writings. Proud and arrogant, it claimed to have attained "perfect knowledge," while regarding the Christian knowledge of the unlettered as a second-rate, "adult catechism" kind of knowledge. Irenaeus vehemently reacted against this mentality.

> It cannot be said that [the apostles] preached before having perfect knowledge (Gk., *gnosis*), as some brazenly assert.

No, after our Lord rose from the dead and the apostles were clothed in strength from on high by the sudden coming of the Holy Spirit, they were filled with all gifts and had perfect knowledge, and only since then have they gone forth to the ends of the earth proclaiming the good news and the benefits God sends us and proclaiming to human beings the peace of heaven. They possessed, all equally and each in particular, the gospel of God. [*Adv. Haer.*, III, 1, 2][25]

Irenaeus qualifies this arrogant "knowledge" as "heresy" and combats it in his best-known work, *Against the Heresies* (*Adversus Haereses*).[26] This composition, then, is a defense of the knowledge available to the poor. The poor were looked down upon as persons of little literary formation. But among the poor were — at that time — the bishops, presbyters, and doctors. For Irenaeus, however, the great enemy of the faith was not "those of little learning," *oligomatheis* in his adversaries' contemptuous terminology, but precisely this contempt for them. Irenaeus cites the contrast between "gnosis," or perfect knowledge — the goal of the intellectual efforts of the heretics — and an apostolic tradition handed down by way of simple knowledge, but consisting in the expression of a life lived in the discipleship of Jesus. The apostolic tradition was simple indeed: "One God, creator of heaven and earth, proclaimed by the Law and by the prophets; and one Christ, God's Son" (*Adv. Haer.*, III, 2, 1).[27] Irenaeus poses the entire question of the apostolic tradition from the standpoint of a need to safeguard a popular knowledge of salvation, and develops his argumentation throughout book 3 of the *Adversus Haereses*. The precious treasure of the apostolic tradition is preserved in the hands of poor, uncultivated folk. Irenaeus is sure that the moment this tradition (or "memory") fell into the hands of the high and mighty it would be altogether emptied of its content. Hence his defense, tooth and nail, of the "apostolic tradition" against the "wisdom of the perfect," and the "disciples of truth" against the "sophists of the word" (*Adv. Haer.*, III, 24, 1), "who are not founded on the one rock, but on sand, and sand mixed with a great deal of clay."[28]

As a result of his meticulous, painstaking investigations,

Irenaeus is in a position to denounce once and for all the false "gnosis" he regards as much too full of chatter and theology. Here is his basic text:

> It is better and more profitable to know little or nothing but to live close to God by charity, than to imagine that one knows a great deal and has had a great many experiences but to become a falsifier and enemy of God. Therefore does Paul proclaim, "knowledge puffs up, but charity upbuilds." It is better, I say, to know nothing, to be ignorant of the cause of all that exists, but to believe in God and persevere in his love, than to be puffed up by knowledge and condemn the love that makes us live. It is of more value to abandon all search after knowledge in order to know Jesus Christ alone, God's Son, who was crucified for us, than to be drawn into impiety by the subtlety and hair-splitting of learned debates. [*Adv. Haer.*, II, 26, 1]

This is a highly charged text. Irenaeus' emphasis on charity must have stemmed from some familiar, concrete reality. Doubtless he was only all too personally familiar with the heretics' contempt for the poverty of the learning demonstrated by the presbyters, doctors, prophets, and other individuals guiding the communities. Marcion, Valentinus, Mark, and Simon Magus are only the vanguard of a veritable ocean of adversaries who threaten to drown the life of the communities in a flood of theoretical speculations, sterile discussions, and arrogant propositions. Irenaeus judges that the hour has come to say "Enough!" to these usurpers of Christian knowledge who say they know so much more than others.

> The Apostle exhorts us "not to know more than is fitting, but to know with prudence" (Rom. 12:3), lest we be expelled from the paradise of life for having eaten of the fruit of a knowledge like that of the heretics, which is calculated to "demonstrate" more than is suitable. [*Adv. Haer.*, V, 2, 20][29]

We need know only what God communicates to us in God's grace. Holy scripture teaches us everything necessary for salvation. But it is not a question-and-answer column, or an oracle, or a secret doctrine reserved to the knowledge of a special few endowed with superior holiness or intelligence. The truth offered to us by God is a truth for life, an orientation for our practice. The whole of Irenaeus' reflection centers on action, not on sterile theorizing. What is important to him is not the scriptures as such but the faith to which these scriptures testify (*Adv. Haer.*, III, 4, 1). It is not a matter of discussing texts, then, but of practicing acts of charity and justice. Truth is the fruit not of the lucubrations of theory, but of real contact with the Jesus event, by way of the apostolic tradition—that is, by way of the faithful memory of the Apostles, bishops, presbyters, and doctors. Thus the true church is founded on the practice of the life of the Apostles, and not on written texts. "Suppose the apostles had left nothing in writing. Should we then not have to abide by the content of the tradition bequeathed by them precisely to those to whom they entrusted the churches?" (*Adv. Haer.*, III, 4, 1).[30] The apostolic tradition is a practice, a behavior (*Adv. Haer.*, II, 22, 5; III, 3, 4; IV, 27, 1–32; V, 33, 3). The true church is any church founded on the practice of an apostle and his successors. This is why the ecclesial point of reference for Irenaeus, who lived in Gaul, far from apostolic churches like Antioch, Jerusalem, Ephesus, and Corinth, was perforce the church of Rome, which had likewise been founded by apostles. This is the burden of Irenaeus' celebrated text in *Adversus Haereses,* III, 3, 1–3, where he speaks of a convergence of the entire church upon Rome—a passage that later came to be interpreted entirely out of context. Irenaeus saw Rome as the defender of the knowledge of the marginalized against the arrogant "knowledge" of the high and mighty. Rome for him was the advocate of the humble learning of the "ignorant" in the face of the onslaughts of the heretics, who despised such a simple faith in the name of a superior revelation reversed to the perfect. Irenaeus views Rome neither as the capital of the empire nor as the head of a Christendom, but as a sister church with solid roots in the apostolic tradition.

Tirelessly our author repeats: "Faith is one and self-identical.

It can neither be swollen by the one who can expound upon it at great length, nor shrunken by the one who cannot" (*Adv. Haer.*, I, 10, 2–3). God bestows revelation on all, just as God makes the sun to shine upon all: "As the sun is one for the whole world, and always self-identical, so truth is preached in every corner, enlightening all who seek to come to a knowledge of the truth" (*Adv. Haer.*, I, 10, 2). As Irenaeus sees it, theological speculation should confine itself to questions of genuine concern to humanity, rather than on purely theoretical questions that are of interest solely to those who "preach to themselves" (*Adv. Haer.*, III, 2, 2).[31] But the latter speculation was all the rage, at least in the circles of the sophisticated. With irony, Irenaeus refutes this dubious approach to God and his Christ.

> Would someone know the manner of the Son's proceeding from the Father? Then let him listen well. This prolation, or generation, or pronunciation, or revelation—that is, this ineffable generation, by whatever name it be called is known to no one: not to Valentinus, not to Marcion, not to Saturninus, not to Basilides, not to the angels, not to the archangels, not to the principalities, and not to the powers. It is known to the Father alone, who has generated the Son who has been generated. [*Adv. Haer.*, II, 28, 4–6]

The irony of history, however, running precisely counter to that of Irenaeus, has contrived that, ever since the third century of the Christian Era, theology has immersed itself in the very speculation he condemns. We see this as early as the fourth century, with the appearance of an Arian heresy that, as Cardinal Newman observed a hundred years ago, had no connection with the faith of ordinary people.[32]

Tertullian

The third mighty exponent of a theology of the poor and marginalized is Tertullian. Born in Carthage about A.D. 157, Tertullian was a lawyer. He was converted to Christianity in the year 190 and died about 224. In Tertullian we have the vigorous expression of the most striking phenomenon of the earliest

Christian centuries: African Christianity. I shall examine this phenomenon more systematically in the next chapter. For the moment we need only recall the words of the eminent specialist in Roman history, Theodor Mommsen: "In the evolution of Christianity it is Africa that plays the most important role. Originating in Syria, Christianity achieved the status of a world religion only in and by way of Africa."[33]

The prodigy to which Mommsen is alluding is the Latinization of Christianity by way of the translation of holy scripture. Latin had come to be both the official language of the Roman Empire and a means of communication of crucial importance to the world of commerce. The translation of the scriptures into Latin, effected by nameless Christians over the course of the second century, altered the face of Christianity. Now the seaports of the *orbis terrarum* were open for good and all to this movement sprung from among people of low estate. It was at the service and in the defense of these lowly folk that Tertullian placed both his talents as an attorney and his extraordinary resources as a man of letters. As Mommsen, once more, reminds us: "It was in Africa that the infant church found its most fervent witnesses, its most talented representatives."[34] Among these, Tertullian occupies a place in the front rank, alongside Cyprian and, later, Augustine. Paradoxically, African Christianity was more Latin than its Roman counterpart. Until the middle of the third century Christian communities in Rome used Greek (that known as *koinu*, "common"). Words and expressions like "sacrament," "Trinity," "incarnation," "confession," "sacred scripture," "pagan," "gentile," even "pope" (a presbyter or bishop of whom the people were particularly fond) emerged from the historical experience of African Christianity, only later coming to be employed throughout the extent of Western Christianity.[35]

What does Tertullian do to secure for the poor a place in a culture continually threatened by manipulation on the part of the learned? He draws on his legal training and elaborates a most resourceful line of argumentation. A time-honored article of Roman legislation provided that anyone continuously occupying a piece of land for ten years or more could repel all claims and remain in peaceful possession of his property in virtue of what was called "prescription." This ancient law was profoundly in the popular interest, as it defended "possessors" against "proprietors." Brilliantly, Tertullian applied the legal principle of prescription to the use of the scriptures by Christians. His *On the Prescription of the Heretics* dates from the year 200.[36] There Tertullian propounds the thesis that Christians are the "possessors" of the sacred scriptures of the New Testament because it was they who first developed and used them. In vain, then, do the learned, the "heretics," appeal to them in support of their positions. They lack all prescriptive right to these scriptures. Far from constituting a sophism or other artifice, Tertullian's argument represents the intuition of a profound truth. Christians are seen to have occupied areas presumably belonging to the "wise and prudent." Having thus taken possession of these areas, they now have proprietary rights to them. The areas in question are those of discourse, doctrine, philosophy, wisdom, and the art of living. It had always been the learned who had taught the ignorant. With the advent of Christianity, however, things had suddenly been turned around. Suddenly the lowly are more knowledgeable than the wise. Suddenly the humble find themselves in serene possession of this new knowledge — in virtue of having been the first to occupy, by way of the apostolic succession, the "territory" of the reading of the Bible.

Thus the apostolic succession is interpreted within the framework of prescription. The Apostles were the first possessors in the history of this homesteading, this "invasion" of a territory traditionally constituting the property of the powerful and erudite. Tertullian's indictment is a powerful one:

> From the moment that Jesus Christ, our Lord, sent the apostles to preach, no other preachers are acceptable, as these alone have been constituted such by Christ. After all, no one knows the Father but the Son and the one to whom the Son may have revealed him. Now, Christ cannot have made such a revelation to any but the apostles whom he had sent to preach, and to preach precisely what he had revealed to them. This is the prescription to which we appeal. [*De Praescriptione*, 20] [37]

Here, as in other passages of Tertullian's masterpiece, we sense the contempt in which preachers were held in certain more erudite Christian circles. The ministers of the gospel frequently lacked all humanistic or classical formation, and hence failed to conform to the prevailing concept of what it was to be a teacher. But just as Irenaeus had defended the "ignorance" of the presbyters against the arrogance of the heretics, so Tertullian defended the knowledge of simple Christians against the false claims of the learned.

Tertullian's reasoning is reminiscent of Irenaeus in another passage as well. Refusing to yield an inch to an erudite knowledge he regards as the sheerest uselessness, curiosity, and vainglory, he inveighs against the presumption of the "knowers":

> Provided the content remain unaltered, delve and discuss all you like. Vent your curiosity. If some [scriptural] point seems ambiguous or obscure, race to some one of the bretheren who is endowed with the charism of knowledge, or who associates with capable folk, and who is as curious as you are. After all, he is making his own 'investigations'! But really, now: is it not better to be ignorant of what need not be known, once one knows what one ought? "It is your faith," said the Christ — and not your assiduity and versatility [*exercitatio*] in the interpretation of scripture — "that has saved you." Faith is a rule, it has its law, and salvation is in the observance of that law. *Exercitatio*, on the other hand, is merely curiosity, and has its glory in its reputation for sophistication. Then let *exercitatio* give place to faith, and glory to salvation. To know nothing against the rule is to know all things. [*De Praescriptione*, 15][38]

From what we read here, the Christian communities must have been without "capable folk," or even a "brother endowed with the charism of science" and fond of delving into the scriptures. And yet Christianity had gained such a rapid and broad popular consensus. In fact, in North Africa it constituted a genuine popular church. Tertullian rejoices:

> We came but yesterday, and already we occupy your land — all your domains, your cities, your suburbs, your forts, your townships, your assemblies, your barracks. We

have your tribes, your *collegia* [associations for mutual assistance], your court, your senate, and your forum. The temples? These you may keep. [*Apologeticum*, 37]

And Tertullian mounts a defense of this popular church through his writings. His works spread like wildfire and provided a solid basis for endeavors at the grass roots. "Every Christian artisan knows what is at stake and what truly matters: he finds God, and all theoretical questions about God he solves in practice and by action" (*Apologeticum*, 46). There is nothing in common "between a philosopher and a Christian, between a disciple of Greece and a disciple of heaven" (*Apologeticum*, 46), "between Athens and Jerusalem, between the Academy and the Church" (*De Praescriptione*, 7, 9).[39]

The workings of Tertullian's mind become crystal clear in a lesser-known work—the work that, nonetheless, is the "most taking" of his writings, to borrow von Campenhausen's expression.[40] We refer to the *De Testimonio Animae* ("The Testimony of the Soul"). The "rude and simple, uncultured and uncomplicated" soul finds God with greater ease than the one "formed in the schools and spouting the wisdom of Attica." The latter is all but a hopeless case, as it will never understand Christianity (*Testimonio*, I, 6). Simple, unsophisticated pagans demonstrate by their "longings" that, deep within them, they believe in God and eternal life. We see this in their expressions, Tertullian tells us. They say things like: "God sees us," or, "*Requiescat in pace*" ("May [the deceased] rest in peace").[41] Otherwise Jesus would have made a serious mistake in sending "simple fishermen rather than sophists" to be his missionaries (*Testimonio*, III, 3). Jesus must have understood faith to be a practice, a way of living and acting, and not a theoretical exercise, a line of reasoning. A philosopher knows only the "God of the philosphers" (*Adversus Marcionem* ["Against Marcion"], II, 27, 6), whose abode is afar off in a world of transcendency. A philosopher is shocked to hear of God's nearness to us in Jesus—in the humility of Jesus, in the cross of Jesus. To the philosopher, those who would ascribe to God such an abasement commit an offense against the divine majesty. It is utterly beyond the grasp of the heretic that the salvation of humankind is God's most glorious accomplishment and attribute (*"Gloria Dei, salus hominis"*); that the soul is "naturally Christian" (*"anima naturaliter Christiana"*) if it preserves its simplicity; that faith is founded on the philosophically absurd (*"Credo quia absurdum"*); or finally, that Christianity is "hidden from the learned" and "revealed to the merest children" (Matt. 11:25). Tertullian's compendious expressions still ring with the passion with which this giant of the past embarked on the defense of a church in which "the poor evangelize the poor," as we would put it today. It is impossible to imagine two more diametrically opposed pieces of writing than Tertullian's *Testimonio* and the work of another African, written just two hundred years later: the *De Catechizandis Rudibus* ("Catechizing the Unlettered") of Augustine of Hippo. Augustine's thinking is just the opposite of Tertullian's. According to Augustine the *rudes*, the uneducated, are necessarily without the Christian knowledge of which they have need, and so must be "catechized." Tertullian and Augustine's catechist are worlds apart, then. They are completely contrary models of church. Manifestly, between A.D. 200 and 400 the church was to have undergone a Copernican revolution.

Commentators like to attribute Tertullian's passion to his temperament. Doubtless there is something to be said in favor of this hypothesis, since on one occasion Tertullian himself confessed his lack of patience. But surely there was more to it than that. After all, social and political reasons for Tertullian's bruising discourse abounded. The church was genuinely in danger of succumbing to an elitist thinking. It was on the point of becoming a "grand church," with precious little memory of its origins and a great deal of compromise with society. When Tertullian writes, with such conviction: "Where three are present, even if they are laity, there is the church" ("Ubi tres, ecclesia est, licet laici)," he is defending the prehierarchical, community model of church in which no one claims to "know" any more than anyone else, provided all know Christ's cross.[42]

Thus Tertullian's niche in the vast hall of apologists for primitive Christianity is secure. He is another great defender of a popular knowledge against the knowledge that vaunts its imagined superiority and calls itself by the name of "gnosis," knowledge par excellence. For Tertullian, the philosophers are the "patriarchs of the heretics" (*Testimonio,* III, 1), who threaten to dilute Christianity into just another spirituality bereft of a recollection of God and the covenant with the poor.[43] Philosophers, in Tertullian's judgment, place more trust in their own "inspirations" than in the historical, objective word of God handed down by way of the prophets and apostles. They are vain. They are dragged hither and yon by "curiosity"—an expression of superiority that was fostered by the Greek tradition. St. Paul himself had warned Christians against philosophy (Col. 2:8), and scripture recalled that Christians are to seek God "in integrity of heart" (Wis. 1:1)—not go running off after a "new Stoic, Platonic, or dialectical Christianity" (*De Praescriptione,* 7, 11). Tertullian's principal text to this effect is also the clearest expression of his thinking as a whole:

> What can Athens and Jerusalem have in common? Or the Academy and the Church? Or heretics and Christians? Our teaching has come from the Porch (*Stoa*) of Solomon, whose doctrine is that God is to be sought in the simplicity of the heart. We pity those who have invented a Stoic, Platonic, dialectical Christianity. We have no need of "curiosity": Jesus Christ has come. We have no need of scholarly investigations: we have the Gospel. From the moment we believe, we have no need of any knowledge but that of faith. After all, the first article of our faith is that faith alone is worthy of belief. [*De Praescriptione,* 7, 9-13][44]

PART TWO

THE MISSION

CHAPTER VI

A Great Popular Movement

The most impressive thing about the history of primitive Christianity is the astonishing speed with which the movement spread within such a short period of time. It is no exaggeration to say that the first Christian centuries were the greatest missionary centuries of all. Never have Christians been more strongly motivated to propagate their faith than immediately after the birth of their church.

THE GEOGRAPHY OF THE MOVEMENT

Let us briefly examine the geography of this expansion, following the study by Norbert Brox.[1] By the close of the first century, Christian church communities were already in existence in Palestine, in Syria (in the region around Antioch), on Cyprus, throughout Asia Minor (first Ephesus, then elsewhere), in Greece, and even in the capital of the empire, Rome. Any Christian presence in Alexandria (the great seaport of Egypt), Illyria and Dalmatia (today's Yugoslavia), Gaul, or Spain so early in the missionary endeavors of the church is something of a matter of conjecture. By the end of the second century, however, the geographical picture of Christianity was truly impressive. Not only were there new communities in the regions just mentioned, but Christianity was being established in eastern Syria (moving outward from Edessa, in Osroene), Mesopotamia, Egypt, southern Italy, Gaul, Germany, Spain, and especially northern Africa, in the regions around Carthage, such as Numidia, Mauritania, and Proconsular Africa (today's Tunisia, Algeria, Morocco, and Libya). Not Rome but Asia Minor had been the launching pad for the western expansion of the church, as we may gather from the cases of Irenaeus, Justin, and others.

From the end of the second century to the beginning of the fourth, the principal documented development of the church was in the field of organization. The church of Alexandria, at the mouth of the Nile in Egypt, was extending its influence not only along the Nile Valley but to more remote regions as well, and had established its hegemony over the important Coptic sector of Christianity from which the monastic movement was soon to spring. The influence of the Alexandrian church actually reached northern Arabia, along the eastern bank of the River Jordan. Another focus of expansion was Syria, with its "theological school" of Antioch and its important synods. The missions of the Antiochian church extended as far as Armenia, Mesopotamia, and, beyond the frontiers of the Roman Empire itself, Persia. Armenia especially, in the early part of the fourth century, was the land of a vigorous Christianity. A third mission center was Asia Minor, with its burgeoning rural Christianity overflowing from the cities. In Greece, in the Balkan regions, and in the valley of the Danube, progress was less impressive. But in Rome the Church now grew to number tens of thousands, and a central Italian (Neapolitan) Christianity sprang into being. As for northern Italy, we hear of pockets of Christianity in cities like Milan, Aquileia, and Ravenna. There were Christians in some of the cities of Sardinia and Sicily. The rise of Christianity in northern Africa, where a missionary awareness was particularly strong, is especially noteworthy in the period from the closing decades of the second century to the early years of the fourth. We have little information about Spain, Gaul, Germany (Xanten), or Britain. Tertullian proudly asserts that Christianity has now outdistanced the mighty Roman armies themselves.[2]

The euphoria generated by this sensational expansion occasioned the belief among Christian generations of the fourth century that the whole world, or at least the whole urban or civilized world, had now heard the word of the gospel. Thomas Aquinas would echo this conviction as late as the thirteenth century, and claim that any who had not yet heard that word must live "in the bush, among brute beasts" (*"in silvis inter bruta animalia"*).

SOCIOLOGICAL PROFILE OF THE MOVEMENT

Christianity's sociological penetration was no less impressive. Scholarship suffers from a dearth of monographs on the sociology of primitive Christianity. Most authors, then, simply repeat that Christianity penetrated among rich and poor, among owners and workers alike, without attempting to develop these assertions in any detail. To a limited extent, I will attempt to make up for this lack of monographic information by examining some of the data of the Roman martyrology, whose characterizations of the saints of the first four Christian centuries are of indisputable sociological value. Here I perceive the following sociogram: The Christians (or the saints, at any rate) are laborers, poor hermits, soldiers (in the reign of Diocletian), women who have fled society to repair to the desert, married couples, rich persons who have been converted and have embraced the eremitical life or the service of others, bishops, charitable persons, the Fathers of the desert.[3]

The lives of all of these saints — men and women, rich and poor, educated and uneducated — are linked by a common trait: the experience of marginality, especially the marginality of martyrdom or life in the desert. Martyrdom and the desert are the two sociological models of the Christian mission that prevail in the early centuries, as we may gather from the repercussion of the lives of the saints (the "examples" so precious to early Christians) on the Christian people. The saints could not have had this effect on the Christian memory had their special experiences not struck a responsive chord in the general Christian sensibility. Christians everywhere must have been undergo ing the same types of experiences. Thus the martyrology is a mirror of the sociology of Christian mission, and this is the reason for its value in the study of Christian origins.

CONCEPTIONS OF MISSION

Christians have perceived mission in various ways through the course of history. In the third and fourth centuries the notion cropped up in the church that not only revelation but mission itself had closed with the death of the last apostle. A literal understanding of Jesus' words concerning the apostolic mission (Matt. 28:19; Mark 16:20; Acts 1:8) led to an understanding of mission as the specific task of Christ's Apostles rather than one of the post-apostolic church. It was supposed that the Apostles had already reached the "ends of the earth" and thus prepared the world for Jesus' glorious return. The concept was a long-lived one. We find traces of it as late as the sixteenth century, with the myth of the apostle Thomas' journey to India and Brazil. No one today any longer entertains such a notion explicitly. But we must observe that this way of regarding things has frequently clouded, even in modern times, the actual, concrete data of the first Christian mission. We like to attribute everything to the Apostles. The facts of the ancient post-apostolic mission are often forgotten. Even today this constitutes an obstacle to the reconstitution of the ancient missionary reality.

Another faulty understanding of mission is the one that projects upon the mentality of Jesus and the Apostles the image of the "great church" that Christianity would of course one day be. This outlook on mission is roughly the following: As he was bent on founding an institution destined to outlast the ages, Jesus was concerned, at least from the beginning of his public life, with gathering a group of twelve Apostles, to whom he would entrust his church after his death, resurrection, and return to the right hand of his Father. As his hour approached, he invested St. Peter with the hierarchical power of "binding and loosing." That is, he authorized St. Peter to take command. At the Last Supper he conferred upon his Apostles priestly ordination, complemented after the resurrection with the power of forgiving sins. Finally, before ascending to heaven he dispatched the Apostles to preach his gospel throughout the world, enjoining them to transmit their functions and powers to successors, that the church might never deviate from its institutional foundation. In this perspective the purpose of the mission of Jesus and his Apostles was to found a new religion, complete with institutional framework and, especially, with a hierarchical priesthood as the necessary means for the functioning of the church in particular and of the Christian religion in its totality.

There is an interesting article on this question by J. Moingt, himself a priest, who asserts: "There is no longer to be found any exegete who would recount the origin of Christianity in this fashion."[4] And yet one has to admit that it is on this anachronistic model, based on our experience today rather than on an analysis of the documents that have come down to us from early Christian times, that we continue to conceptualize early Christianity. The eschatological climate pervading the early Christian literary production, the primitive Christian enthusiasms for the perceptible action of the Holy Spirit that glows on every page, the force of the Jesus event in all its detail, stand in stark contrast to any description of the church as a planned, premeditated institution. The contrast between Jesus with other religious geniuses, even with the Buddha or Zarathustra, is crisp and clear: unlike the founders of religions, Jesus was unconcerned with preserving his project in writing, with establishing prescriptions or rules, or with instituting rituals and worship.[5]

How, then, should we conceptualize the first Christian mission? Eusebius of Caesarea gives us the answer in a beautiful passage:

A very large number of disciples were—in those times—marked in their spirit by the Word of God with a most lively love of wisdom (*philosophia*). First they heeded the Lord's counsel to go and distribute their goods to the poor. Then they left their country to carry out the mission of evangelists, preaching the word of faith to those who had not yet heard it and handing on the Scriptures and the Good News. . . . We should find it impossible to list the

names of all those who, as the first successors of the
apostles, became shepherds and evangelists of the communities of the entire world. We record the memory only of
those who have written for us the Tradition and teaching
of the apostles.[6]

The missionaries were, then, largely anonymous. It would be
difficult, if not impossible, to understand the Christian mission
without reference to the anonymous agents of that mission. The
propagators of Christianity were not only Saints Peter and Paul
but the centurion Cornelius, Lydia the dye merchant, Saints
Priscilla and Aquila, fishers, seafarers, merchants, mistresses of
households, artisans. Humble, lowly folk who had opened
themselves to conversion by the memory and imitation of Jesus'
practice gave away all they owned and went out to the mission.
How else might we explain the electrifying rapidity of
Christianity's expansion, in the absence of support from the
state, official financing, and friendship with the great ones of
the world?

But equally, mission was not the sole prerogative of these
"specialists" who left all things to go and preach in the cities of
the empire (Matt. 10:9–14). In the beginning, everyone was a
missionary — by the simple fact that the Christian way of life, the
new community life of sisterly and brotherly love ("See how they
love one another!") had a challenging and contagious effect on
the environment. It is in the events of everyday living that we
must search for the secret of primitive Christianity's rapid
expansion. The Apostles had died. The question of the Christian
memory, then, had become more pressing. Now all Christians
were concerned to revive the practice of Jesus and the Apostles
and to solve, in community, the problems that arose in their
everyday lives. This is not to deny the appearance in the
community of new "specialists" — persons "sent," like Paul,
Barnabas, and others. But the wellspring of these very specialists
was the living, converted community of the followers of the lord
Jesus. Thus the mission organized itself in a way that is called
"charismatic," and this is a subject to which we must return
later. The mission was not at first the monopoly of specialists. It
belonged to the entire community. The history of the church in

those times was nothing more nor less than the history of mission. Mission was a way of conceiving one's whole life, a way of bestowing meaning on the whole of life, as José Comblin emphasizes in several of his works.

An important part of this non-specialist mission consisted in the mission of the elderly. These were the great communicators in the beginnings of Christianity. Their part in mission was merely a prolongation of a phenomenon that had already begun to manifest itself in the synagogues and Jewish communities in which "elders" (the older men) had a relevant role. Primitive Christianity made admirable use of these "presbyters," defending these elderly persons against the contempt of those who regarded them as ignorant and unlettered. Primitive Christianity was unconcerned with a sophisticated culture. It was centered on the preservation of a memory. The Christian life has never been exempt from the threat of the "uprooting" of its memory, and this was as true in ancient times as it is today. A forgetfulness of what we are about has frequently managed to infect the living social body of Christianity. The meaning of tradition becomes distorted, and Christians begin to lose an awareness of their historical roots. Then Christianity petrifies in laws and juridicisms, dogma and dogmatisms, sacraments and a closed, codified, rule-ridden, dead sacramentalism.

At such times, Christians are starved for Christianity. Their only spiritual food is what they receive from systems that have managed to install themselves in the Christian social body and rob it of its meaning. In these cases the best antidote is the memory of the elderly, who have been the witnesses of these processes of the uprooting of the Christian social body. The elderly remember. "This is not the way it used to be." This is the approach taken by the Gospel of St. Luke. Luke seems to have been written for a middle-class community with precious little understanding of the theology of marginality. The third Gospel is a powerful demonstration that, "of old"—two or three generations earlier—the question of marginality and sharing among Christians was a serious one. Thus, for example, Luke cites the case of Zacchaeus, someone from the middle class who had given "half of his goods" to the poor.[7] This is very much how the Gospel of St. John functions as well. Its elderly author had interiorized his precious memories of Jesus in long years of Christian experience. Later, Papias of Hierapolis would write his five-book work entitled *Exegeses of the Words of the Lord* (*Logion Kuriakon Exēgeseis*), a collection of information on the practices and words of Jesus as gathered in the discipleship of the apostle St. John.[8] Here, then, the memory of one "presbyter" relied on that of another, earlier one, and the great current of the apostolic tradition was under way.

Primitive Christianity treated its elderly with great tenderness. True, they were no longer "useful" for the heavy work of producing food or providing for their children's security. But they found a special community service all their own in catechesis, in counseling, in the preservation of the community tradition. Thus the solidity of the Christian social memory rested on the individual memory of the elderly, who formed as it were the root of the community life. The elements of this social approach to the construction of the Christian memory in ancient times are still available to us today not only in the literary sources, but also, and especially, in the liturgy, both the eucharistic and the baptismal. The eucharistic liturgy included that texture of commemorative material that eventually received the name of Liturgy of the Word. It was originally a free conversational exchange, with discussion, counsels, and readings. In this manner Christian groups created for themselves a universe of Christian discourse that may not have been overconcerned with "what really happened," literally and physically, in the days when Jesus walked the earth, but which was certainly concerned to preserve the memory of Jesus in a way that would nourish the evangelical life and the new Christian lifestyle in society. The transmission of this universe of discourse was, then, "formally" faithful. That is, it faithfully recalled Jesus' manner of being and acting.

As for its "material content," many elements that were de facto available to Christianization, and later would indeed be Christianized, were not present from the outset, such as feminism, black consciousness, or the various shapes and forms taken by the authentic Christian life down through a long history to come. These are later themes. They did not flourish in the universe of discourse developed by the first mission because the objective conditions for their perception were lacking. But conversely, certain themes of this discourse were later to be "forgotten," as for example the incompatibility between Christianity and economic exploitation. The subject of a great deal of discussion in early times, this theme began to slip out of the Christian discourse with Clement of Alexandria, as we shall see.

There is a wonderful passage concerning the non-specialist, anonymous agents of the Christian mission in a letter written by one of their number to a certain pagan, one Diognetus. Diognetus had expressed curiosity on three points. First, why did Christians keep their distance from both the Jews and the pagans? Second, what was this "charity," this Christian love of neighbor, about which he had heard so much? And finally, if the Christian religion was indeed the religion of God, why had it appeared so late in the history of humanity? The *Letter to Diognetus* dates from the latter part of the second century, and was found among the works of Justin in a library in Strasbourg, the original having perished in a fire in 1870.[9] Here is the passage in question:

Christians are no different from the rest of men as regards their country, language, or customs. They have not their own cities, they are not distinguished by their foreign languages, they lead no extraordinary life. . . . Rather, living in cities Greek and barbarian alike, as is the lot of each, and observing local usages as to clothing, food, and customs, they manifest the wonderful nature of their life, which all look upon as extraordinary. They live indeed in their native countries, but as if they were foreigners. They share as citizens in all things, but endure what aliens must. Every foreign land is a country to them, and every country a foreign land. They marry and have children, but they never expose their infants. They share a common board, but not a common bed. While living in the flesh, they do not live according to the flesh. They live on earth, while enjoying the citizenship of heaven. They conform to the law, while going beyond it in their lives. They love all persons, though all persecute them. Strange and unfamiliar as they are, they are by that very fact concerned. But when

they are handed over to death they receive life. In poverty,
they enrich many. Deprived of all things, they abound in
goods. They are condemned, but in the midst of dishonor
they sense their glorification. Vilified, yet are they just.
Outraged, yet are they blessed. Insulted, they honor others. They do good, yet are punished as malefactors. When
punished, they rejoice as having received a new birth of
life. Jews are hostile to them as being not of their race.
Greeks persecute them. But none of their enemies can
name the reason for their hatred. In sum, what the soul is
to the body, that Christians are to the world: as the soul is
diffused throughout all the members of the body, so are
the Christians distributed throughout the cities of the
universe.[10]

The text stands in no need of commentary. Still, let us point up
the theology of marginality underlying it.

MARGINALITY AND REASONS FOR THE SPREAD OF CHRISTIANITY

Christians today constantly ask questions about the primitive
Christian mission. They wonder whether it went hand in hand
with an economic movement, as it does today in Latin America.
Or they ask whether mission was exclusively the work of the
poor. They ask what it was about the Christian life that exerted
such a powerful attraction on the pagans of the Roman Empire
and converted them in such great numbers. Let us try to make
some response to these questions.

As to the first: Not much has been done in the way of an
investigation of the relationship between the spread of Christianity and the economic expansion of the Roman system. The
question is asked from the standpoint of an experience typical of
later Christianity, where the expansion of Christianity went
hand in hand with the spread of capitalism, for example in the
formation of the Latin American Christendoms. The rulers of
Spain and Portugal fostered the Christian mission by way of an
alliance between the ecclesiastical estate and the expansionist,

militaristic civil state. The early Latin American mission, then, represented the cream of society, while the primitive Christian missions were authentically popular movements in civil society, maintaining no alliance with the power brokers of political society. In and of itself, it is altogether normal that economic movements and religious movements should go together. Irenaeus belonged to a movement of "Greeks" who colonized the region of the Rhone in Gaul. Justin traveled to Rome within an economico-commercial movement that brought "Greek" colonies to the capital of the empire. Many missioners were also artisans, like St. Paul. They were slave and free, they were merchants, fishers, small property owners, mistresses of households, soldiers.

The second question raised by today's Christians can be formulated thus: Will it not be something of an exaggeration to assert that the primitive Christian mission was carried on by, and addressed to, the poor and marginalized alone? Did Christianity not likewise spread among folk of the middle or even wealthy class? This image of a proletarian church, then, a church of slaves, a church of the poor alone, is challenged. True, the oldest Christian documents certify clearly enough that members of the privileged classes were converted to Christianity from the beginning. Some owned goods and property, others had a literary formation evincing their bourgeois origin, others again owned slaves. What is forgotten in posing the question is that the acceptance of Christianity in those times meant a conversion, and not only a "spiritual conversion" but a conversion of one's whole lifestyle. When we call the primitive church a church of the marginalized, we mean that any members of the upper class who were converted to Christianity had to be converted to marginality as well, becoming what Antonio Gramsci has called "organic intellectuals" — persons committed to a genuinely popular movement. The four figures of Christian tradition briefly presented in part 1 of this book — St. Paul, St. Irenaeus, St. Justin, and Tertullian — show what is meant by this. They are respectively a Pharisee, a bishop, a philosopher, and an attorney. But they are all committed to their option for the poor. Jesus himself, who had made an option for the "mass of those of no account" (*'am ha 'arets*) — for those who did not belong to his own class, according to the analysis of Father François Houtart quoted above—gave the definitive example. Being rich, he became a slave and "took on the condition of a slave."[11]

Finally, why did the Christian life exert such a strong attraction in those early days? Were conditions especially favorable to such a rapid expansion? If so, what were they? Modern authors cite a number of such conditions. These are five of them:

1. Unlike the other mystery religions of the age, none of which survived late antiquity (or indeed the third and fourth centuries), Christianity bore the stamp of universalism. It issued its call to all humanity without regard to nationality or national origin. "At bottom, Dionysus and Orpheus remained Hellenic, Atis Anatolian, Adonis Syrian, Isis and Osiris Egyptian—ever bound up with their peoples. Christianity was addressed to all."[12] By reason of its supranational orientation, Christianity formed natural ties with a form of the Greek language called *Koine* ("common" to all parts of the empire). *Koine* was the vehicle of Hellenistic culture and, at least in the cities, it unified minds and hearts. Thus Christianity could be propagated from Palestine to Spain, and from Ethiopia to Ireland, in a single "urban language." In the countryside, as it happens, innumerable languages were spoken. We call them "vernaculars," or "dialects." Only from the fourth century onward did the church attempt to respond to the challenge of rural culture by creating parishes in the modern sense. At first the Christian mission was, for all practical purposes, bilingual. On the level of universal or "catholic" communication, Greek was used. On the level of communication with local communities, the many local languages were used. Thus Irenaeus relates that he attempted to learn Celtic, and Tertullian says that the presbyters who struggled at the side of the people had to learn not only Latin but the indigenous languages of northern Africa as well.[13]

2. A second circumstance particularly favoring the Christian mission was the mobility enjoyed by merchants and artisans of the Roman Empire. The empire had an excellent infrastructure at its disposition in terms of transportation by sea, river, and land (the famous *viae*, or ways). Christianity had these same commercial and military routes available for its propagation.

First was the Mediterranean Sea, a veritable maritime highway connecting the rivers that led deep into the continent, such as the Nile, the Danube, and the Rhone. This mobility resulted in certain particularities in the formation of Christianity. The church of second-century Gaul spoke Greek, as it had been formed by Greek colonists. The African church spoke Latin, the language of the central administration, which suppressed the African languages, or at least attempted to do so. The church of Alexandria spoke Greek. On the other hand, the people who dwelt along the valley of the Nile were Coptic and never willingly accepted Hellenization. Thus the great Roman communication and transportation network entailed a negative consequence for Christianity as well. Missionaries did not always speak the language of the people and so were tempted to mold an elitist Christianity wafting above the heads of poor folk. We perceive this danger as early as the age of Irenaeus. "The world is at peace because of the Romans," he says, "and we [Christians] may move about without fear, by highway and by sea, whithersoever we wish."[14] The celebrated "Roman Peace," the *Pax Romana*, was actually only an authoritarian peace, one maintained with an iron fist and a sharp sword. Various sectors of the Christian mission regarded this "peace" with sympathetic eyes, however. It furnished their apostolic labors with mobility. Two great periods of the Roman Peace proved to be especially profitable to the mission: the period from A.D. 177 to 202 (to the persecution under Septimius Severus), and again from 260 to 304 (between the peace of Gallienus and the great persecution of Diocletian). But in fact, as we shall see, these periods of peace were times of crisis for the Christian memory, periods in which important elements of the Christian message were forgotten.

3. Another extrinsic reason for the success of the primitive Christian mission is to be found in Judaism. Christianity was a branch on the living trunk of Judaism. As such, it benefited from the structures created by Jewish tradition and known under the names of diaspora, synagogue, rabbinical pedagogy, biblical reading, and the already mentioned ministry of the presbyters. We should not forget the great contribution of the Judaism of the diaspora to the Christian mission.

Another value inherited from Judaism by primitive Christianity was the shift in the accent of the community experience from worship and ritual to ethics. Judaism presented itself to the eyes of the world as a "philosophy," a way of life for people who think, rather than as a cult. Hence the accent on "the Book," or the reading of the Bible, on the discussion of problems and on the formation of community, which prevailed over ritualism and attachment to worship for its own sake, so typical of other religions of the age. From the outset, then, Christianity inherited a worship that was not "overdone." In vivid contrast with the other mystery religions, Christianity was typified by moderation in its "religious" expressions.

Another element of enormous value for the facilitation of missionary labors was the synagogic principle, based on the autonomy of the local community. We shall focus on this more explicitly later in this book. Meanwhile, the theology underlying this organizational principle was that of the full salvific potential of each and every community. Every Christian community is self-sufficient when it comes to leading its members to salvation. This theological groundwork enabled the communities to tolerate, with all equanimity, the pluralism prevailing among them. The movement of local churches was always pluralistic, for there were always peculiar accents and particular problems. But all of the churches remained basically bound to the one Jesus. The Christian movement was intolerant only of breaches in the communion prevailing among the churches. How this insistence on unity functioned in practice is verifiable in documents that have survived the centuries. We refer to the quarrels that took place around A.D. 190 concerning the date of the annual celebration of Easter. The thinking of the communities was altogether clear. Pluralism, yes. Breach, no. St. John's Gospel, alluding to the inevitable disagreements among communities, but insisting that these need not sunder the unity of these communities with one another, tells us: "In the Father's house are many dwellings." Side by side with Johannine communities were Pauline and Petrine communities. Each had to recognize the legitimacy of the pluralism of the other, lest the unity for which the Lord had prayed at the Last Supper be shattered.[15] Understandably, this pluralism in unity facilitated the practice of mission. Bureaucratic centralization was absent. All Christians felt a responsibility for the spread of the Reign of God in this world.

4. Still another circumstance that smoothed the way for the Christian mission was religious tolerance on the part of the Roman bureaucracy. No contemporary author any longer questions the fact of this tolerance. The controversy begins when we inquire into the relative importance for the development of Christianity of the persecutions on the one hand and the spirit of tolerance on the other. Until recently, a maximalist appraisal originating with Eusebius of Caesarea and tending to speak of the first three centuries of Christian history as an "age of persecutions" has predominated. But this interpretation is scarcely compatible with the incontestable fact of religious tolerance on the part of the Roman civil authorities, or with the celebrated "syncretism" that the Roman bureaucracy not only permitted but fostered, in order to win popular consent to the imperial structures. Recent authors are more discreet in their appraisal of the persecutions and their influence on the Christian mission. A recent work by André Mandouze discusses the question, and I shall return to it when treating the martyrs.[16]

5. Finally, Christianity laid a solid foundation in civil society by fostering "colleges"—the associations of mutual assistance that meant so much to the poor populations of the Roman Empire. The colleges enjoyed a secure juridical status, and we have good reason to think that the communities organized these associations for the defense of the daily interests of the people wherever they managed to establish themselves. This attachment of the Christian mission to the everyday problems of the people surely facilitated the spread of the new religion.

All of the reasons listed here, as well as others perhaps equally important, surely contributed to the spread of Christianity throughout the Roman Empire. Yet all of them, even taken together, fail to provide an adequate explanation for that spread. The main reason for the spread of Christianity lay not in a convergence of favorable circumstances, but in the nature of the Christian message itself. That message shifted the whole of human living into an altogether new context. When all is said and done, it was the Christian message itself that so many persons seeking the meaning of life and the world found so irresistibly attractive. What was it specifically in that message that proved so powerful? Its eschatology. Christian tradition refers to the "last things"—*novissima* in Latin, the *novissima tempora*, the "last times," the "last hour" (in Greek, *eschatē hora*). What was special about the Christian message is that it endowed the "last age" or "last hour" with a crucial importance. Christianity transformed life into a historical drama. In earlier religions of the empire, life had been only a movement of the "eternal return of the same," a cycle analogous to the cycles of nature. But in Christianity, the life of the individual as well as that of any collectivity is marked by the drama of the time to come, by the Reign to be realized, by the hour that will be the last.

On the individual plane, eschatology soon came to be confused with the perspective of personal salvation, which acquired such importance in Christian reflection with its themes of judgment after death, resurrection, and eternal life or immortality. These are surely important matters. But they are not the only, or even the most important, themes in primitive Christianity. Early Christianity laid its heaviest stress on the theme of the Reign of God to be built in this world. Emphasis, then, was on the collective aspect of eschatology. This is what was singled out by the Jewish and Jewish Christian prophetic writings describing an "apocalypse" (a revelation) of the events of the end of the world. The purpose of this apocalyptic literature was to establish the urgency of the mission and its importance for all creation. It was composed in the last centuries before the Christian Era and in the first Christian centuries. One of the writings of this genre, the Book of Revelation, or Apocalypse of St. John, came to be included in the New Testament canon.[17] The Book of Revelation has many aspects, but one of them is its reprobation of all of the power of this world, as well as the theological necessity, as it were, of the persecution of Christians by the powers of this world.

The apocalyptic writings had a decisive influence on early Christian mission. They demonstrated that that mission is the work of God, God's labors in the building of the Reign (John 10:1-16; Mark 12:1-12; Luke 4:2-3; Matt. 15:52). The whole world lives the eschatological drama, and all can share in it by the cross. Jesus' resurrection is the sign of the victory of his cross over time and history, the anticipation of the future resurrection of women and men and the definitive establishment of the Reign of God. This eschatological, apocalyptic vision of mission predominated among Christians until the third and fourth century. Then it was gradually marginalized and replaced by a less powerful vision. The latter, reaching its highest expression in St. Augustine, diluted the traditional emphasis on the end-time and reduced eschatology to a doctrine and a "spirituality."[18]

CHAPTER VII

Mission Cycles of the First Two Centuries

The Christian mission proceeded in cycles. It could not have been otherwise. The particularities of eras, places, and persons make it impossible for any historical movement to exempt itself from history's diversified, intermittent character. Thus the first Christian mission cycle was brusquely interrupted by the Christian flight from Jerusalem (A.D. 70), the city that had been the center from which that cycle radiated, just as the Arab invasions in northern Africa would later destroy the Christianity that flourished in that region. Jean Daniélou emphasizes the cyclical nature of the apocryphal New Testament writings, which seem to come from a series of different geographical locations: "The apocryphal writings of the New Testament are divided into cycles: the cycle of Peter, the cycle of Thomas, the cycle of Philip, the cycle of John. These cycles seem actually to refer to determinate geographical environments."[1]

THE FIRST CENTURY

The Palestinian Cycle

The apostolic cycles of the first century, then, were four: the Palestinian, the Antiochian, the Asian, and the East Syrian. In Clévenot's felicitous phrase, the first missionary cycle began with a "new Jewish community in Jerusalem" between A.D. 35 and 40.[2] This community of Christian Jews was made up of devout Galileans, persons with more affinity for the Pharisaic milieus than for those of the Sadducees, and resembling to a certain extent the Essenes of Qumran—without, however, the obligatory celibacy entailed in a thoroughgoing contempt for time and the temporal, and especially without the a-historical ideology so important to the Essene experiment. Acting "in the name of Jesus," this new community had aroused public discussion by an incident at the Beautiful Gate of the temple (Acts 3:1–10). The discussion centered on the question of power. Who was this Jesus in whose name this "wonder" had been worked (Acts 4:17–20)? What was unsettling for the community at large was obviously a power that could get out of control. Rabbi Gamaliel, a respected Pharisee, closed the discussion and opened the gates of history to the new community (Acts 5:35–39). On the internal level, one of the central issues was the financial question. This community claimed to heal even breaches in a brotherly and sisterly communion by taking financial relationships in hand, and Peter placed his authority behind this orientation (Acts 4:32–5:11). As for the question of Jews who had adopted the Hellenistic culture, however, the solution was not as ready to hand, and we must await Paul's intervention to discern an evolution in this delicate matter.

The Antiochian Cycle

The second mission cycle is Antiochian and takes shape between 43 and 49. Stephen, of the Hellenistic group, perceived that the church was more than merely a Jewish community and dared to confront the priests of the Sanhedrin, the usurpers of the popular religion (Acts 7:52), with his view. And we have the first formal indictment of clericalism in the history of the church, antedating the very coining of the term. Stephen was stoned to death in 36 or 37, and a persecution broke out against the Hellenists. The latter fled to Antioch, capital of the Roman province of Syria and center of the Hellenistic East, Alexandria's great rival and the seat of an important Jewish colony. Barnabas, from Cyprus, was Jerusalem's delegate to the new experiment in Antioch, the place where Jesus' followers first received the name of Christians (*Christianoi*). With the establishment of the Christian community of Antioch, the church properly so-called sprang into being—the *ekklēsia*, the assembly of Christians dwelling in the Greek cities of the Roman Empire (Acts 11:26). Barnabas went in search of Paul of Tarsus, and between A.D. 45 and 48 the pair embarked on the first great missionary journey "to the pagans." While Christians in Jerusalem were experiencing times of tension with the central power of Rome, and using circumcision as a symbol of resistance, the Apostles in Cilicia were insisting on the rights of the uncircumcised and thereby provoking the crisis of the year 49 and the so-called Council of Jerusalem (Acts 15:19). But Paul was imbued with a strong missionary spirit and founded communities in Thessalonika (A.D. 51), Corinth (50), Philippi (50), and many other locales. And Western European Christianity was born.

The Asian Cycle

Beginning in the year 70—when the Roman emperor had the city of Jerusalem and its temple destroyed—the center of the Christian mission shifted to the city of Ephesus, in western Asia Minor, called by the Roman administration the "Proconsulate of Asia." The Roman proconsul resided in Ephesus. Here the Pauline and Johannine currents converged, creating a Christianity closely bound up with Hellenized and Orientalized popular religion, and thereby contrasting with the faith of the "pillars" of Palestine (St. James, St. Peter), which was colder and lacking religious experiences. In Asia Minor religiousness was altogether lively and had the general tenor of a quest, a journey or pilgrimage. Here religion was a philosophy of life. The thinking and feeling of Christian writers were in tune with this environment, where good acts were judged to emanate from good spirits and evil ones from "demons" flitting about in the air. Astrology and the horoscope flourished. This was all assimilated by Christianity, which dug in its heels only when the uniqueness of Christ and of the "folly of the cross" was impugned. Typical of this Asian mission were the New Testament Letters to the

Ephesians and to the Colossians, which constitute the first attempt at a reinterpretation of Christianity in a new cultural environment.[3]

The East Syrian Cycle

Still in the first century, we have a fourth missionary cycle, in the interior of Syria. Daniélou insists on the importance of this cycle, unfamiliar as it is because of the constant penchant of Christian sources to emphasize the Hellenistic dimension. But "there exists an Aramaic Syria, in Phoenicia with Damascus, in Osroena with Edessa — a Syria that plays an important role, while the canonical documents scarcely mention it. Here again we must seek to readjust our outlook."[4] Antioch, in western Syria, was always a focus of Greek culture. But eastern Syria constituted Christianity's sturdiest bulwark against Hellenization. And for certain historical reasons, this region, constantly invaded, constantly oppressed, ever marginalized, was the scene of a Christian resistance that may be unique in the history of the church. Syria, the crossroads of three continents, was the point of convergence of the empires of Babylon, Egypt, and Greece. Previously occupied by Semites, the region was successively invaded by the Egyptians, the Hittites (both sixteenth century B.C.), the Assyrians (eighth–seventh centuries), the Persians (539 B.C.), the Greeks, (fourth century), the Romans (first century), the Arabs (seventh century A.D.), the Ottoman Turks (1516–17), Napoleon Bonaparte (1799), the Ottomans (1841), the English (1917–18), and the French (1920). More recently, since the end of World War II, Syria acquired its independence. But like Lebanon, it is far from knowing peace.

The age-old history of Syrian subjugation and resistance explains much of the character of Syrian Christianity. In the first century it was a Jewish Christianity from Palestine that penetrated eastern Syria, and the apostle Thomas is linked to this tradition, along with the *Didache*, a Jewish-Christian catechism and one of the earliest extant Christian writings. This cycle always maintained its independence of the empires and had given persecution a theological interpretation as early as the end of the first century.[5] The literary cycle surrounding Thomas includes the Acts of Thomas, the Psalms of Thomas, and the Gospel of Thomas.[6] Like a later African Christianity, Syrian Christians organized a catechumenate in preparation for baptism—a sign of the seriousness with which they took their commitment. From this catechumenate we have the *Didascalia Apostolorum*—the "Teaching of the Apostles," a third-century Syrian writing. According to one belief, the Syrian missionary cycle reached as far as India. "This is by no means impossible," writes Daniélou. "Later tradition connects the evangelization of the Indies with the name of St. Bartholomew."[7]

The rapid development of the Christian mission in its first four cycles entailed a problem that we can sense in a number of documents—the First Letter of St. Peter as well as, especially, the seven letters of St. Ignatius of Antioch. We refer to the isolation felt by the Christian communities. There was a physical isolation, of course, by reason of the sheer immensity of the territories across which the communities were scattered. But there was a moral isolation as well—the solitude of a Christianity awash in a culture that rejected and despised the Christian lifestyle. The response to this challenge would have to consist in more contact among the communities. And so the Christian mission initiated the gradual process of further developing a ministry that up until now had been but one among many: the episcopal ministry.

The communities of the first century were mainly presbyteral. That is, their Christian memory relied mainly on the memory of the Apostles, or the elderly among them who had had contact with the Apostles. This was how the rabbinical tradition decreed that a community memory ought to be maintained. Over the course of time, however, and with the dissemination of the communities over such great distances, the need arose for greater contact *ad extra* among the communities, along with a more urgent need for the preservation of concord *ad intra*, within the communities.

We readily perceive this evolution if we compare the letter of Clement of Rome[8] with the letters of Ignatius of Antioch,[9] the former from the year 96 and the latter from around 110. The contrast is arresting. Clement presents us with a helter-skelter list of various ministries in his community, as high priest, priest, levite, deacon, lay person, apostle, and bishop (Clement of Rome, *Letter to the Corinthians*, nos. 40–44). For Clement, God is a "bishop" of sorts (ibid., no. 59).[10] Here is his description of the function of bishops in the Christian mission:

> [The apostles] went about preaching, through countryside and city, baptizing whoever submitted to God's designs and establishing the first fruits among these, after having tried them in the Holy Spirit, bishops and deacons of those who would come to believe. Nor was this a novelty, since such bishops and deacons have long been described in writing. Indeed, scripture says in a certain place: "I shall establish their bishops in justice and their deacons in faith" (Isa. 60:17).[11]

Far from constituting a new invention of any kind, then, for Clement the designation of members of the community as bishops and deacons was only a continuation of the usages of Judaism. And yet, just as the function of the diaconate was occasioned by a specific challenge — the need to render assistance to Hellenistic widows in the Palestinian communities — so it was with the episcopate, which was conceived in terms of the altogether specific function of mediating a closer contact among communities suffering from isolation and lack of comradeship. The Christian mission generated its specific ministries in response to challenges posed by society along the course of its historical journey. Today we tend to visualize these ministries as if they had been planned in advance, mapped out, and carved in stone. Nothing could be further from the truth. Mission is life, adaptation, and sensitivity to the "signs of the times."[12]

Ignatius of Antioch — who is referred to not as a bishop but as a "theophore," a God-bearer — was incontestably a leader of the community of Antioch and had been arrested in the persecution of Trajan, which reached the communities of Italy and Palestine in the years 107–108 and those of Asia Minor some years later. Antioch was affected only for a comparatively brief period. But Ignatius was one of the victims, and he was taken from Antioch to Rome by sea. The voyage was a long one, and the vessel carrying Ignatius docked at various seaports along its route.

During one of these stops, at the port of Smyrna, Ignatius received the visit of three delegates, or "bishops," from the churches of Ephesus, Magnesia, and Thrales respectively. Ignatius writes: "It was thus that I received all your great community [of Ephesus], in the name of God, in the person of Onesimus, a man of unutterable charity, your bishop according to the flesh."[13] To the church of Magnesia he likewise writes: "God has granted me to contemplate all of you in the person of your bishop Damascus, one truly worthy of God, and in the persons of your worthy presbyters Bassus and Apollonius, as well as my brother the deacon Zotion."[14] To the Christians of Thrales he exclaims once more: "By the will of God and Jesus Christ your bishop was here in Smyrna. So greatly did he rejoice with me that I am in chains for Jesus Christ, that it seemed to me that I contemplated in him your whole church."[15]

In these delegates, or "bishops," then, Ignatius sees the "churches"—his brothers and sisters living far off and unable to come to see him. Bishops, then, are emissaries entrusted by the Christian communities with the task of establishing contact with other Christians, expressing solidarity with persecuted and imprisoned Christians, and thus combating the terrible isolation that occasioned such downheartedness and abandonment of the mission.

At a later stop, at the port of Troas, likewise in Asia Minor, Ignatius received word that the persecution in Antioch was at an end. He promptly wrote to the communities of Philadelphia and Smyrna, as well as to Polycarp, asking them to send one of the brothers to Antioch to congratulate the community there on the glad occasion of the restoration of peace. Ignatius' words betray an eagerness for communication and communion among these far-flung groups of Christians. Here are the texts:

> It would be well for your church were you to send, to the glory of God, some holy ambassador to Syria, to relay your congratulations to those who have recovered their peace and regained their grandeur by the re-establishment of the very body of the church. I am certain that it would be an act worthy of yourselves thus to send one of

your number. [Ignatius of Antioch, *Letter to the Phila-delphians*][16]

It would be a righteous and beautiful thing, were you who make up the church of God to select a deacon to go to that church [of Antioch] as an ambassador of God, there to gather those good faithful in one place and to congratulate them, glorifying the Name [of Christ]. Happy in Jesus Christ the one who would be judged worthy of such a ministry! [*Letter to the Smyrneans*][17]

And in the letter to Polycarp, the person he calls "bishop of the church of Smyrna, inasmuch as he himself has as his bishop God the Father and the Lord Jesus Christ," Ignatius insists on the same point.[18]

It would be fitting, Polycarp, most happy one in God, to gather the assembly, as befits God's glory, and to select someone dear to you, and zealous, who might be called God's courier, and entrust to him the honorable burden of going to Syria and manifesting, to the glory of God, your charity with all its rich works. [*Letter to Polycarp*][19]

The conditions of those times imposed a special necessity on the churches. The churches stood in need of ambassadors of God, "couriers of God," delegates that could be dispatched from the communities to those far off or in trying circumstances. "After all, Christians live as nailed to the cross of the Lord Jesus Christ" (*Letter to the Smyrneans*).[20] For his part, Ignatius feels "near the sword and close to God" (ibid.).[21] In such circumstances, charity demands that the communities be more committed to communication, and that they keep contact with the persecuted in order to encourage them. Seeing this need, the churches both at Smyrna and at Ephesus sent one of their number to accompany Ignatius to Rome—to be with him on his way of the cross.[22] They likewise established contact with the church of Antioch. This is the context of the episcopate as a ministry of special importance in and among the Christian communities. The reason for insisting on this point, and treating it at such great length, is that so many Christians have a "prefabricated" picture of church structures in their mind. We imagine that everything had been worked out beforehand, without having to pass the test of the course of history and the challenges encountered along the way.

THE SECOND CENTURY

Three principal mission cycles mark the course of the second century. They are the Asian, the Syrian, and the African. (The Egyptian cycle, which has certain unique characteristics that merit separate treatment, will be dealt with in the next chapter.) Let us begin with the Asian cycle, doubtless the most dynamic and most influential of the three.

The Asian Cycle

When the Roman power had overwhelmed Asia Minor, it had found a complex of autonomous urban communities practicing a democracy in the renowned Hellenistic, elitist manner and attempting to Hellenize the rural populations of the interior. This ancestral population was accustomed to domination, then, at the hands first of the Greeks and then of the Romans. An appreciation of this fact will make it a good deal easier to understand the development of Christianity in the region, as well as in other parts of the Christian world, such as Rome, Gaul, and Spain.

Asia Minor had no central metropolis analogous to Egypt's Alexandria, Syria's Antioch, Africa's Carthage, or Italy's Rome. The Romans thought of Asia as the "province of the sixteen cities" that lay scattered over the regions of Bythinia, Paphlagonia, Galacia, Mysia, Lydia, Pisidia, Pamphilia, Cilicia, Licaonia, Phrygia, Cappadocia, and Pontus.[23] Each of these regions had its own particularities, inherited from its pre-Hellenistic populations (the peoples living in these regions before the invasion of Alexander the Great), who now found themselves under the domination of Hellenes and Celts.[24] The process of Hellenization succeeded in unifying these regions in the use of a single language ("common" Greek, *Koine*) and a single, populist emperor-worship, winning by these means a popular consent to the structures of the empire and the benefits of the celebrated Roman Peace—a "tranquillity of order" indeed (*tranquillitas ordinis*), to use the terminology of St. Thomas Aquinas. In order to reinforce this popular acceptance of the Roman hegemony, the imperial administration was most anxious for the people to be content, and its rule was not a harsh one. Times were tranquil, facilities for travel and shipping well organized, the paths of commerce smooth, the public security assured by a police force. The Roman administration was careful to maintain the tributary system based on farming in the countryside and commerce in the cities, but without imposing crushing financial burdens on small producers. To many eyes, the region seemed to be living in peace and prosperity.

There are indications, however, that all was not sweetness and light. The Roman administration, which repeatedly proscribed popular associations, did so "with particular severity in Asia Minor."[25] It is in this context that we must interpret the well-known counsels of Pliny, Governor of Bythinia, to the Emperor Trajan in the course of the years 110–12, concerning "a great number of persons, of every age and condition, and of both sexes" who "assemble on fixed days, before sunrise" to pray, "in alternating choirs, hymns to Christ as a god."[26] These gatherings took place not "only in the cities, but in villages and in the countryside," Pliny reports.[27] This is Christianity's first contact with the bureaucracy of the Roman Empire. It affords a good example of the means taken by that administration to control the Asian communities—to all appearances "democratic" on the Hellenic model. All authority for making decisions was in the hands of a bourgeois elite, lest any uncontrolled association on the part of the bourgeoisie provoke rebellion, or even demands, on the part of groups of the oppressed. Another disquieting indication is the Roman policy of fostering a religious syncretism, especially in Asia Minor. The Roman power tolerated the widest variety of popular religions, provided the latter did not oppose the high religious symbol of popular consent to the system, worship of the emperor. Roman religious policy bore no resemblance to the great legal principle of the "religion of the prince," whereby peoples would one day be constrained to embrace the religion of their respective rulers (*"Cujus regio, illius et religio"*) in both Europe and America. All religion was tolerated, so long as it was not "political."

Christianity surged with life in this Asian world. Second-century Asia, according to Daniélou, "was the most intense focus of the life of the church."[28] Indeed that life radiated all the way to Rome, the capital of the empire. Roman Christianity can be said to be Asian in origin. Eventually, by reason of its central geographical location, Rome absorbed the tendencies of all the various missionary cycles of the empire. Marcion (A.D. 140), Justin (160), Irenaeus, and Hegesippus had all come to Rome from Asia. "By the end of the second century, schools abound in Rome,"[29] comments Daniélou, and "by the end of the second century the place of Rome is salient in the life of the church."[30] It was in Rome that Tertullian, an African, encountered Montanism, an Asian movement. It is out of this historical reality that the specific role of Rome in the life of the church emerged. "I can appreciate the value of having the local church of Rome, whose leader or bishop has the function of Peter, keep watch that the local churches maintain their union," explains Edward Schillebeeckx. "But this is its only function—to be a 'last instance,' as it were, to which local churches can appeal."[31] Later, local churches would come to be almost entirely under the domination of the Roman power. Rome would gradually arrogate to itself all ecclesial authority, appointing bishops and frequently ignoring the concrete needs and capabilities of the local churches in other ways as well.

This phenomenon not only worked to the prejudice of mission, it was alien to the function ascribed to Rome by the primitive church. The Christian movement originally came to Rome from without. We observe that none of the first great personages of the primitive church are Roman. The first imposing figure of the Roman church is Callistus, who was bishop there from 217 to 222. Before Callistus it is Polycarp of Smyrna, Denis of Corinth (A.D. 170), Ignatius of Antioch, Irenaeus of Lyon, Justin of Palestine, Marcion of Sinope, Montanus of Phrygia, Tertullian of Carthage, and Clement of Alexandria who are the giants among Christians, expressions as they are of missionary cycles that antedate the Roman establishment.[32]

If we are to form an adequate picture of the Asian mission cycle, we must begin by emphasizing its Jewish character. Then we must stress its Paulinity—which will explain both its singular moral rigor and its extraordinary experience of interior liberty. The best way of illustrating the nature of the Asian church is to present two particularly typical second-century products of Asian Christianity: the movements known as Marcionism (or the Marcionite church) and Montanism.[33]

Marcionism

Marcion, son of a wealthy Christian shipowner, was born in Sinope, in Pontus in the north of Asia Minor. Around 140 (some say around 120 or 130), he took up residence in the capital of the empire and began to frequent the Roman community. This must have been poor, for Marcion, following the counsel of Jesus given in Matthew 19:21, sold his goods and donated the proceeds to the Roman church. At first he won the hearts of the people. But then, around 144, some confusion arose. The exact nature of the problem is difficult to specify. A tangle of contradictions and preconceptions surround the figure of Marcion. None of his writings has been preserved intact: we know them only from citations by his adversaries, Justin, Irenaeus, and especially Tertullian in his *Adversus Marcionem*—"Against Marcion," a five-book composition, twice revised by its African author and constituting the latter's most extensive work. We have it today in its A.D. 207 edition, in which Tertullian portrays Marcion as one of the worst, if not the worst, of all the enemies of Christianity.

What can we learn of the Christian way of life as practiced by Marcion and the Marcionites? To all indications Marcion was a staunch champion of the theology of marginality and of a practice consistent with that theology. This impression comes simply from the way in which Marcion regards Jesus. Jesus, in Marcion's understanding, needs no documents of divine authentication, such as the Old Testament prophecies o typologies. Jesus has no need of proving his divinity by an appeal to the Old Testament. He is accepted because of his manner of acting, or more specifically, in virtue of his miracles in favor of the marginalized and the sensitivity toward the poor these miracles evince. According to Tertullian, Marcion speaks as follows: "Through the facts of his miracles, [Jesus] offered an immediate demonstration that he was the Son, the Missionary, the Christ of God" (*Adv. Marc.*, III, 3, 1). We may translate: Jesus' sensitivity and action with regard to the poor and rejected is the greatest proof of his divinity. Only God glimpses the small, and all of our efforts to gather allegorical or typological readings drawn from the Old Testament (as the apologetes do so frequently) in proof of his divinity are superfluous. A "literal" reading of Jesus' miracles suffices to prove his divinity. Marcion was not the last Christian in the history of the church to insist on a literal interpretation of the Gospels. For example, St. Francis of Assisi was one day to repeat that we must read the scriptures "*sine glossa, sine glossa, sine glossa*" ("without glosses, without learned commentary").

Pauline in the extreme, Marcion understood and valued the stubbornness and depth of the apostle's reflections on Jesus and Christianity. But he did not very well see how these reflections could be related either to the data of the Old Testament or to the post-Pauline Christian writings. Accordingly, availing himself of methods of analysis very like ours today, he succeeded in trimming the catalog of authentic Pauline letters as far as ten, rejecting the pastoral epistles and the Letter to the Hebrews as spurious, just as do modern exegetes, and limiting the other acceptable writings of the New Testament to those of St. Luke. Everything else was to be rejected as fabrication. Thus—at a time when the canon had not yet been fixed—Marcion stripped the New Testament to a list of writings consonant with the Pauline vision of Christianity. For Marcion the message of Paul was simply identical with the Christian gospel.

The Old Testament seemed to him to proclaim a very different God—a power-hungry "Lord," creator of evil itself, the defender of dominators and the violent who had imposed obedience and subservience upon "his" people. Marcion's God is a God of Love, the sole foundation of ethics and the sole support of the Christian institution, which may not permit itself to appeal to fear in order to control the Christian social body. It was this aspect of Marcion's thought above all that aroused Tertullian's irritation. Marcionites, the great African complained, "have no fear of their God whatever. They pretend that evil is to be feared, and good is to be loved." And he goes on to mount the attack: "How can you say that the one you call 'Lord' is not to be feared, when the title itself indicates a power to be revered?"[34] What else but fear, asks Tertullian, will keep Christians from the games and circuses, the theaters and the houses of prostitution? Little by little, they will lose their Christian memory![35] Marcion thinks just the opposite—not out of any laxity, surely, but because he represents the authentic spirit of Asian Christianity—fervent and rigorous, but based on love and not fear. Tertullian and Marcion represent two very different ecclesial experiences, both limited in time and space, and their confrontation demonstrates the difficulty of pluralism in a movement that is necessarily plural and diversified.

Only by relating Marcion with the historical experience of Asian Christianity can we understand his various positions. Marcion's rejection of the Old Testament is not strictly theological in tenor but historical and "situated." Marcion rejects the law of violence and oppression, embracing the law of a communion of brothers and sisters instead—the law of solidarity and freedom prevailing in the communities of Pontus. Hence his predilection for the New Testament. The distinction between an evil God of the Old Testament and a good God of the New Testament is Tertullian's absolutization of the thought of Marcion and the Asian church. Marcion finds that the genuine, simple Christian memory is being clouded over by a thousand compromises and is in danger of disappearing completely. This is the reason for his radicalism, a naive, utopian radicalism, to be sure, in for example his wholesale condemnation of marriage. But the Christian memory cannot simply reject Marcion, who posited certain fundamental truths. "New wine cannot be stored in old vessels" (Luke 5:37), he loved to say, for he had a clear, convinced perception of Christianity's absolute novelty, as contrasted with the legalism of the Judaizers and their nostalgia for the Law of Moses. For Marcion, to be a Christian is not to follow the Law of Moses, but on the contrary to live the new freedom to which Christ has delivered us. For Marcion, the "Law" is error, while the gospel is truth.

On this, as on other points, he falls short of the equilibrium of a St. Paul, who articulates the relationship between Law and gospel more profoundly than this. Concerned with the question of the Christian memory and the dangers of deviancy therefrom, Marcion was opposed to anything suggesting pact or adaptation, compromise or conventionalism. His drastic "antithesis" between the God of creation and the God of Jesus underlay some crass errors, such as the Marcionite condemnation of marriage, an asceticism based on contempt for the world (the long-lived theme of *contemptus mundi*), and an exaggerated eagerness for martyrdom (already present in the writings of Ignatius of Antioch). Marcion's radicalism forced Christian communities to think seriously about drawing up a canon of the New Testament, which they did, in an indubitably anti-Marcionite gesture, at the close of the second century.[36] That effort was a mightly profession of faith in the compatibility of the canonical New Testament with the Old, and a rejection of the strident dissonance that Marcion wished to see between the two. The church finally opted for openness before the God of creation, for optimism with regard to human nature (via a rejection of the notion of *natura corrupta*), and for the theme of creation as a basic one for all theology.[37]

What befell Marcion in Rome? Around the year 144, the presbyters of the Christian community, recognizing the actual scope of his program, returned his money and expelled him from the community. Marcion then returned to Pontus, where he organized the so-called Marcionite church, an organization with so powerful a framework that it endured to the sixth century. This crisis of leadership in the church had the effect of preoccupying the communities more and more with the apostolic succession. Gradually Christians came to be of the opinion that the "charismatics," or spontaneous leaders, must be subject to some mechanism of control on the part of the Christian social body. But the Marcionite communities are interesting for the study of Asian Christianity from several points of view. Women in these communities performed the important ministries of teaching, exorcizing, and baptizing, as Tertullian testifies.[38] The Marcionites recited prayers, in the form of hymns composed by Christians themselves, with the whole community standing and facing the East. Their ministerial offices were those of the Jewish tradition: bishops, deacons, priests, lectors, deaconesses. They maintained a dynamic missionary movement, and the Marcionite church succeeded in establishing numerous communities in Mesopotamia, where they preceded Manichaesim.[39]

Montanism

A second Asian missionary movement of great internal dynamism was Montanism, which had arisen in Pepua, a small hamlet near Philadelphia in southern Phrygia, around A.D. 156. It was to be associated with the persecution under Antonius Pius in 155, which cost the life of Polycarp, bishop of Smyrna. Like Italy, Asia Minor was particularly threatened by the various religious persecutions of the second century—more than Syria, for example, which suffered almost no persecution apart from a brief episode around 112 (see the material on Ignatius of Antioch, above), or Africa, which was finally affected in 180. But four persecutions struck at Asia Minor over the course of the second century: one under Trajan in 112, another under Antoninus in 155, and two under Marcus Aurelius, in 165 and 185 respectively. Rural Christians and Phrygian slaves, already living in harsh conditions of poverty, came to interpret persecution as a sign of the imminence of the end, and of the revelation of the Spirit of God at the end of history. Montanus, Maximilla, and Priscilla were the prophets of Montanism, which achieved publicity in 172 and was discussed in Rome in 177—when Irenaeus came from Gaul to speak in its behalf to the authorities of the church of Rome. By the end of the century Montanism was agitating all of Asia. The sources indicate its powerful feminism, which would seem to have had its basis in the servile and rural condition of so many Christian women. It is difficult to be certain, however, as we are almost entirely ignorant of the internal life of the Montanist communities.

The prestige of Montanism made a quantum leap when Tertullian of Carthage joined the movement at the beginning of the third century. Clearly, Montanism was somehow the outgrowth of problems entailed in the structure of the churches grouped around bishops. The bishops tended to seek an alliance, or at least peace, with political society in the interests of the protection and development of the communities. Montanism fostered opposition to political society, especially in a moment of persecution. Caught between the bishops and the church of the Montanists, Tertullian made his option for the latter, convinced that it "represented the true Christianity."[40] In his Montanist period Tertullian prompted an out-and-out campaign against everything representative of the political society of his time: the imperial propaganda (in his *De Pallio*), the restoration of the family to Roman molds (*De Exhortatione Castitatis*), and military service, indeed patriotism generally (*De Corona*). The writings just cited are directed against the ideology of the Roman Empire as also against that of bishops who wished to "make a deal" with Rome. At the beginning of the third century, during the harsh persecution under Emperor Septimius Severus, Montanism emerged in all parts of the empire as the party of the martyrs. It is a matter of historical record that the persecution by Septimius Severus was directed especially against Montanists and Marcionites, the two expressions of Christianity regarded by the Roman Empire as the most dangerous, and both movements numbered many martyrs.[41]

Modern authors point out that Montanism did not really represent a departure from original Christianity. The novelty was not in Montanism, but in the times themselves, which no longer tolerated traditional radical Christian forthrightness in the face of the political authorities. As Donini says: "Basically these ridiculous-looking Pepusans were not very different from the Christians of the apostolic era, or indeed from the apologetes themselves."[42] They lived a popular Christianity of extreme moral rigor and great apocalyptic enthusiasm, and saw in the city of Rome, as in the structures of the Roman Empire as a whole, the city of Satan, locked in mortal combat with the "city" of God, exactly as had the Christians of the milieu that had produced the Book of Revelation.

This "explosion of propheticism" (Daniélou) in Asia Minor

taught that, the age of the Paraclete having been ushered in with Montanus, the New Jerusalem would now be established and last a thousand years. To prepare for this utopia, Christians were to live in sexual continence, practice a number of prescribed fasts, and if need be, provoke their own martyrdom by self-denunciation. As we see, then, while seemingly so strange and exotic, the movement has deep roots in marginality. And it awakens an echo down through the whole history of Christianity. A unifying thread traverses the warp and woof of Montanism, Novatianism, Donatism, and then the medieval movements of the Cathari, the Bogomils, the Albigenses, Joachim of Floras's "spiritual ones," St. Francis of Assisi's "little brothers and sisters," and down to modern times, with the movements of the Hussites, Anabaptists, and others. Beneath all the superficial strangeness, beneath the millenarianism and the exaltation of virginity, one senses the presence of an oppressed class unwilling to formulate a discourse acceptable to those in power and fashioning practices of resistance.

Some of the characteristics of Montanism call for special attention, owing to the influence they exerted on the later development of Christianity. There is, for example, its "encratism," or the notion that married life is incompatible with the fullness of the Christian experience. The markedly encratistic character of Montanism springs from its roots in Jewish Chris tianity, as Daniélou has shown.[43] One of the outgrowths of the basically pessimistic view of the whole order of creation as maintained by certain segments of Jewish Christianity in Asia Minor and Syria was the condemnation of marriage. Encratism was condemned in Rome in the latter part of the second century. But in the Christian East it had a stubborn life and reappeared in "distortions of eremitism and cenobitism."[44] By this route it penetrated the vast current of Christianities Eastern (Constantinople) and Western (Rome) alike. Even today it influences the behavior and thinking of large numbers of Christians with regard to sexuality and the conjugal relationship.

In the encratistic mentality, marriage, like death, has come into the world only in consequence of original sin. The Montanists and the other champions of encratism, who taught that sexual abstinence constituted a moral obligation for all Christians, have exerted a remarkable influence on the formation of the Christian conscience in our day.

Another historically important characteristic of Montanism is its Johannine emphasis. It has been said that, as Marcionism is an exaggerated Paulinism, so Montanism is an exaggerated Johannitism. The very term "Paraclete" as used by the Montanists betrays their Johannite posture. Millenarianism, the thirst for martyrdom, the conflict between Rome and Jerusalem, and the exaltation of virginity are all among the themes of the canonical Johannine writing known as the Book of Revelation, as of apocalypticism in general. In Montanism, as in the Book of Revelation, we discern a Christian hatred for the entire cultural complex represented by the Roman system, which is presented as an oppressive, crushing culture. Along these same lines, Montanism can be understood in terms of a response on the part of the poor rural class, not only in Asia but throughout the extent of the empire, to attempts at conciliation with the powers of the empire on the part of, especially, the bishops of the various churches. The collision of Montanism with the episcopal church was inevitable. We observe that the first synods in the history of the church were organized to combat Montanism and its influence on Christians of the poor class.

The Syrian Cycle

A second missionary cycle of the second century was the one that spanned Syria. We have observed that Syria stood at the crossroads of the great empires and zones of influence of the ancient Western world, and that this was a major factor in determining its historical lot. Second-century Syria was a state under Roman control. The Romans actually controlled two nations here. There was the Hellenized nation surrounding the capital, Antioch, and the Syrian nation of Semitic origin, with its Arameans, Phoenicians, Hebrews, Philistines, Assyrians, even Arabs. These two nations were in constant, mindless conflict with each other. Two Christianities sprang up as a result, the one more Hellenized and "Antiochian"; the other, in the vicinity of Edessa in Osroene, more Syrian. One was

Western, then, while the other was Eastern. The Christianity of eastern Syria constituted Christianity's staunchest bulwark against Hellenization in a subsequent era, and in the Middle Ages would launch a truly remarkable movement of Christian expansion, reaching India, Tibet, Mongolia, China, Indonesia, and Japan. For political reasons (the Turkish invasion), eastern Syrian Christianity lost this influence in the fourteenth century. In the Middle East today only a few small groups continue the tradition of ancient Syrian Christianity. Daniélou's observation is very much to the point: the extraordinary vitality of eastern Syrian Christianity obliges us to "change our perspective" in studying the history of the ancient church and go beyond our current, Westernized view to appreciate the Eastern mold of a Christianity in its first beginnings.[45]

The most important Roman stronghold in Syria and in the East as a whole was the Hellenic city of Antioch, at the bend of the River Orontes, a city built not on industry or commerce but on the geopolitical considerations of both the Macedonians (the empire of Alexander the Great and, later, of the Diadochi) and the Romans. The Hellenization of Syrian culture by way of Antioch was thoroughgoing and profound. We still have a sense of this today when we read the New Testament and find certain names doubled—Christ/Messiah, Thomas/Didymus, Tabitha/Dorcas, and so on—Greek and Syriac words conjoined. Cultivated milieus spoke Greek. The army spoke Latin. But to reach the people one had to speak Syriac. Christianity, accordingly, in the dynamism of its missionary thrust, resurrected the Syrian language, which had been marginalized by the administration and the bourgeoisie as a vulgar, oral, unwritten tongue. A clear proof of the intimate involvement of the second-century mission cycle with the people of Syria is the fact of the translation of the scriptures into Syriac. The center of this translation work was not Antioch, but Edessa, the east Syrian city on the silk route from China to Mesopotamia by way of Samosata.

Antioch never really became a thoroughly Syrian city. When the emperor traveled in the East he stayed at Antioch. The coinage of the eastern empire was minted at Antioch. The arms industries of the eastern empire were there. The city bore the indelible mark of its military and strategic function. Voluptuous and ostentatious as it was, its roots were in the people. "Throughout all antiquity, no other city invested the pleasures of life with the capital importance" attributed to them by "Antioch with its Daphne."[46] Daphne was a complex of gardens eight kilometers in circumference, rich with ornamental trees, fountains, a temple dedicated to Apollo, and a center of attraction for the military and the various functionaries of the empire. "No city of the empire could vie with Antioch for first place in luxury and splendor," writes Mommsen, the great historian of the Roman Empire.[47] Antioch's main thoroughfare was flanked by porticos to protect pedestrians from the sun and the rain— something even the capital, Rome, did not have. By night the city was completely illuminated, something recorded of no other city of antiquity. The life of the Antiochian elite was a worldly one indeed, and the artists of the city were renowned throughout the empire: dancers, actors, theater personnel of all types. Truly they lived Horace's familiar *"Carpe diem!"* ("Reap the day"), giving no thought to the morrow.[48]

It is at the base of this social edifice that we must look for the Christians—in the linen, dyeing, silk, and glass industries, for example, which brought such wealth to the shipowners who transported merchandise back and forth across the world, whether via Antioch's port, Seleucia, or by the land route that linked the city with Arabia by way of Palmyra and in the other direction with Mesopotamia by the above-mentioned cities of Edessa and Samosata. Some of the characteristics of Syrian Christianity can be explained in terms of an opposition to the lifestyle of the Antiochian rich, with a particular emphasis on self-denial, poverty, and humility.

An interesting detail of this attitude on the part of Syrian Christianity is to be found in the iconography of Christ. Hellenized religious thought regarded it as repugnant to represent Christ's passion and humiliation. The religious style of a Hellenized environment recommended that the "God of the Christians" be represented as a figure of serenity, majesty, even haughty arrogance. Even in the catacombs of the great cities of the empire we find a beardless Christ (the beard being a sign of an uncivilized "barbarism"), young, with short hair like stylish young gentlemen of Rome.

Later Byzantine art, of Hellenistic inspiration, perpetuated this elitist iconography of Christ, as can be seen in a detail of one of the oldest extant Roman icons we have, from a convent in Rome around A.D. 1000. There Christ is represented as seated on the imperial throne of the entire world, holding in his hand a globe inscribed with the words, *Ecce vici mundum*—"Behold, I have overcome the world." Even Jesus' cross has become a kind of imperial scepter, and his throne is the rainbow. The representation appears to suggest that Christ has conquered not by the humility of the cross, but by a power very like that of the emperors themselves. Syrian Christianity reacted against this tendency to elitization and represented Jesus Christ with a beard and long hair, suffering on a cross in humiliation and agony. Underlying this "iconographic option" we may discern a Christian experience based on the values it expresses.

Syrian Christianity was a Jewish Christianity of pronounced ascetical tendencies. Many of its converts renounced marriage, and "the church was made up essentially of ascetics."[49] It was the latter who formed the nucleus of the community, received the spiritual gifts, and proclaimed the gospel against the world. A consequence of the encratistic character of a Syrian Christianity so attached to sexual continence was the "spiritual marriage" of a male ascetic with a virgin known as *virgo subintroducta*, a usage that occasioned an enormous amount of discussion in the fourth century, as we shall see below. In Syria as in Asia Minor, martyrdom was regarded as the highest honor that could fall to a Christian's lot, as we may gather from the apocryphal *Ascension of Isaiah,* a composition dating from the same time as the Book of Revelation and preaching the most absolute independence vis-à-vis the empire.[50]

As we shall see in the next chapter, a theological movement arising in Alexandria in the third century gradually gained control of several mission cycles, Hellenizing them and altering their mentality on certain basic points of the Christian mission. The only region to succeed in mounting a reaction to this Hellenization was eastern Syria (Edessa, Samosata). This is why the study of the Christianity of eastern Syria has such importance for Latin American Christians, who perceive that the Hellenization of Christianity had some disastrous consequences for Christianity's authentic memory. An excellent representative of non-Hellenized theology is St. Ephrem the Syrian (A.D. 373). Let us briefly examine how he presents Christianity, based on the study by de Halleux.[51] St. Ephrem's activity arose in a particular context. The churches of eastern Syria were in hostile territory. Christians here dwelt beyond the confines of the Roman Empire, in that of the Sassanids. They became the victims of violent persecutions, beginning especially in the year 340. However, the autonomy of the eastern Syrian Christian communities made it very difficult to uproot the new religion from the region, since Christians would simply reorganize after any persecution. In order to survive, the base communities relied on the so-called "school of the Persians," which flourished primarily in Nisibis, later withdrawing to Edessa (A.D. 363). This "school," which provided the communities with theological and liturgical support, reached its peak expression in St. Ephrem the Syrian. Ephrem, then, was an "organic intellectual" of the base communities scattered throughout the Sassanid Empire of the fourth century, writing in the language of his forebears and maintaining the Christian memory in particularly difficult situations.[52] To a certain extent Ephrem expressed the themes of the second-century Syrian missionary cycle in all its Aramaic originality. Hence our interest in him.

Ephrem composed hymns that were to be sung in the Syriac communities for centuries. These hymns had their doctrinal basis in a theology of marginality, the theology of the school of the "poor for God." Ephrem himself regarded the "poison of the wisdom of the Greeks" as the source of all error.[53] The Hellenistic disputes on Christology, pneumatology, and the Holy Trinity that so vexed Christian intellectuals in the Hellenized cities were of no interest to Ephrem whatever. His work was addressed to the people; it was *didascalia* (instruction), catechesis, advising and encouraging the communities. His Hymns of Paradise lead us to conclude that paradise was an extraordinarily meaningful archetype in the life of these non-Hellenized Christians. Paradise in Ephrem's hymns corresponds to the Neo-platonic heaven. The difference in terminology is important, however. "Paradise" suggests a historical, material reality, a journey through time. "Heaven" had come to denote a "spiritual," non-historical, individual salvific state. For Ephrem humanity is on a pilgrimage, a journey. Expelled from a primordial paradise by sin, the human race is on its way to an eschatological paradise. The historical meaning of Jesus is conceived in terms of the restoration of paradise. Jesus' own body is the new garment of paradise, prepared by the Virgin Mary. The Christian communities are the sacramental locus of paradise restored. Only at the last judgment will the restored paradise be established in its fullness. In this theology, the theology underlying Ephrem's hymns, the entire history of salvation is bound up with the body. Ephrem does not adopt the anthropological dichotomy between "body" and "soul" stemming ultimately from Plato and the philosophers rather than from Christ or the scriptures. Contrary to Hellenized thinking, the creation of the material universe is in no way conditioned by the "fall" of pure or spiritual intelligences. On the contrary, "Ephrem conceives paradise in a manner as 'incarnational' as that of the actual law of its perfection, which forbids the soul's entry there without the body."[54] In the sacramental anticipation of the eschatological restoration of paradise—the Christian communities—the great enemies are "the lying of the powerful, the ostentation of the rich, the superstition of the simple, and the license of custom."[55]

Ephrem developed a Christian anthropology on a Semitic base. Thus spirit is the "subtlest form of matter." On the principle that the soul needs the body to live, Ephrem is most insistent that the soul can neither sense nor act without its body.[56] Deprived of its companion by death, the soul is paralyzed in its activity and thinking, like a fetus in its mother's womb were its mother to die. Hence between death and the resurrection "of the body" the soul can acquire no new cognition, for lack of any organ of perception and sensation. This anthropological view has the good odor of a wholesome materialism, far removed from a spiritualism that would discriminate against the body. For Ephrem, salvation is to be understood not as the intellective soul's escape from its material prison, but as the crown and term of a journey of soul and body in tandem. Death is painful by reason of the separation of two companions who will meet again in the hour of the resurrection. Ephrem has such a high sense of the body that he attributes to it its own will and freedom. The soul is immortal not in virtue of any "spiritual essence," but solely by the will of the Creator.

This is not the place for an elaborate exposition of this beautiful theology, so akin to its biblical sources, so far removed from any philosophic lucubrations, and so germane to the life of the communities. It will be enough to indicate the bibliography listed by de Halleux.[57]

The African Cycle

A third region where Christianity encountered favorable conditions for a rapid expansion in the second century was the region around Carthage in northern Africa. From one point of view the rise of Christianity in this part of the Roman Empire, which no apostle had visited, is a surprise. But it is also a confirmation of the fact that mission in those times was a great popular movement carried on by nameless, humble folk. When the labors of Tertullian finally revealed African Christianity to the eyes of the world, that Christianity was already solidly organized.

The Africa reached by Christianity was precisely where, in the third century B.C., there had been the terrible contention between Carthage and Rome for control of the Mediterranean: the actual Punic region around Carthage—Numidia and Mauritania. But by the time the Christians had begun to organize in the region, all of the old Carthaginian pride was gone. The region had become typical of the periphery of the Roman system. That is, it was valued for its natural wealth and its cheap labor. There, as we may gather from Tertullian's writings, a popular Christianity of working families came into being. Another indication may lie in the fact that the oldest martyr in living memory was a slave of Punic name and blood, one Namphanus of Madaura.[58] And in the *Martyrdom of Saints Perpetua and Felicity*, the account of an event occurring in the persecution under Septimius Severus (202), we find interesting information about the social class in which Christianity moved.

In order to have established a solid church as early as the end of the second century, the first Christians must have arrived in

Africa by the turn of the previous century, as Daniélou suggests.[59] Some authors say that these Christians were Jews from Syria and Egypt. Others are of the opinion that the first Christians to land in Carthage were Greeks of the Roman community. At all events, the first African Christians were the anonymous persons who performed the Herculean task of translating the Christian message into Latin, thereby definitively universalizing and internationalizing the Christian movement. Not that the Latin language was spoken by the local populations. On the contrary, various tongues were used, so that until the fourth century the gospel had to be preached in the local languages of the people of the base, who spoke no Latin. But Latin facilitated the rapid expansion of Christianity in the military, administrative, and judicial elements of the Roman administration in Africa.

While the Christians of Rome continued to speak popular Greek until at least the beginning of the third century, those of Carthage were already using Latin, at least in their liturgy. Long before the appearance of St. Jerome's celebrated Latin Vulgate, the anonymous African translators of the Bible into Latin introduced the Christian social body to words that we still use today to express our Christian faith, as we have seen — including the title "pope," which denoted a presbyter or bishop and was repeatedly used of St. Cyprian of Carthage. Tertullian was the first Christian author to make use of this translation, the work of earlier pioneers, and he thereby constitutes "a crucial link between Greek and Latin Christianity."[60] It was through Tertullian that the controversies of Greek Christianity, such as the Montanist and Marcionite questions, came to be expressed in Latin and so were universalized. Rarely in the history of the church has the influence of a single individual been so decisive as that of Tertullian, standing as he did at the crossroads of Greek and Latin Christianity.

So African Christianity was markedly popular, in the cities (especially Carthage) and in the countryside. At the same time, it used Latin and was quickly molded into an episcopal structure. As early as A.D. 198, Bishop Agrippinus of Carthage convoked a council, the first in the history of the Latin church, with no less than seventy bishops from Proconsular Africa and

Mauritania in attendance. At another Carthaginian synod, this time in the year 220, once more seventy bishops gathered. In 240 and again in 256 (under St. Cyprian of Carthage), there were ninety. The Roman synod of 250, meanwhile, gathered no more than seventy bishops. So "the church of Africa manifested its particular characteristics in a more pronounced fashion than the church of Rome."[61] Some authors claim that this solid episcopal organization was a sign of an African nationalism vis-à-vis Rome—a reaction of the periphery against the center of the system. At all events the later Donatist movement, originating with the bishop Donatus, would eventually justify this thesis, along with, for example, the heavily ecclesiological positions of St. Cyprian on the question of the *lapsi*, those who had "fallen" or performed a token act of emperor-worship under the persecution of Decius in the 250s.

This thesis on the peripheral nature of African Christianity appears to furnish the interpretative key to a reconciliation of certain seemingly contradictory elements in that church.[62] It happens that from 316 to 411, the space of almost a century, the African church was shaken by a violent social and religious war, occasioned by the appearance of the movement known as Donatism. No sooner was Donatism defeated than the Pelagian question agitated Christian Africa (410 to 412). Only a few years later, in 430 (the year of the death of St. Augustine), Roman Africa fell into the hands of the Vandals, who dismantled the structures of the church. Now the church was maintained in existence, throughout the ensuing period of official silence, by the very poor who had provided it with its original roots. In the sixth century Christian Africa was snatched from Vandal hands, only to fall into those of the Arabs, who eliminated the last vestiges of this so flourishing church, the church that has bequeathed to us the legacy of a Tertullian, a Cyprian, and an Augustine.[63]

By way of concluding this presentation of the mission cycles of the second century, it would seem useful to add a word on the Ethiopian cycle, which to be sure came into being only later—in the early half of the fourth century—but whose dynamism follows the missionary rhythms of earliest times: autonomy vis-à-vis the powers that be, an attachment to the popular culture, and a predilection for the poor and the marginalized. Furthermore, the Ethiopian cycle took shape beyond the frontiers of the Roman Empire—similar in this respect to the churches of eastern Syria, Armenia, and the Egyptian interior—and constituted the sole missionary cycle of black culture. This last characteristic seems to imply interesting suggestions for Christianity in Latin America, where the influence of black culture cannot be ignored. The history of Christian Egypt is steeped in a dialectic: the opposition between Alexandria, symbol of Hellenization and hence of a bourgeois predominance in the church, and Axum, symbol of the popular cultures that resisted Hellenization.

Above the highest cataracts of the Nile, where the river is no longer navigable, at the level of Syene (today's Aswan), the Kesh peoples (their Egyptian name), or Ethiopians (the name given to them by the Greeks) have dwelt since time immemorial. The names are charged with ideology. They define the peoples of these climes as "burnt-skinned," by way of contrasting them with the "clear-skinned" peoples of the North. The Greek word *aither*, "ether," denotes the upper air, the air that burns, the air just beneath the sun and above the *aer* or air properly so-called. *Aithiops*, then, "Ethiopian," a derivative of *aither*, denotes a person who lives in these burning airs, so that his or her face is burnt as a consequence. The notion had carried an ideological connotation since Homeric times. We read in Homer's *Odyssey*:

And now king Poseidon departed,
   to dwell with the burnt-skins afar—
the scattered, the furthest of men,
   in their double domain:
The first to the west, to the east those remaining.
   Regaled all the day
With bulls and with sheep in hecatomb sweet
   did he feast him with joy. . . . [*Odyssey*, I, 21–3]

To the peoples of the North, then, the name "Ethiopian" suggests carousing and indolence. In the *Iliad* (I, 423–7), Zeus, the supreme god, leaves his serious, laborious Olympus from time to time to amuse himself with the other divinities "in the direction of the Ocean," in the land of the Ethiopians. Twelve days later, all are back at work again. Herodotus later writes that the Sudanese (from the Arabic word for "black") have a great table where roast meat is laid before their visitors in all abundance (*History*, III, 17), and he looks on the "kinky-haired ones" with contempt: "Crispissimos inter homines habent crines." This mentality, doubtless general since earlier times, infiltrated the Bible as well, where we read that Miriam and Aaron upbraided Moses for having taken an "Ethiopian" wife (Num. 12:1, cf. Exod. 2:15–21, 4:25, 18:2). The same prejudice pervades the parasitic era and the mentality of the great Christendoms. Here we have one of the main reasons why the Ethiopian missionary cycle was marked by the stigma of isolation, marginality, and contempt.

Early in the Roman imperial period, an independent state came into being around Axum, in the heart of the mountains, on a plateau 1,800 to 2,000 meters above sea level. Axum has good communications with its port, Adulis, the best Red Sea location in terms of commerce and the principal market for the commercialization of the renowned African ivory. Thus Axum is brought in contact with Arabia and the whole Middle East.[64] Commerce brought some degree of Hellenization to the State of Axum, but this was later vigorously combated by Christianity. The Romans never dared penetrate the realm of Axum, surely for lack of the wherewithal to negotiate mountainous country lying so far from sea or river, contenting themselves instead with a mutual non-intervention policy. Given these conditions, Ethiopia, or Abyssinia, escaped till the twentieth century from the invasions and dominations that deface the pages of the human pilgrimage. Here is a land that enjoyed twenty-five centuries of uninterrupted independence, sixteen of these being marked by the Christian presence. What has always united the Ethiopians has been their color, the desert around them, and their mountains.

The gospel was brought to these plateaus by Syrian merchants in the first half of the fourth century. We have the story of the two youths from Tyre in Phoenicia named Frumentius and Edesius who arrived as slaves in the court of King Aizanas, or

Ezana, in Axum, and managed to convert him. However, as Marrou writes, "a deep obscurity shrouds the early developments of the church in Abyssinia."[65] What renders this particular missionary cycle even more mysterious is the legend of the visit of the Queen of Sheba to King Solomon in Jerusalem many centuries before Christ. The realm of Sheba surrounded Lake Tano, source of the Blue Nile, above the sixth cataract. In Ethiopian Christian folklore, a legendary son of Solomon by the Queen of Sheba (1 Kings 10:1-13) carried an Ark of the Covenant to Axum, thereby laying the foundations of Christian Ethiopia. This legend is still very much alive today, and many Christian Ethiopians wear a little vellum scroll around their necks with the words: "This is the writing entrusted by Saint Michael to King Solomon. . . ." Christians themselves wear this amulet to ward off evil spirits, thus demonstrating both the vital partnership between this Christianity and the ancestral beliefs of Africa, and a keen awareness of the antiquity and dignity of Ethiopian Christianity. The amulet may as well read: We are true Christians, and our tradition is as old as any on earth. Another Ethiopian mystery, once dear to the medieval Western Christian mind, is the legend of Prester John, the illustrious presbyter who ruled a great African Christian empire. Twice in its history, Latin Christianity sought to make contact with such an empire—at the close of the fourteenth century with the Venetians, and beginning in 1540 with the Portuguese. Both attempts at the Romanization of Ethiopian Christianity failed.

Ethiopian Christianity had several characteristics of its own. The most important is doubtless its popular nature, evidenced in the use of "animistic" amulets by the Christian faithful. It was Christianity that resurrected Ge'ez, the language of the people, giving it the status of a written language by way of translations of the texts of holy scripture. As with the first Latin translations in North Africa three centuries earlier, the task of rendering the Christian message in Ge'ez was carried out by anonymous Christians, who did their work from the second half of the fifth century to the seventh. Just as it had in eastern Syria and the Egyptian interior, Christianity seized upon the national language and preserved in that language such important documents of Christian memory as the Apocalypse of St. Peter, discovered in

1917,[66] the Gospel of St. Peter, found in 1886–87,[67] and the Discourse of Jesus to His Disciples in Galilee.[68]

The most original contribution of the Ethiopian cycle to the preservation of the Christian memory, however, is its inclusion in the canon of sacred books of the First Book of Henoch, regarded as apocryphal by the great Christendoms and a popular book par excellence. First Henoch, a product of the Jewish tradition from around 150 B.C., is an attempt to provide a theological explanation of the evil in history. Essential in its approach is the legend of Genesis 6:1–4: the fall of the angels, their carnal relations with lovely women, and the resulting race of giants. Every human and celestial creature, the sacred writer explains, has a "guardian angel." Rain, wind, storm, and so on, especially, have their angels. Even nations have their guardian angels, and Israel's is St. Michael. The demons are "fallen" angels, spirits fallen from heaven "into sin."

No very good explanation is offered for how these angels sinned, but one thing is clear: there are angels and there are demons. The angels help and "guard" us, while the demons try or "tempt" us, enticing us to evil. Thus a drama develops between God and Satan, between the angels and the demons.[69] Like the other Jewish literature from around 150 B.C. (the Book of Jubilees, the Testament of the Twelve Patriarchs, the Life of Adam and Eve, the Second Book of Henoch, and the apocalyptic literature of Qumran), First Henoch was eagerly read by the Christians of the first generations, although it was later combated by the structure of the church.[70] This literature not only provided those pondering the question of the evil in the world with an interpretive key but constituted a penetrating social critique as well. First Henoch is "one of the sharpest criticisms of society that I know," confesses Edward Schillebeeckx.[71] In 1 Henoch 98:4–8, wealthy exploiters are cast into hell, to the laughter of the just. Then the rich, "who build their palaces with the sweat of others" and monuments "whose every stone, every fragment of cement is made of the sins of the wealthy" (1 Hen. 99:13), are excoriated. The theme will recur again and again in medieval frescos of the Last Judgment or in the ornamentation that we find carved in the cathedrals. "As no prophet before him, the author [of First Henoch] turns upon the rich," says

Schillebeeckx.[72] The Ethiopian cycle, then, preserves a document of the Jewish-Christian tradition that declares, without any shilly-shallying, that where injustice disappears, there is the Reign of God. This is no longer a theology of marginality. This is authentic liberation theology, based on the theme of the victory of good over evil, the angels over the demons, God over Satan and the powers of hell.

Ethiopian Christianity's popular nature is evident from numerous details of its liturgical, catechetical, theological, and moral life. Church buildings are indistinguishable from the other houses of the village and are known simply as the "Christians' houses." They serve not only for the liturgical assemblies and other meetings but as the central points of nature preserves as well, and it is forbidden to fell the trees around them. The interior of these "Christians' houses" still roughly follows the separation between tabernacle and temple that characterized the sacred precinct of the Jews: the space is divided into a vestibule, where readings are addressed to the people, and the "holy of holies," with an altar that the faithful cannot see. Images are prohibited, just as in Jewish tradition. The liturgy is entirely based on the great musical tradition of Ethiopian Christianity, a tradition that, far from suppressing pre-Christian dances, integrates them harmoniously into the liturgy. The singing is done to the tapping of a pole, which also serves as a support. A kind of metal maraca is used along with a drum. The people accompany the singing by clapping their hands. The music director is the famous *debtera*, the master singer whose training begins at the age of fifteen and lasts no less than ten years. The *debtera* preserves the memory of the community by way of traditional music that once was not written down but transmitted entirely orally. In Ethiopian Christianity, popular traditions were not a question to be debated. Christianity itself was a popular religion here and transcended the verbosity so characteristic of our Western Christianity. Through long centuries of co-existence with Coptic, Islamic, Jewish, and "pagan" religious influences, Ehtiopian Christianity has preserved the most varied traditions: pre-Christian African dances, sacrifices of oxen, sheep, and goats, the precept of the Sabbath rest (observed on both Saturday and Sunday), conjugal taboos, and dietary laws.[73]

The present condition of Ethiopian Christianity reflects the regrettable situation of separation and mutual misunderstanding prevailing among the various Christian confessions generally. Currently there exist no less than four distinct ways of practicing Christianity in Ethiopia. The Ethiopian Orthodox Church is under the jurisdiction of the Coptic patriarch of Alexandria. In 1951 the first Ethiopian *abuna* or bishop was ordained in Cairo, as a progressive independence movement under the tutelage of Alexandria gained influence. This Ethiopian church is referred to as "monophysite," since it rejects the Council of Chalcedon (A.D. 451), which in its time expressed Byzantine domination of the various Christian churches of the East. Other monophysite churches are the Armenian, the East Syrian (called the Syro-Jacobite), and the Coptic. The Ethiopian Orthodox Church is not Coptic and manifests its subjection to the Coptic church only in its episcopal ceremonial. In its daily life, in its liturgy, music, catechesis, and customs it maintains a typically Ethiopian character. It numbers many priests and monks among its faithful, perhaps as many as seven thousand. The faithful total some eleven million. A second Christian body is formed by the Ethiopian Catholic Church, which came into being with the union of a small group of Christians with Rome in the past century. Third comes Catholics of the Latin Rite, and fourth, Protestants. These last two groups lack any deep roots in the reality of the Ethiopian nation.

The Christian history of Nubia is closely tied up with that of Ethiopia. Nubian Christendom met with extinction between the fourteenth and sixteenth centuries, probably for lack of popular acceptance. Certain authors emphasize the fact that the evangelization of Nubia was elitist, proceeding "from the top down," carried out in a strange language, Greek, and appealing predominantly to the old and new Hellenized bourgeois classes. Nubian Christianity furnishes us with an instructive example of the importance of evangelizing in the language and culture of the people.[74]

CHAPTER VIII

Marginalization of the Theology of Marginality

The preceding presentation of the mission cycles of the first two centuries has emphasized not only the popular nature of the Christianity of that period, but likewise the fact of a theology based on the election of the poor and marginalized in God's project for humanity. These various cycles produced intellectuals whose writings bore the mark of what I have called a theology of marginality: in the Syrian cycle, Justin, who later was active in Rome; in the Asian cycle, Irenaeus, who moved to Gaul; in the African cycle, Tertullian. Christianity's concern with the interests and problems of the marginalized classes within and without the Roman Empire was of course not confined to the first and second centuries, but it was the principal characteristic of Christianity in those centuries. The third century ushered in ever clearer indications of an important change of mentality in the Christian communities. The theology of marginality, always under assault at the hands of the elite, was gradually relegated to secondary status. A new theology gained the upper hand. The first signs of this new state of affairs appeared in the Egyptian missionary cycle, which is therefore considered here, out of chronological order.

We must not think that Christianity came to Egypt only in the third century. The Christian presence there is attested as early as the first century. My purpose in looking at Egypt in this chapter is to contrast it with the cycles of Syria, Asia Minor, and Proconsular Africa. Egyptian, especially Alexandrian, Christianity was very different from that of the other cycles. While Irenaeus, Justin, and Tertullian defended the adequacy of the knowledge of the poor in matters of faith, Clement of Alexandria and Origen began to discriminate against such humble knowledge, depreciating it as second-class and insisting on complementing and perfecting it with a higher cognition, a Christian gnosis inaccessible to the simple and ignorant.

SOCIAL, ECONOMIC, AND POLITICAL FACTORS

Situating the Egyptian cycle in time and space will lead to a better understanding of the matter. The ancients called Egypt the "gift of the Nile." At certain times of the year that mighty river overflows its banks to deposit a soil so rich that the wheat harvest from this "black soil" eventually came to feed one-third of the city of Rome. The extraordinarily fertile region in question extended from the Nile Delta, with its sixteen mouths, to the first cataract, at Syene (Aswan). Egypt's strength, then, lay in its production of wheat for Roman commerce. Once Italy stopped growing wheat, Rome itself could no longer live without Egypt, as it literally depended on Egyptian production for its daily bread. When Vespasian wished to seize power in Rome around A.D. 70, he appropriated the wheat of Egypt. Thus when certain Roman rulers—such as Antoninus, Nero, or Geta—proposed to move the center of the empire to the East, the city they had in mind was not imperial Antioch but Alexandria, the great Egyptian metropolis. Egypt also had a very active industry in linen, glass, and especially papyrus. Papyrus served as a foodstuff and was used in making rope, baskets, and boats, but its most important use was as the material on which the entire literate world of the time did its writing. Countless persons made their living from the production and commercialization of papyrus. A third-century Roman writer observes: "Alexandria is a city of wealth and luxury, where no one is unemployed. One works in glass, another in papyrus, a third in linen. Their only god is money."[1]

Socially, from the beginning of the Hellenic rule of Alexander the Great (333–23 B.C.), Egypt had been a state composed of two nations. The state was Hellenistic and part of the Roman periphery. The nations were composed of, respectively, the descendants of Greek colonists (concentrated especially in Alexandria and Ptolemais, the two cities created by the new power brokers) and Egyptian Copts, who lived in thirty-six "districts" scattered over the interior of the country. (The Greek for "district" is *chora*, whence the verb *anachōrein*, to "go out to the country," the desert, said of the "anchorites" or monks of Egypt.) The word "Copt" is itself a corruption of *Aiguptios,* "Egyptian." Traditionally each district was dedicated to a god named after an animal: "Dog," "Lion," "Crocodile," and so on. But unlike the other regions under the domination of the Roman system, the Egyptian districts were completely deprived of any autonomy or organization where the base of the social edifice was concerned. There were no grassroots associations there—no "colleges," no professional guilds such as marked the social life of Asia Minor, Syria, and even northern Africa.

This is the fundamental reason why Christianity in Egypt developed along new lines different from its original course. What Aristotle had recommended to Alexander the Great was accomplished in Egypt: to be a leader (*hēgemon*) to the Greeks and a despot (*despotēs*) to the barbarians or Copts, treating the former as friends and allies and the latter as dogs. Discrimination against a non-Greek nation was more cruel in Egypt than anywhere else in the empire. Nor was this the work of the Romans, who were accustomed to respect the political and social systems of the regions they ruled. It was the outgrowth of structures previously established under Alexander the Great. More than anywhere else, in Egypt Hellenization meant cultural domination—cultural war, in fact, where the Copts were concerned, these peasants, these artisans, these small traders and merchants. The Hellenization of Egypt meant the establishment of a highly hierarchized society in which speaking Greek (*Koine*) opened the doors to higher positions in society, while speaking the venerable ancestral language meant social marginalization and discrimination.

But here as elsewhere, Christianity adopted the popular language and translated the documents of its faith into that language. Up until the middle of the third century, the ancient tongue survived in society. Later it was marginalized and driven to the interior of the country where, owing primarily to the Christian influence, peasants were still using it in the eighteenth century. Today Coptic is only a liturgical language, although it still has its importance in the study of ancient Christian texts. Social pressure occasioned the subjoining of Greek suffixes to names of persons and places, like *-polis*, "city": Heliopolis, Heracleopolis, Aphroditopolis, Panopolis, Diospolis, Hermopolis. Ptolemais and Alexandria were "metropolises" now. Even the gods were Hellenized. This shameful process of cultural domination has received the name of syncretism—a euphemism that hides more than it reveals.[2] Discrimination against the Copts continued through the later history of Egypt, and today 93 percent of Egyptians declare themselves Muslims, while only 5 percent still profess themselves Copts (1,250,000 persons). There is a Coptic Christianity in Egypt, in the Sudan and, as we have seen, in Ethiopia. I shall return to this subject when considering monasticism.

Owing to the absence of any structures of popular representation—the legacy of Pharaonic times—the rural districts of Egypt were left in total dependency on the royal functionaries, and these kept everything in their own hands—the law, taxes, and the police. Not even large cities like Alexandria had a municipal organization properly speaking, in the Greek tradition of popular representation. Rather they were entirely under the control of well-disciplined functionaries who ruled with an iron hand. Romans, accustomed as they were to something like a representative political system in which all decisions were made by the *Senatus Populusque Romanus* (the "Roman Senate and People"), did not feel at home in Alexandria. They never succeeded in adapting to the exceedingly complex royal court ceremonial with its pomp and ostentation after the manner of bygone Pharaonic times. And yet the "Egyptian model" proved its efficiency on the financial level. More than any other province, Egypt funneled its wealth into the coffers of the empire, and it was finally this consideration that moved the Roman emperors, in the wake of the third-century financial, social, and political crisis, to attempt to apply the Egyptian model throughout the empire. This reorganization was ultimately accomplished under Diocletian (284–305) and Constantine (313–37). In the Egyptian model, the purpose of the state is not the welfare of its subjects but simply and solely the reinforcement of the state itself. In this logic there must be a strong army, a popular emperor, great emphasis on methods of popular control, and a secret police. M. Rostovtzeff, a specialist in the social and economic history of the Roman Empire, writes:

> The social revolution of the third century, which destroyed the foundations of the economic, social, and intellectual life of the ancient world, was a catastrophe across the board. Upon the ruins of a prosperous, well-organized state based on the most ancient classical civilization and on regional autonomy, was erected a state based on general ignorance, coercion and violence, slavery and servility, corruption and venality.[3]

The city of Alexandria occupied a strategic position in this evolution and propagation of the Egyptian model throughout the empire. Alexandria had been the scene of a number of crucial encounters at the cultural level, such as that with philosophical Neo-Judaism (Philo of Alexandria, 13 B.C.–A.D. 42),[4] Neo-Pythagoreanism, Neo-Platonism (Plotinus, between A.D. 205 and 270), and Neo-Christianity (Clement of Alexandria).[5] Unless Clement is placed in the context of the city and land of his activity, the scope of his writings cannot be understood.

CLEMENT OF ALEXANDRIA

Titus Flavius Clement was born of pagan parents, probably in Athens. After his conversion to Christianity he traveled a great deal throughout the Hellenized empire. After sojourns in southern Italy, Syria, and Palestine, he finally took up residence in Alexandria as a freelance teacher and philosopher, in the style of Justin in Rome. In the years 202–203, on the occasion of the persecution under Septimius Severus, he was forced to leave

Alexandria, and he died in Asia Minor around 215. Clement was the first intellectual to have a profound literary knowledge of the history of Christianity. He cites no less than 360 pagan authors and demonstrates an equally impressive knowledge of sacred scripture. Of his writings, three full-length works and a homily remain: the *Protreptikos* (the "Admonition" to the Greeks); the *Paidagōgos* ("The Pedagogue"), a handbook of Christian morality; and the *Strōmateis* ("Tapestries"), a series of essays on the subject of the "Christian gnosis." The homily, called *What Rich Person May Be Saved?*, is a commentary on Mark 10:17–31.

From the first lines of the *Strōmateis*, it is clear that Clement is writing in an atmosphere of suspicion on the part of the Christians of the communities with regard to philosophy and dialectics:

> Certain individuals regarding themselves as being of good judgment deny that there is any reason for studying philosophy, dialectics, or the universe at all. They insist on a "pure and simple faith." It is as if they refused to toil in the vineyard, but wished simply to go out to harvest the grapes at the beginning of the season. [*Strom.*, I, 9, 43, 1][6]

This text says everything. Clement belongs to a new current in Christianity, one aspiring to a more elevated knowledge. He is impatient with the "simple" followers of an orally transmitted, inerudite Christianity. "Should nothing at all be written? Or are there persons to whom this right should be reserved?" he asks (*Strom.*, I, 1). "I well know what certain ignorant individuals repeat, frightened as they are by the slightest stirring—that we ought to limit our knowledge of the faith to the 'essentials,' and neglect anything coming from without as superfluous" (*Strom.*, I, 1, 18, 2).[7] Clement then rejects these scruples and embarks on a broad development and exposition of his theses on Christian gnosis.

We readily sense the tenor of Clement's lifestyle in the counsels he gives regarding the Christian life. His is the bourgeois environment emanating from Alexandria, as Michel Clévenot shows.[8] Clement appears to be simply ignorant of the Copts. Nor is he concerned with the peasants who grow the wheat or the humble merchants and artisans that teem in the streets of Alexandria. His environment is that of the celebrated *museion*, the greatest library in the world and sovereign ruler of the scientific thought of the age. His audience is composed of the wealthy, who complain of their servants (*Paid.*, II, 60, 1), dress in white (because "white is the color of truth," *Paid.*, III, 54, 1), and apportion their domestic tasks as follows: Women should busy themselves with embroidery and offer the cook a little assistance (*Paid.*, III, 49, 2); men should see to the fishing. After all, Clement observes, even the noble St. Peter was a fisherman (*Paid.*, III, 52, 1–2). By no manner of means must Christians become involved in politics, that sphere of perilous passions. They must live in the candor of truth symbolized by their white clothing.[9]

What is this "Christian gnosis" of Clement's? Christian gnosis is a "higher" or superior knowledge, an intuition flowing from a special revelation, a comprehension and penetration of the Christian mystery unavailable to the "ignorant masses." The gnostic is a friend of God and the equal, even the superior, of the angels. True, Clement rejects a radical view of gnosis whereby the Christian social body would be explicitly differentiated into the gnostic and the ignorant. But there is an undeniable tone of divisiveness in his writings when it comes to the "masses" and the "enlightened." "This gnosis, coming from the apostles and transmitted orally, has reached by that succession a small number of persons" (*Strom.*, VI, 7, 61, 1). There are two conversions in Christianity: from paganism to the faith, and from faith to gnosis (*Strom.*, VII, 10, 57).[10] The gnostic is presented altogether in the manner of a Stoic sage. He understands everything, has no more passions, and prays ceaselessly. His life is a continuous example to others. He is an apostle and priest, a member of the true hierarchy of the church (*Strom.*, VI, 106–107). To the ignorant the gnostic exhibits the condescension recommended of old by St. Paul, who made himself "all things to all," permitting, for example, the circumcision of Timothy (*Strom.*, VI, 15, 124). The ignorant practice an imperfect Christianity, not only here but even in eternity. In the house of Jesus' Father are many mansions, but they are separated by an abyss (*Strom.*, IV, 97–114). It is the lot of the ordinary Christian forever to remain at a greater distance from God and Christ than his or her gnostic brother.

Who can ignore the social separation that this manner of discourse presupposes and attempts to conceal? Unlike the great text of Matthew 11:25, which tells of a secret revelation to the little that remains hidden from the wise, Clement of Alexandria proclaims a secret revealed to the wise (*Strom.*, VI, 115, 1). It is astounding that a doctrine so clearly contradicted by the gospel should not have been condemned by the church. Jules Lebreton states: "This Christian is impregnated with a haughty, aristocratic Hellenism that has precious little to do with the gospel."[11] Clement touches the heart of the matter when he claims to be able to harmonize the Bible with philosophy. The Bible is the memory of the poor, a memory of liberation and deliverance from the land of Egypt. Philosophy had been born and remained a practice of the privileged classes. Clement managed to join the two traditions, the biblical and the philosophical, only by attempting to read the Bible in the light of philosophy, as Philo, the great Alexandrian Jew, had done. In order to be able to combine Judaism and Hellenism—an imperative task in the city of Alexandria, where Jews occupied two of the five great quarters of the city—Philo created an exegetical tool in the Greek spirit known as allegorical interpretation, "which consists essentially in an effort to extract a deeper meaning than the one immediately given in the text."[12] But what might this deeper, this higher, this more spiritual sense be? Must we not now admit that everything in scripture has a "spiritual" sense but not everything has a historical sense? Will not this quest for an allegorical sense tend to de-politicize and de-historicize the revealed text? In the difficult attempt to harmonize the "God of the philosophers" with the "God of Abraham, Isaac, and Jacob," Philo opened the door to a subtly deceptive, and therefore all the more dangerous, method of interpreting the scriptures. The attribution of a variety of meanings to the revealed word is the exegete's license to bypass the actual historical meaning of the text. Clement cites Philo numberless times. He is especially fond of Philo's allegorical interpretations of the Pentateuch. In fact, Clement regards Philo's writing as authentically "patristic."[13]

It has to be said that Clement of Alexandria embarked on a brand-new course where Christian theology is concerned. He invested the Greek tradition with a supernatural character. The writings of the philosophers acquired a dignity comparable to that of the Judaic Law. Both the Old Testament and Greek philosophy providentially paved the way for the coming of the gospel. But the fact is that the Greek philosophy of which Clement speaks is an elitist practice. It discriminates against the faith of the simple. It tends to posit the co-existence of two distinct kinds of Christian, the ignorant Christian of the people, destined to attain to perfection neither here nor in eternity, and the authentic Christian, learned, cultivated and, at least by innuendo, assimilated to the Christian of the privileged class (*Strom.*, I, 99, 1).

Upon reflection, of course, it is not fair to saddle Clement with sole responsibility for the distortion of Christianity wrought in Alexandria at the beginning of the third century. When all is said and done, Clement was merely being realistic. He was only attempting to mount an adequate response to a crisis arising in the Alexandrian Christian social body, the crisis of a new class that had begun to share the Christian mission, the bourgeois class. This class reacted to the Christian message with a sensibility of its own, a cast of thought dubbed "gnostic" in all of the documents we possess. Clement himself asserts that he is only attempting to build a dyke to protect the "Lord's vineyard" from the waves of "human sophism" — in other words, from the bourgeois mentality itself (*Strom.*, I, 20, 100, 1). He is in no position to reject gnosis across the board. Its presence is a *fait accompli* with his audiences. And so he hit upon the solution of a "Christian gnosis," which somehow would not scorn the knowledge of the simple. But he is aghast at a fundamentalist interpretation of the scriptures, and his humanistic training holds him aloof from a daily association with the poor. Clement's perspective is the outlook of one who does not participate in popular practices but judges them from the posture of an erudite, classicist self-sufficiency.

Historians have correctly observed that Clement of Alexandria helped prepare for the Constantinian reversal and the inauguration of Roman Christendom.[14] Clement laid the theoretical groundwork for a bourgeois Christianity. This new orientation could scarcely pass unnoticed in the eyes of the imperial administration, which began to see in Christianity a tool for the reinforcement of the new imperial project so anxiously pursued throughout the course of the second century. Clement had opted for a path calculated to secure the broad acceptance of Christianity on the part of the political powers. We can scarcely say the same of his contemporary, Tertullian, who, two thousand kilometers away, revived an altogether different approach, one that remained suspect in the eyes of the power brokers of the age. The writings of Clement of Alexandria favored the rise of a "great church," heterogeneous in social class, hierarchized, and capable of harmonizing, indeed collaborating, with the political model then prevailing in Egypt, an authoritarian, power-centralizing model. By way of Clement of Alexandria's allegorical reading, the Bible no longer represented the memory of the poor, the memory of a deliverance. On the contrary, now it sought to bridge the gap between the Christian message and the dominant culture of Alexandria. To this end the Bible must be depoliticized. Allegory prevails. Typology has gone by the board.

Today, so many centuries later, we need to ask certain questions: Was the evolution of the Christian mission in Alexandria at the beginning of the third century inevitable? Was it irreversible? In its encounter with the long history of complex societies with their mutually antagonistic internal interests, has Christianity been in any position to escape the "bourgeoisization" of its message and consequent manipulation of the memory of Jesus, the prophets, the Apostles, and the Reign of God? Unfortunately, it is difficult to answer such questions with any very great degree of certainty. It is a *fait accompli* that Alexandrian Christianity became bourgeois, and that the influence of that cosmopolitan city, the second most important in the Roman Empire, was such that its reading of the Christian message gradually penetrated the Christian social body as a whole.

ORIGEN

The other writer of enormous importance for the fortunes of the Alexandrian reading of the Christian message was Origen (d. 253–4). Origen is the most prolific intellectual of Christian antiquity.[15] Born around 185, probably in Alexandria, Origen for years headed the Christian catechetical school of that city, later moving to Caesarea in Palestine where he founded a school in the Alexandrian mode. Arrested and brutally tortured in his old age, he nevertheless survived several years, to the ripe age of seventy, before at last succumbing to his injuries.

Origen was the first intellectual to rethink the new religion from a point of departure in basic principles. He bestowed upon the religion of the marginalized and simple the respectability of a philosophical and theological system. His contemporaries regarded him as a phenomenon, and St. Jerome would later exclaim: "Can anyone have read all of the writings of Origen?" Origen created a new science, the one we call biblical theology, subjecting every sentence in holy scripture to a systematic analysis. He also created Christian philosophy itself, approaching that discipline not by way of an appropriation of the Greek philosophers, as Justin had done, but by constructing it scientifically, out of whole cloth. He created the first theory of knowledge based on Christian premises, thereby erecting Christianity into an autonomous intellectual universe of its own. He was the first theoretician of clericalism—criticizing the clergy, to be sure, but systematically exalting the ecclesiastical state as invested with a special dignity and power, and positing an absolute distinction between clergy and laity. He understood the church as a social reality bound up with the sacred as the state is bound up with the profane or secular. The task of the laity in the church is to demonstrate "reverence and obedience."[16]

This is not the place to put forward a comprehensive picture of Origen's thought. My concern here is to set in relief the aspects of that thought that bear on the Christian mission. The latter, in Origen's thinking, takes two forms: one common and imperfect, the other "secret" and perfect. Origen applies this reading key to the writings of St. Paul who, we are given to understand, preached a "common" Christianity "to the common" while reserving the loftiest secrets for his favorite disciples. Origen claims that when St. Paul wears his hair short, or permits Timothy to be circumcised, he does so out of condescension, becoming a "Jew with the Jews to win the Jews." But the upshot of this missionary method of adaptation and condescension was a "fleshly" Christianity, one not yet "spiritual" (*Commentary on John*, I, 7, 43). Origen passes a severe judgment on "carnal" or popular Christianity:

> The second category of Christians is that of those who know nothing but Jesus Christ and Jesus Christ crucified. They are persuaded that the Word made flesh is the totality of that Word. Thus they know Christ only according to the flesh. I refer to the mass of those who are regarded as Christians. [*On John*, II, 3, 29][17]

"Fleshly" or "common" Christianity imparts only the shadows of the mystery, not its secret light. Christians who embrace it know only the Christ debased on the cross, not the Christ exalted in glory. They worship only the Christ who became a slave, not the Christ who entered into his glory (*On Matthew*, XII, 30). Origen provides Christianity with a further development of the "secret-tradition" theory, a theory of gnostic origin broadly accepted by educated Christians of the age.

To draw the lessons of the secret tradition from the scriptures and apply them to missiology, Origen uses the allegorical method developed by Philo and Clement. This is a "matter of life and death" for him, as Lebreton puts it.[18] The allegorical interpretation of the scriptures is a religious duty of the highest importance, and Origen's writings are steeped in it. Indeed it constitutes the spiritual nourishment of Origen's deeply religious soul. Allegory rules all. How does Origen regard the Christian message? Wafting high above the common faith accessible to all Christians, a special Christian knowledge issues from a secret tradition. This knowledge is immediately intuitive in nature and transforms one's life for good and all.[19]

Conceptualizing the Christian message in this way, Origen is no longer interested in Christians' everyday problems, which he regards as "vulgar" or "fleshly." What interests him are problems of more cosmological proportions — how the Father generates the Word (in order to create the world — the God of creation, then, not the God of the convenant with the people), or the mechanics of the incarnation of the Word in Jesus Christ (from a Neo-Platonic viewpoint — Jesus Christ the Lord, then, and not

thc liberator), or the intra-trinitarian procession of the Holy
Spirit, or the freedom and responsibility of the human soul.
Origen focuses his attention exclusively on the explanation of the
world and life. He is blissfully unconcerned with the questions
that plagued Christians living at the base — health, land, trade,
daily nourishment, destitution. In Origen's writings, Christianity, which up to the beginning of the third century had presented
itself as a religious faith, takes on the features of a metaphysical
doctrine, thc stuff of erudite discussions among persons of
culture. The irritation experienced by our aristocratic Christian
speculator in the presence of the Christian "ignorant" is alto-
gcther reminiscent of Clement of Alexandria:

> The attentive reader will see that the gospel text is not as
> simplc as some think. It was presented to the simple in a
> simple way. But to those who aspire to a deeper under-
> standing, and are capable of such an understanding, it
> conceals realities charged with wisdom, and worthy of the
> very Word of God. [Origen, *On Matthew*, X, 1][20]

Origen has had to pay a price for his two-layer theory of the
Christian social body, with its simple and ignorant on the
bottom, and its wise, its educated, its initiated on top. Modern
authors have begun to judge that theory rather severely.
Lebreton writes:

> When we think of the wealth of the intellectual, moral, and
> religious values of these great thinkers [Clement of
> Alexandria and Origen], and contrast it with the poverty of
> any contribution they may have made to the progress of
> dogma and Christian worship, we feel a sadness at seeing
> such magnificent trees, and such pitiful fruit.[21]

PART THREE

THE BASE CHURCH COMMUNITY

CHAPTER IX

The Synagogical Model

It is not easy to find models or prototypes for the current Latin American experiment with base communities by looking at church history after the fourth century. The profile of today's communities seems to have been anticipated neither in the confraternities, nor in the "third orders" and other lay associations of medieval origin, nor in the movements of the high Middle Ages emphasizing poverty, nor in the first monastic movements of Egypt, Syria, and Palestine, nor in the numerous heresies that accompanied every stage in the history of the church. A search for parallels between the church of the past — at any rate from the fourth century onward — and today's base communities has been pretty much in vain. Today's base communities discover startlingly relevant models, however, in the very early Christian communities — those of the first three centuries. At least this is the enthusiastic finding of Christians today who belong to a base community and seek to compare their experience with that of the first Christian centuries.

Without claiming to have the last word on the question of an affinity between the current experiment and the life of the first Christians, it is possible to bring certain observations to bear on the matter, especially with regard to the similarity between the ecclesial model lived by the first Christians and the synogogical model. Many difficulties in interpreting life as it was lived in the earliest years of Christianity owe their origin to the fact that

Christians today are without adequate knowledge of the Jewish roots of Christianity—to say nothing of our need for a new radication of Christian history in the soil of the Judaism from which the church originally sprang.

As Conzelmann reminds us again and again, the first Christians were all Jews, and Jews they meant to remain. Their intention was not to inaugurate a new religious movement but to follow the Jewish religion.[1] They did not propagate a new notion of God. They accepted the God of Israel. Their sacred scripture was what we today call the Old Testament. Their world-view was Jewish and, together with the other Jews who participated in the apocalyptic movements of the age, they expected the imminent end of the world, the resurrection of the dead, and the Last Judgment. Like other pious Jews of the day, they regarded themselves as sinners and believed in a heaven peopled with angels, a hell full of demons, and an earth that was the scene of the combat between the heavenly and the infernal powers. In fact, like the other Jews of the time, they believed in certain intermediate powers between God and the world, such as Wisdom, and the Word.

Faced with Jesus, they defined him both as the Messiah (the Jewish term and concept) and as the "Son of Man" (an expression calculated to impress Greeks). Being Jews, Christians practiced a rereading of the Jewish religion in function of the novelty of the Jesus event. That novelty, however, completely reshuffled the deck. Now all the themes of traditional religion had to be reorganized. Traditional speculation on angels and devils, the endless questions concerning the end of the world and the Last Judgment—all of this vanished, eclipsed by the great novelty: faith in Jesus. Interest in a nationalistic Messiah and an apocalyptic "Son of Man" collapsed before the person of Jesus. The whole of the Old Testament was now subjected to a "typological" reading in terms of the "good news" that was Jesus (1 Cor. 15:3-4). The "scriptures" now confirmed the history of Jesus and "prophesied" of him. Even the God of Israel, the God of Abraham and Moses, was reinterpreted as the Father of Jesus.

In sum, then, we have a fresh understanding of the whole of history—an interpretation of history in terms of "old" and "new." The same thing occurred with the sociological model of the new faith: the synagogical model. The first base communities had sprung from the synagogue and found there the atmosphere they would need to grow and develop. It is difficult to comprehend the primitive Christian ecclesial model without an acquaintance with the synagogue as its vehicular sociological model, its model of congregation and communication.

THE SYNAGOGUES

If we are to have an adequate understanding of the synagogue, we must plunge into the bloody events of 38 B.C. In that year, in Alexandria, the Egyptian capital, the Romans carried out a violent repression of the Jews, who occupied two of the five quarters of the city and thus constituted a considerable segment of the population. Thirty-eight members of the Council of Elders were trampled to death before the crowd gathered in the circus, four hundred houses were destroyed, and Jewish commerce was outlawed. Some of the victims of the repression were now enclosed in a ghetto of the city, while others were driven to the outlying slums.[2] What can have motivated such hatred of the Jews on the part of the Roman system? Mommsen explains: in large part, the synagogical system. Between the Roman system, which cultivated a popular consent centered around the worship of the emperor — for the purpose of the maintenance of its structures of servitude and tribute — and the synagogical system, with its deep roots in the people, there could be neither peace nor harmony: "Hatred and repression of Jews are as old as the diaspora itself — those autonomous Oriental communities subsisting in the more general Hellenized social context."[3] The synagogues, scattered over the entire "diaspora," or dispersal, systematically developed a theology of opposition to the Roman imperial system. Knowing but one God, the God of Israel, the Jews regarded the Roman system as a radically atheistic one and looked upon the worship of the emperor as an intolerable abomination. Some pious Jews felt that they would be rendered impure merely by touching the Roman coin on which the image of the emperor was stamped. (Hence the question posed by the rabbi in the gospels, "Is it permitted to pay tribute to Caesar?" and Jesus' ironical and actually somewhat evasive response.) The same theology was expressed in vivid colors in the Book of Revelation — an expression of both the Jewish synagogical mentality and the attitude of various sectors of Christianity.

The synagogical system demonstrated this sovereign autonomy, however, not only where the Roman Empire was concerned, but vis-à-vis the Jerusalem temple itself. No one knows for certain where and how the synagogue originated in Judaism itself. In any case it was after the Babylonian Captivity.[4] The synagogue was an unofficial phenomenon, surviving in the underworld of large Hellenized cities of the Roman Empire like Alexandria, Rome, and Antioch, as well as in the lesser cities of Asia Minor, as in the interior of Syria, Africa, and even Gaul. In order to hold on to their "memory" — lest they lose their identity, awash as they were in a world of such total hostility — the Jews of the diaspora clung more faithfully than ever to the Torah, the five books of the Mosaic Law. The authorities of the Jerusalem temple, who represented Jewish religious officialdom, refused to support the synagogical movement, with the result that this took shape and form with an autonomy rarely seen in the history of religions.

Each synagogue was a genuine church — an *ekklēsia*, or autonomous assembly. The very condition of its survival as a people was the "memory of the fathers" — the memory of the patriarchs and prophets. After all, the members of a synagogue were a people. Hence the synagogue's traditionalistic character. At stake was fidelity to the revelation codified in the Law of Moses and implemented in the everyday life of the community. In this fashion the synagogue came to be, and remains today, Judaism's most resistant institution. Its twenty-five-century-old structural and ideological schemata are still practically intact. The synagogue is a house of prayer, the place of counsel, "parliament," and even the "university," all based on the Torah and its rabbinical interpretation. The synagogue testifies to the community model of a social congregation. What ultimately defines it are the strategies of survival that it has incorporated throughout its historical experience — the experience of its life and persistence in a climate of such hostility. This is the art of the synagogue, which primitive Christianity simply inherited.

Two aspects of the synagogue were particularly important for nascent Christianity: its non-territorial or group aspect, and its family aspect. First, the synagogue implies no local sociological insertion, as in a city, town, or territory. Rather it implies a relationship with a determinate human group. This can still be seen today in cities like New York, Paris, or London, where some synagogues fall into disuse while others are built in other parts of the city. The group migrates and takes its synagogue along. The synagogue is not a local but a group phenomenon and belongs to a community on the move, as the needs and circumstances of life may dictate. The visible, physical place deteriorates, and the community is reborn elsewhere. This is much less the case with our parish churches, for example, which maintain a strongly territorial character even when the population migrates and leaves the church empty. The ecclesial models underlying the two realities are very different, as can be seen in everyday life. One is the group model, the other the local or territorial model.

A second aspect of the synagogue that marked the life of the primitive church is connected with the first. The synagogue maintains close ties with the family. We may even say that the essence of the synagogue or base community consists in the relationship obtaining between the "house of prayer"—where a symbol of the Ark of the Temple is preserved, containing the scrolls of sacred scripture—and the family home. The great Jewish festivals, such as Passover, Pentecost, Rosh Hashonah, the Great Reconciliation (Yom Kippur), or the Festival of Tents (Sukkoth) are domestic festivals in which alimentary traditions are of great significance (Lev. 11; Deut. 14). Furthermore, they are related to circumcision, which is a family rite (Gen. 17:9–14). On the Feast of Passover, for example—originally an ancient agricultural festival concerned primarily with the first-fruits of the barley harvest, and celebrated after the flight out of Egypt as a symbol of that exile—the father of the family is the priest who sees to the selection and ritual purity of the foods, the general cleanliness or purity of the house, and the overall progress of the eight-day festival. It is important to observe that primitive Christianity inherited the essential family character of the synagogue. We need only examine the Acts of the Apostles and the Letters of St. Paul, which afford an insight into the significance of the correlation between *ekklēsia* and *oikos* ("house")—a correlation that we shall examine in chapter 11.

THE SYNAGOGUES AND PRIMITIVE CHRISTIANITY

Understanding the Judaism of the synagogues gives us a fairly accurate picture of the life of primitive Christianity. Christianity in earliest times was a network of communities scattered over enormous territorial expanses, principally concentrated in the coastal cities, both the metropolises and the smaller urban centers. Common to these communities was their faith in Jesus Christ. But they lived that faith according to the "synagogical experience." This experience shows itself in both the ministerial structures and the religious practices of these communities—as for example in the ministries of presbyter, bishop, prophet, teacher, and deacon, or in the practices of fasting, communion and excommunication, the catechumenate, the Eucharist, prayers, hymns, and homilies. Everything in original Christianity bears the stamp of the synagogue. Only with the passing of time and separation from Judaism did Christianity develop its own ways of living and expressing its faith. Of course we must not forget that that network of communities was considerably diversified, for reasons explained in part 2, in our consideration of the mission cycles. In the Latin, Western tradition of the history of the church, we have a picture of a Christianity that was always centralized, dependent on the bishop locally and the bishop of Rome universally. This image must not be projected upon the primitive church. It arose as a result of later developments of one particular ramification of Christianity, the Western ramification. Let us not lose sight of what Jean Daniélou observes in this respect:

> The documents we possess have been redacted in Greek
> and for Greeks, whose interest was in the development of

the church in the Western pagan world. But the Christian mission likewise developed in the Eastern pagan world, whose cultural language was Aramaic—in Transjordan, Arabia, Phoenicia, Coelesyria, Adiabene, Osroene. There the Jewish mission [the synagogue] preceded it. Syrian Christianity took on a considerable importance in the first two centuries . . .[5]

Is it possible to formulate some of the special traits of a Christianity so diversified and scattered throughout so many communities? I think so. One characteristic that disappoints certain readers today who look in vain for stronger pronouncements issuing from primitive Christianity with respect to the unjust structures of the Roman Empire and the surrounding society in general stems precisely from the character of frailty and helplessness of communities living in a state of diaspora. The Christian communities were scarcely in a position to transform the social structures of the age. These were communities of marginalized, of poor, of manual laborers, of slaves, of homemakers, artisans, and small merchants. Powerless to act on the large structures of society, Christians concentrated on the formation of communities and, in these communities, on *metanoia*—a change of attitude and lifestyle. The silence of the New Testament on the subject of politics does not mean that historical Christianity must sidestep the political question forever, especially in circumstances where Christianity does enjoy some form of political power. What the first Christians knew very well and sought to live in their communities was this basic principle: among Christians there can be no master-slave relationship. In the communities, the equality of brothers and sisters must prevail. This is the salient trait of the first Christian communities.

Another trait is that of communion (in Latin, *communio*; in Greek, *koinōnia*). In its original sense, "communion" denoted the Christian's union or oneness with Christ. But the word soon came to indicate the union of Christians among themselves as well. The evolution of the Christian social body entailed many cases of conflict, divergency, and even open strife within or among communities. These cases were resolved not in authoritarian fashion but by "synods" or meetings among representatives, who would gather precisely in order to solve problems. A famous instance is that of the controversy over the date of Easter, which flared up in the year 190. Here it was not the opinion of the Roman bishop that prevailed but respect for a variety of traditions.[6] The ancient church practiced not uniformity but unity, in all respect for the autonomy of each community, which was regarded as fully and authentically "church." This is the *modus procedendi* that typifies the synagogical diaspora, Jewish and Jewish-Christian. A visible, reiterated sign of the communion of Christians with Christ and with one another was the Eucharist, which itself came to be called the "communion" (*communio, koinōnia*) in church documents from the fourth century. (In the Middle Ages, surely under the influence of popular religion, the Christian meal acquired yet another name that has survived to our own day: it came to be called the "Mass," from the words of the deacon as the celebration ended, "*Ite, missa est!*" — You may return to your homes, the moment of the *dismissal* has arrived.)

A third trait characterizing synagogical or rabbinical Christianity, also called the Christianity of the circumcision, was the seriousness of the Christian commitment.[7] This same dedication permeated the Jewish life of the diaspora, for example in the way it distanced itself from its environment through special clothing, diet, home furnishings, child-rearing, and a thousand details of daily life. This alone, in the big cities of the West, would have sufficed to enclose the Jews of the synagogue in "ghettos," or closed neighborhoods. A number of the institutions of primitive Christianity, such as the catechumenate, excommunication, fasting, and prayers, recall that same special dedication. It is not by chance that eastern Syria, where Christianity was so markedly synagogical, retained the rigorous catechumenate in an age when many churches had abandoned this requirement for admittance to Christianity and decided on an easier, softer way: infant baptism. I shall return to this point.

As for excommunication, it signified a breach of "communion" when someone lapsed into sin or heresy. In the *Didascalia Apostolorum,* the document produced by the churches of northern Syria in the early part of the third century,[8] we observe that excommunication at that time was a rigorous, protracted process consisting basically of three moments: expulsion from the community of the "saints" (since the church is holy and Christians are holy, are saints), a rigorous penance, normally consisting of fasting and prayer, and reconciliation through the laying-on of hands by the bishop and other members of the community.[9]

Who excommunicated whom? In theory, any Christian had the right to excommunicate, provided he or she presented arguments that the community could accept as valid. So while there were cases in which a bishop excommunicated a lay person, a presbyter, or another bishop, there are also examples of laity excommunicating the bishop.[10] As can readily be understood, such a typically synagogical, "democratic" practice of excommunication made for a great deal of confusion when communion and excommunication came to be used as weapons in the struggle for power in the communities or hegemony in doctrinal authority. And so with the passing of time, excommunication came to be reserved to the bishop, who was already monarchical, as the *Didascalia* shows.[11] The demanding, intransigent practice of excommunication, which took no account of a person's social position but acted solely in function of the model of the Christian life, would undergo a profound modification in the course of the third century, when communities would have to discuss the question of Christianity's openness to the *lapsi*, the "fallen"—finally electing to swing wide the gates of Christian mercy to those who had not succeeded in living holiness to the hilt.

ABANDONMENT OF THE SYNAGOGICAL MODEL

These must be only provisional observations on the difficult question of why and when historical Christianity abandoned the synagogical, community model; the observations will draw attention to certain elements essential to any future discussion. The crucial question is why the church abandoned the model of the autonomy of the base church communities. Three elements were likely to provoke conflict between the Christian church and the synagogue—a conflict extending through several generations and resulting in the transposition of the Christian organizational model to new bases. First, the Christian mission's thrust toward universality was ill reconcilable with the proselytism of the synagogue. Second, the Christian social body adopted an ideological rejection of the entire Jewish people, whom Christians charged with responsibility for the death of Christ. Third, Christians were gradually succumbing to a fascination with the sheer organizational efficiency of the Roman imperial system. Let us examine these points one by one.

The Christian mission knew no frontiers. It was addressed to everyone without discrimination: Jews and proselytes, men and women, slaves and freepersons, Greeks and barbarians, whites and blacks. Jesus had made it perfectly clear that salvation was not the private property of members of the Jewish culture. He had offered it to Samaritans and Romans, Canaanites and Galileans. And so before long Christians ran headlong into the question of "uncircumcision," which occasioned a veritable persecution of gentile proselytes by Christians of the synagogue, who were persuaded of the absolute superiority of the chosen Jewish people in the matter of salvation. The synagogue as such failed to confront the question of openness to the various cultures. Christianity did not. Its decision in favor of uncircumcision opened the door to the acceptance of the popular culture, which involved various risky adaptations and translations of the Christian message.

Christianity adopted an open attitude toward other religions—toward the problems of peoples who found in their religion their symbolic self-expression in the task of confronting problems of marginality, oppression, suffering, death, survival, work, family, housing. The synagogue, on the other hand, remained culturally and religiously closed. It failed to open to "popular piety," continuing to practice purity in the midst of the impurity of the environment, piety in the midst of an impious world, and so forth. Christianity began to practice "impurity." Christians shared their lives with those whose "lips were unclean." That is, they shifted the line between clean and unclean to other levels than those of ritual and legalistic observance, such as circumcision or the dietary laws. This behavior enabled Christianity to become a channel for the expression of the religious problems of peoples generally, and not only of those who shared its community life. Thus Christianity began to have an appeal beyond the borders of its own communities. This characteristic was fraught with constant danger. It could happen—and it did—that one group would arrogate to itself the whole of Christianity's new social function vis-à-vis the general population, transforming that function into a stepping-stone to the creation of a religious bureaucracy destined eventually to suppress the autonomy of the base communities.

Another element in the explanation of why Christianity abandoned the autonomous community model is the fascination that the organizations of the Roman Empire have always held for Mediterranean peoples, even today. It is by way of these organizations that the legacy of Greek culture has come down to us. Marrou, who has made such an exhaustive study of the history of late antiquity (the third to the sixth centuries of our Christian Era), goes so far as to assert that "no other periods in the history of Europe have bequeathed to later centuries so many or such enduring institutions" as the period of the late antiquity of the Roman Empire.[12] One of these "enduring institutions" is undoubtedly Western Christianity, based on the principle of territoriality—organization by territory instead of by human group. This was the Emperor Diocletian's guiding principle at the close of the third century, when he sought for a better control of the grass-roots society through the implantation of the so-called Egyptian model, one based no longer on democracy and popular representation but, quite the contrary, on a territorial subdivision that would make rapid and effective military action possible in case of social unrest. Under this policy Diocletian divided his empire into 4 prefectures, 17 "dioceses" (*dioikēsis*, a distribution of homes), and 101 provinces. Each of the dioceses was governed by a "vicar" and each province by a governor, with a military authority in each province called a *dux*, or leader, who was independent of the civil power. The very adoption by the church of the terminology emerging from this territorial reorganization of the Roman Empire, such as "diocese" or "vicariate," shows how fascinated organizers were with the administration of the empire. This emerges all the more clearly from a comparison of the organization of Latin

Christendom with that of non-Romanized Christendoms, the Irish, for example, which took shape in the fifth and sixth centuries along Celtic lines and in a non-diocesan form—a case of great interest for anyone wishing to investigate the relationship between the episcopate and territoriality.[13]

The age in which the principle of territoriality began to influence the church came long before Diocletian, manifesting itself in the transition from the primitive community church, the family church, to the local church—the church of a city, territory, or neighborhood. Now the church "of the Corinthians," the community of the Christians sojourning in Corinth, became the church of Corinth. Historically the church adopted the territorial principle, which was an organizational principle of the Roman Empire. This acceptance had enormous consequences at the pastoral level, of which the first was the gradual replacement of the catechumenate, which had been based on the principle of a group church requiring the conversion of individuals, with infant baptism, based on the principle of the conversion of "cultures." Pastoral attention now shifted from preparation for baptism to a concern with reiterated penance, the religious instruction of those who were already Christians, and "canonical obligations."

It was easier to enter the Christian social body now, and the church had to make a radical change in its pastoral instruments. There is a logic leading from infant baptism to frequent penance, rural parishes (to serve Christian populations living at a distance from the episcopal center), obligatory Sunday Mass (since Christians baptized in infancy without a personal conversion will have a tendency to relax their religious observance), Easter communion and the Easter "duty," and then—although this came much later—religious instruction in schools and a system of Catholic schools. Once it decided to withdraw the community model, the church had to create new instruments to maintain its fidelity to its original project. So it struggled, and still struggles, with the unavoidable danger of decharacterization and uprooting entailed in this withdrawal. Some authors regard the shift from the community model to the local model to have been a necessary, inescapable evolution, imposed on the church by developments in society as a whole. Adequate historical data upon which to base a solid argument are scant, but the matter is so important for the future of Christianity that some elements need to be touched on here.[14]

Christianity's abandonment of the synagogical or community model did not occur peacefully. Various movements appeared, especially from the second half of the third century onward, which were marginalized and persecuted, but still hold great interest for those seeking to snatch the authentic Christian memory from oblivion. In Latinized Greek these movements were called by the generic name of *cathari*, "pure" — a term that was constantly to recur, especially in the Middle Ages. There was no authentically Latin equivalent. One of these movements was Novatianism, named after its founder, Novatian (d. ca. 257), who was active in the community of Rome and the first theologian — an excellent one, incidentally — to write in Latin there.[15] The ecclesial model championed by Novatian was the one the primitive church had maintained — that church of saints who brooked no compromise with the structures of the Roman Empire. The burning question of Novatian's day was that of the *lapsi* (the "fallen") — the Christians who had denied their faith in the persecution under Decius (251) — and the demand for the excommunication of these sinners, which Novatian upheld. In this he was holding to the more traditional position of the community church as found in St. Paul, Tertullian, Hippolytus, Marcion, and Montanus.

As it happened, however, the community model was being marginalized and discriminated against at the moment, and the upshot was Novatian's condemnation by sixty bishops gathered in Rome.[16] We know little of the exact content of Novatian's teaching, as the same fate befell him as had befallen Marcion before him: his works were destroyed, and we know him only through his adversaries — or else, equally indirectly, by way of the movement that took his name and propagated itself in the East, as also throughout Africa (where it later fused with Donatism) and Gaul, with such a force and tenacity that the Roman emperors themselves, in the fourth and fifth centuries, saw themselves constrained to issue successive decrees against the Novatianists. And despite all, the movement was still alive in the sixth century. In the question of Novatian and Novatianism, then, two models of church came into conflict: the synagogical, community model, and the model gradually taking shape on the basis of the principle of territoriality. Ineluctably, Novatian represents church tradition. The Catholicism that condemned him was a novelty. This is not to make a value judgment on the concrete validity and legitimacy of this Catholic innovation. It may have been valid and legitimate, but it must be said that it had no roots in primitive Christianity or any affinity with the primitive, original themes of a "church of the saints" a "church of the martyrs," or a "church of the perfect." The innovation is a sign of the historical evolution of Christianity, and constituted a realistic response to the new challenges encountered by Christianity along the course of its pilgrimage. But it seems important for Christians today to perceive that this evolution was not the only possible road to have taken, nor even the one more faithfully corresponding to the historical memory of the Christian people. To be sure, the Catholic solution flung wide the gates of the history of Christianity. But at the same time it posed serious problems of the preservation and recollection of an authentic Christian memory.

CHAPTER X

Some Documents from the Base Communities

Lovingly and tenderly, the memory of the Christian people preserves various documents attesting to the life that sprouted up in the base communities. These documents afford us an insight into the nature of relationships prevailing both within and among the various communities. These writings are exceedingly heterogeneous. They include letters, gospels, acts of apostles, apocalypses, homilies, apologias, treatises, commentaries, professions of faith or creeds, liturgical texts, acts of martyrs, lives of monks and ascetics, acts of councils and synods, decretals, catechisms, and more. But in all this vast literature, certain genres stand out as more readily used by the first Christians, such as letters, or treatises on specific subjects, or the group constituted by the trio of gospels, acts of apostles, and apocalypses (one of these last-named groups constituting the New Testament). These genres are dealt with in the present chapter, leaving liturgical texts, homilies, and hymnals for a later analysis.

LETTERS

A written and personal correspondence sprang up among the Christian base communities of the earliest times that was marked by two characteristics: its volume and its egalitarian manner. In the years 160–70, for example, Denis, Bishop of Corinth, dispatched a series of letters to the widest variety of churches — to Lacedemonia, Athens, Nicomedia, Crete, Asia Minor, Rome — without the least trace of authoritarianism. Denis simply encouraged his sisters and brothers to remain steadfast in the faith, to combat the heresies, to seek communion with Christ and among themselves, and finally, to reactivate the Christian memory (Eusebius, *Hist. Eccl.*, IV, 23, 1–11). Let us examine some of the better known letters of the early communities.

The first is the very early letter of Clement of Rome to the church at Corinth, before the close of the first century, A.D. 96–8, dealing with important questions pertaining to the internal organization of the communities.[1] Clement still belongs to the generation of Christians who contemplate the whole of the Christian mystery from the outlook of the marginalized, in the hope of the poor, without speculation. All is cross, salvation, liberation, and Christ's resurrection as token of these Christians' own resurrection. These first Christians know "only Jesus Christ and Jesus Christ crucified" — Origen's very reproach at a later date, part of the great Alexandrian's attempt to depreciate this kind of knowledge and thereby establish his own superiority to it. Origen will be concerned with the enigmas of the universe. The first Christians simply wish to solve community problems — the problems of a life of fellowship in community — in the earnestness of a joint commitment. The first Christians related everything to concrete community life. They dealt with the "givens" of their faith not as themes for abstract speculation, but as concrete realities having a bearing on the life of their communities. Only much later did theologians come to form a kind of exclusive, closed club, at times totally unrelated to the real problems experienced by the church as a social body. In the time of Clement of Rome, Christians' literary production maintained a living relationship with the life of the communities, in conformity with the principle posited by Clement himself: "Let each be subject to his neighbor" (Clement of Rome, *Letter to the Corinthians*, 38:1).

Next, from the first part of the second century we have the seven letters of St. Ignatius of Antioch, upon which I have already commented in these pages.[2] We likewise have the two letters of Polycarp, bishop of Smyrna,[3] and the letter Barnabas[4] issued from an Alexandrian environment around 130. So these well-known examples show the communities of Rome, Antioch, Smyrna, and Alexandria making themselves known and communicating with other communities. These extant letters bear witness to a most lively practice of hospitality and intercommunication on the popular level. Obviously the first Christians had no postal service at their disposal. They had to send their letters by couriers—personal ambassadors from church to church.

NEW TESTAMENT AND "APOCRYPHAL" LITERATURE

A second series of documents that circulated in the base communities of the infant church consisted of the literature that gradually came to be called the "New Testament"—to distinguish it from the scriptures of Jewish Christianity now referred to as the "Old Testament." The New Testament includes the oldest extant Christian writings of all. It was redacted between A.D. 51-2 (First Letter of St. Paul to the Thessalonians) and A.D. 120-30 (Second Letter of St. Peter; Letter of Jude). Gradually a canon of books of the New Testament was drawn up—a fixed, inalterable list established for the purpose of preserving the Christian memory from innovations and fantasy. But the first Christian generations made no clear distinction between what would later come to be regarded as the canonical New Testament literature and the apocryphal literature. The apocryphal books (Gk., *biblio apokruphoi*) were "books hidden away" for fear they might be discovered and destroyed.

We must not forget that before the invention of printing every book was unique and precious. Communities did see their books destroyed by enemies, and Christians themselves destroyed books they regarded as heretical. Hiding books was a typical popular procedure. Christianity itself was "apocryphal"—under cover from the beginning and having to hide everything in its early stages.[5] The term "apocryphal" underwent significant changes in meaning, however, as attitudes in the Christian social body toward the various popular cultures changed. At first, the use of the word in the sense of "hidden" demonstrates that this literature was not being rejected. The apocryphal production spans some four centuries, from the second century B.C. to the second century A.D., the age of the development of an important Jewish popular literature in imitation of the books of the Old Testament.

Christian apocryphal production imitated the New Testament, with apocryphal gospels, acts of apostles, apocalypses, and letters, all crammed with miracles, as they were intended to demonstrate the truth of Christianity as against the claims of pagans and Jews. Then, quite early, Irenaeus bestowed a new meaning on the expression "apocryphal." These writings were spurious and unreliable, he maintained (*Adv. Haer.*, I, 20, 1). At a third stage, "apocryphal" came to denote writings of unknown origin—pseudonymous and hence false in their doctrine. In a last stage of the evolution of the meaning of the term, the apocryphal books were excluded from the canon of sacred scripture. It was mainly theologians influenced by the new Alexandrian orientation (the school of Clement and Origen) who discriminated against the apocryphal writings, such as Eusebius of Caesarea, who wrote of the apocrypha (A.D. 310–12): "They are the fabrications of heretics, totally absurd and impious, totally in disaccord with genuine orthodoxy" (*Hist. Eccl.*, III, 26, 6–7). Other theologians were more moderate, such as St. Augustine, who thought that the apocryphal books ought to be read "with discernment," but that they still ought to be read.[6] With the official condemnation of the apocrypha in the West by Pope Leo I in 449, these documents fell into disuse for good and all. In the East, apocryphal *Acts* continued in official favor until 787, when the Second Council of Nicaea dealt with them most severely, ordering them to be burned.

Today there is a revival of academic interest in the apocryphal literature of the first base communities.[7] Scholars have changed their attitude toward these writings. Until now they have rejected the literature of "miracle and wonder" as foreign to the modern spirit of scientific verification. But today a different "scientificity" is being discovered in the apocrypha: that of the cultural rooting of a marginalized popular movement—infant

Christianity—forced to employ a popular tactic to preserve the memory of the people. The tactic? Recourse to the wondrous, the heroic, the miraculous. A study of the apocryphal literature has shown historians of Christian beginnings that extant Christian literature—fragments, with only occasional complete works—is but the flotsam of a gigantic shipwreck. So many manuscripts have been destroyed or lost that we really ought to be surprised that we have as much as we do. An edict of the Emperor Diocletian, for example, decreed the destruction of Christian books. But then the conversion of Constantine brought about the production of a new and abundant Christian literature. The vigorous practice of a grass-roots Christianity gave new birth to Christian literature after each persecution, with a view to encouraging the communities in faith, steadfastness, and the ways of "perfection."

These writings were encratistic, ascetical, rigoristic, then— the product of a reaction to Christian laxity in the face of persecution. For these reasons, among others, we ought to love and respect the apocryphal writings of the early Christian communities. They are an expression of the faith life of the marginalized. The picturesque, fabulous, miraculous, wondrous, and fantastic elements in this literature ought not to put us off or be allowed to blur our appreciation of the fact that the apocryphal writings indicate, vaguely and in a fragmented way, the presence of nuclei of resistance to the dominant cultural aggression. They are evidence of the small-scale, "underground" labors that permitted the survival of impoverished, exploited sectors of the society of that time, precisely the sectors in which Christianity moved.

The people, who only rarely emerge to the level of our direct historical knowledge, found the apocryphal literature to their taste and used it to nourish their faith. It is understandable that the Apostles should be presented as all but superhuman figures whose miracles humiliated the enemies of the faith. The figure of the apostle in the apocryphal literature assumed in the common, anonymous Christian the function of a symbol of courage and resistance, of faith and hope. It is not by chance that the apocryphal literature includes hymns, poetry, recollections of those great heroes Andrew, James, Philip, Thomas, Peter, and

Paul, and accounts of martyrdom. This "heroization" was a mechanism for the preservation of the Christian popular culture. The apocrypha are the authentic productions of a poor people in their quality as Christian believers. No wonder they appear so strange to the eyes of erudite theologians, who have frequently lost all sensitivity to the questions raised by the deep needs of the common people.[8]

WORKS OF THE SYRIAN MISSION CYCLE

Three writings of the Syrian mission cycle, which spans three centuries, testify to the popular, comradely, fervent spirit that animated Christian life in Syria. These are the *Teaching of the Twelve Apostles* (in Greek, the *Didache*, the "doctrine"), from the first part of the second century;[9] the *Didascalia Apostolorum*, dating from the first half of the third century;[10] and the *Apostolic Constitutions*, redacted or at least compiled in 380.[11] The factor common to all three works is indicated by the use of the adjective "apostolic" in their titles. These are community productions, so the "apostolic" reference does not indicate that the Apostles themselves ordered or directed the composition of this literature, but shows the intention — typically popular — of placing community documents under the protection of the apostolic name and authority. "Apostolic" had come to connote the cohesion and persistence of the community memory, the warranty of community fidelity to the pristine Christian project, the radicating element of the Christian identity. The meaning of the term "apostolic" underwent a substantial change the moment the groups of organizers of the great Christendoms appropriated it as a bolster and support for their hegemony over the Christian social body.

The first of these three writings, the *Teaching of the Twelve Apostles* (also known as the *Didache*), is "easy reading" even today. It reveals the very roots of Christianity. The expression "teaching," or "doctrine," repeatedly occurring in the text does not denote a "doctrine" in the sense in which we use it of later catechisms — let alone anything like "indoctrination" — but simply expresses Christian practice, the Christian way, the Christian life.

The "doctrine" of the first six chapters is simply this: "There are two ways. One leads to life, the other to death. The difference between them is enormous" (*Didache*, 1, 1). In a simple, warm style, bordering on the colloquial, the *Didache* maps out the way or road of life—the "way of the doctrine" (6, 1)—along with the way of death. Chapters 7 to 10 deal with the baptismal liturgy, fasting, and the Eucharist and contain a Eucharistic prayer (10, 1-6). In chapters 11 to 15 the document treats of the respect that the community ought to show for itinerant apostles or prophets, the missionaries of Christianity:

> Any apostle coming to join you, receive as the Lord himself. But he shall not stay more than a day with you, or two, if necessary. If he stays three days he is a false prophet. [11, 4-5]

Why? The reason is simple. The communities lack the resources to offer lodging over a prolonged period to persons who neither work nor participate in some other way in the effort to provide food and housing. "Doctors" (teachers), prophets, and apostles were lodged in family homes. There were no special places for them to stay. Hence the oft-repeated advice:

> If the one who seeks you out is a traveller, help him as best you can. He will stay with you only two, or, if necessary, three days. If he should wish to stay longer among you, and is an artisan, let him earn his bread. If he has no trade, see to it in good conscience that a Christian not live in idleness among you. If he is unwilling to abide by this principle, he is a Christ-monger. Be on your guard against him. [12, 2-5]

Primitive Christianity's trademark was work. There were no Christians who did not live by their labor, other than the itinerants who devoted their full time to the mission and to travel, as we may gather from the following text:

Any true prophet, if he wishes to abide with you, deserves his sustenance. Likewise the authentic teacher is worthy, as is the laborer, of his sustenance. Take the first-fruits of the wine press and the threshing floor, of the oxen and the ewes, and give them to the prophets, for they are our high priests. If there are no prophets, give them to the poor. . . . Likewise if you open a cask of wine, take the first draught and make a gift of it to the prophets. [13, 1–6]

The reason for this altogether special predilection for the prophets lies in the conviction that mission is the prime Christian task, as observed above in part 2. "Seek ye first the Reign of God, and the rest will be added unto you." And indeed the prophet demonstrated his charism not only in words but in life:

Not everyone who speaks in the spirit is a prophet, but only the one who exhibits the behavior of the Lord. It is by his life that he will be known for a true prophet or a false one. . . . Any prophet who teaches the truth and fails to practice what he teaches is a false prophet. [11, 8–10]

One of the great paradoxes of the history of the church is the fact that this principle of legitimation of authority by works and manner of life eventually came to be combated by ecclesiastical authority itself, as in the case of the English "doctor" John Wycliff (1320–84), the Oxford professor who taught that an authority merits respect and obedience only if it practices what it preaches. This principle of "righteousness" or veracity is in conformity with the principle of the *Didache*: "Any prophet who fails to practice what he preaches is a false prophet." And yet the highest authority of the church, gathered at the Council of Constance in 1415, ordered the burning of Wycliff's mortal remains, that his memory might be obliterated from the mind of the Christian people forever.[12] Chapter 15 of the *Didache* teaches that the charismatic model of the Christian ministry centers on the missionaries, be they apostles, prophets, or teachers, and that the standard by which ministers who abide in the communities and do not travel are endorsed or rejected is the criterion precisely of the itinerants:

Let them establish bishops and deacons, worthy of the Lord, humble men, not ambitious for money, truthful and experienced, since they too, along with yourselves, exercise the ministry of the prophets and teachers. Do not condemn them: they should be honored by you as prophets and doctors. [15, 1-2]

The prime authority, then, is constituted by the prophets and teachers, and itinerants.

A century later, these recommendations of the *Didache* were broadened and made more explicit, in Syria, by way of a text entitled *Didascalia Apostolorum*. On one point especially the *Didascalia* proclaims an innovation. In the matter of authority in the communities, this document repeatedly insists on the authority of the bishop, to the detriment of that of the prophets and teachers. The bishop is regarded as holding the place of God in the community. He is the image of God and a mediator between God and the faithful. He is the "voice of God," calling all to justice and good works and proclaiming God's kindness and wrath alike in the coming judgment.[13] With an energy unknown to any other pre-Constantinian text, the *Didascalia* insists on the qualities required of a bishop. First of all he must be altogether familiar with sacred scripture. Next, he must have certain moral qualities and be at least fifty years of age. Finally, he may not have two wives or have been married twice. The conduct of a bishop's wife and children are to be in keeping with the episcopal responsibility. The presbyters—absent from chapters 11 to 15 of the *Didache*—have a relevant place in the *Didascalia* as the bishop's counselors and advisors. They function as advocates in the civil courts where the defendants are Christian. All of this insistence on the episcopal structure of the Christian ministry is a sign of the emergence of a proto-Catholicism that will gradually replace the practices of primitive Christianity.[14]

In the year 182 in Rome, during the episcopacy of Callistus (217-22), the important document known as the *Apostolic Tradition* appeared. Attributed to the presbyter Hippolytus, it has been reconstituted, only recently, by slow and patient scholarship.[15] The intent of the *Apostolic Tradition* is to defend the liturgical traditions of the Christian communities against innovation. The document is fundamental for our knowledge of the Christian liturgy at the beginning of the third century, as it furnishes, for the first time in the history of the church, precise descriptions of the liturgy, giving the text of certain liturgical prayers besides. It records the liturgical prayers for the ordination of bishops, presbyters, and deacons (now mentioned in this order), and then cites other ministries, such as those of widows, lectors, virgins, subdeacons, teachers, acolytes, exorcists, porters or doorkeepers, and ministers of the sick. The teachers, so important in the *Didache*, are now relegated to the category of the lower ministers. The prophets are no longer so much as mentioned. The *Apostolic Tradition* is likewise important for our knowledge of the blessings used by the ancient church, as well as for the processes of community acceptance of new members, such as the catechumenate, baptism, chrismation, and the baptismal Eucharist.

While it claims in its title to be traditional, Hippolytus' work introduces important innovations vis-à-vis earlier base-community writings. First of all it shows a basic change of outlook with respect to ministries, which are now articulated no longer in terms of "service" but in those of "government" and power in the communities. As a result, the concept of the church as charismatic now yields to the concept of a hierarchical church. Now the community is divided into clergy and laity (8–10, 19). The power of officiating at the liturgy is now in the hands of the clergy—specifically, the bishop—while the remaining ministries are arranged in terms of their subordination to the episcopal office. Or rather, all ministries are arranged in a kind of ladder, from the lower ministries up to the episcopacy.

Another novelty consists in the attention bestowed on worship, at the expense of a service of fellowship. The concept of "liturgy" (in Greek, *leitourgia*, sacred "service" as distinguished from profane) forms the focus of the considerations of the *Apostolic Tradition*. Consequently the ministries of the bishop and the presbyters come to be defined in function of Old Testament concepts of the Levitical priesthood and the offering of a "sacrifice." This analogy between the Christian ministry and the Old Testament priesthood opens the door to demands for ritual purity in the ministers "of the altar," and we are now but one step away from ministerial celibacy.[16] Alexandre Faivre emphasizes the new meaning bestowed by the *Apostolic Tradition* on the "imposition of hands"—the laying-on of hands (in Greek, *cheirotonia*).[17] At first, says Faivre, the laying-on of hands represented an *acknowledgment* of the presence of the Holy Spirit, while at the beginning of the third century it came to be the sign of the "transmission" of the Holy Spirit. Now the gift of the Holy Spirit is bestowed by the intermediary of the laying-on of hands.

This evolution in Christian practice posits the entire tradition of "apostolic succession" in new terms. That succession now ceases to be a community succession and is reserved to a group within the community, the group known as the clergy. The new formula apportions the roles of the members of the Christian community in the following schema: The bishops of the neighboring communities ordain (*cheirotonein*) the local bishop (also called shepherd, high priest, the one who teaches, or the one who offers the Eucharist), who in turn ordains the presbyters and deacons, below whom come confessors, and then widows, lectors, virgins, subdeacons, ministers of the sick, and finally the simple faithful, who represent the base or floor of the new social edifice, the Christian community. In the *Apostolic Tradition* the Christian social body takes on the detailed division of a hierarchized social edifice, complete with graduated echelons of power. The episcopate becomes the "charism" par excellence, the complete function that, circumstances requiring, could meet all community needs simply by itself.[18]

The *Apostolic Tradition* is surely the fruit of a long dispute within the Christian communities, in the course of which documents representing the opposing view, like the *Peri ton charismatōn* ("On Charisms"), were obliterated from Christian memory.[19] The insistence with which documents of the third and fourth centuries speak of "apostolic" and "tradition" is of itself a demonstration of the climate of controversy and discord at the heart of the communities as to the legitimacy and apostolicity of the two conflicting models of church—the community model and the hierarchical model. Wherever that legitimacy and apostolicity may lie, at all events Hippolytus' *Apostolic Tradition*

marked the subsequent evolution of power in the church profoundly—some would say irreversibly. By way of the so-called
Egyptian Ecclesiastical Ordination, preserved in Latin, Arabic,
and Ge'ez (the language of the Ethiopian church), the "apostolic
tradition" passed into the *Apostolic Constitutions* (380), and
from there to the vast current of church traditions in the
Christian East and the Latin West.[20]

THE *SHEPHERD* OF HERMAS

This summary presentation of certain documents of the base
communities of Christian antiquity must include mention of one
of the most ancient written works of Christianity, The *Shepherd*
(in Greek, *Poimēn*), published under the authorship of a certain
Hermas, a petty merchant of very narrow cultural horizons but
profoundly pious and conscientious, humble and joyful, and
certainly typifying the ordinary Christian of his time. The
Shepherd was written in Rome around A.D. 150.[21] One of the
lengthiest writings in primitive Christian literature, it is divided
into three parts, comprising five apocalyptic visions, twelve
commandments, and ten "comparisons." The content of these
divisions, however, does not always correspond to their head-
ings, and some are probably later interpolations. So great was
the authority of the *Shepherd* in the ancient church that various
writers—such as Irenaeus, Tertullian, Clement of Alexandria,
and Origen—looked upon it as a canonical book of the New
Testament.

The "Shepherd," in Hermas' allegory, is the guardian angel of
the church. Just as Michael was the angel of the people of Israel,
so the "Shepherd" was the angel of the new Israel who comes on
the scene as an angel of penitence. The end of the ages is drawing
near, Hermas tells us, and the angel has come to warn Christians
to do penance while time remains, for the hour of judgment is at
hand. In the celebrated vision of 3, 1–7, the church is compared
to a tower under construction.[22] The stones of which it is being
built symbolize sinners who, after doing penance, can still be
reintegrated into the community. This penance will consist in the
practice of the "little virtues," those of hearth and home, such as

patience, faith, fear of the Lord, truth, and humility, as opposed to impulsiveness, anger, sadness, or discouragement. The environment must have been that of the family communities of the first age of Christianity, where conversion to Christianity meant a conversion in daily life—the conversion of husband to wife, of rich to poor, of parents to their children. There is an excellent example of this conversion in the manner in which Hermas deals with female adultery (Commandment IV, 1, 1):

> But if he dismisses his wife and then marries another, he too commits adultery . . . If the husband refuses to receive [his repentant adulterous wife] he will sin. He will commit a grave sin, for he must welcome her who has sinned and repented. He must not do so repeatedly, however, since for the servants of God there is but one penance. It is the thought of [her possible future] repentance that will dissuade the husband from marrying anew. Indeed this attitude of mind must rule husband and wife alike.[23]

Aline Rousselle asserts that this is an innovation vis-à-vis prevailing Roman law and certain to place Christian marriages at risk. Hermas is contradicting the Roman juridical system on two points. First, he cites the possibility not only of the wife's repentance but of her husband's forgiveness and reacceptance as his lawful spouse. This was a "juridical impossibility" in Roman law, Rousselle reminds us, and must have rendered the Christian husband liable to indictment for proxenetism (the activity of a procurer—enticement to prostitution).

> The commandment proclaimed by Hermas' "Shepherd" demands of the husband not only the personal effort of a life of celibacy as he waits in hope for the return of his adulterous wife. It also demands he have the courage to risk indictment for moral laxity, for which he could have to suffer the public infamy of having countenanced adultery, and for which he could even be sentenced to exile (if he happened to be wealthy) or hard labor (if he were poor), since an accomplice in an act of adultery was liable to the penalty for adultery itself.[24]

Further: Hermas' text presupposes the concept of male adultery, a concept unknown to Roman law. A husband enjoyed a great deal more sexual freedom than did his wife, and the wife of an unfaithful husband had no legal grounds to repudiate him. The husband had the "right" to promiscuity with slaves or servants, entertainers, prostitutes, and the poor in general, nor might his wife repudiate him for such behavior. By positing the "single standard," Hermas' *Shepherd* created the concept of adultery on the part of the husband by infidelity to his wife. This was something new, and it placed the Christian wife in a delicate situation where her financial security was concerned. Roman law did not restore her dowry. Thus unless she received aid from her family, a Christian woman who had had the courage to repudiate an adulterous husband would have to be helped and protected by the community. Now we understand why there were so many "widows" in Christian communities. In the primitive Christian mentality, still charged with the memory of Jesus and his own actions, the practice of the faith must surely include this specific, original practice, contrast though it might with the prevailing, anti-feminist ideology.

CHAPTER XI

The Christian Life in the Base Church Communities

The documents bequeathed to us by primitive Christianity leave no shadow of a doubt: to be a Christian, in those times, did not mean primarily embracing a new doctrine. Primarily it meant living a new life. The New Testament, the letters of leaders like Polycarp, Ignatius of Antioch, or Clement of Rome, texts like the *Didache,* the *Shepherd,* and the *Didascalia Apostolica* are at one on this point.

VIRTUES BASED IN THE HOUSE AND FAMILY

Christianity stressed living the "little virtues" of home and family in the midst of a hostile environment that demonstrated no sensitivity for such virtues. What did these documents recommend? Gentleness, peace, humility, patience, temperance — virtues little esteemed in a Greco-Roman world that extolled discipline, nobility of spirit, bravery, and courage! The New Testament is altogether clear on the matter of the Christian virtues. It extols not grand, heroic virtues, but a capacity to perceive God in the small things of daily life (1 Cor. 10:31). It extols a readiness to pass unperceived and not to attract attention (Luke 14:7–10; Mark 10:45; Rom. 12:10). It inculcates sincerity (Matt. 5:37), discretion in speaking and in keeping silence (James 3:3–10; Matt. 18:15), an absence of preoccupation with the morrow (Matt. 6:32–34), a pleasant manner (Matt. 6:16), benevolence (Rom. 12:15), punctuality (Matt. 25:1–13; Luke 12:1–16), a struggle with indolence and sloth (Matt. 20:1–16), and perseverance to the last (Luke 9:62; Matt. 24:13; 25:21). In other words it encourages the virtues of familiar, intimate social dealings, which require no monasteries or seclusion from the world. It calls for the virtues of everyday living. These rarely emerge in historiography in the grand manner. Still, they form the warp and woof of authentic history, as emerges from an examination of primitive Christianity—a popular movement borne aloft on the shoulders of the anonymous and marginalized and having the power to transform society from within. Let us glance at one example among many, the letter of the bishop of Smyrna, Polycarp, to the Christians of Philippi:

> First let us teach ourselves to walk in the commandment of the Lord. Next let us teach women to walk in the faith given to them, in charity and chastity; to love especially their husbands with all sincerity, and then all equally, in perfect continence; and to rear their children in the discipline of the fear of God. Let us teach widows to be wise in the things of the faith of the Lord, to intercede ceaselessly for all, and to live far from backbiting, slander, false witness, and the covetousness of anything, knowing that they are the altar of God, where all offerings are scrutinized meticulously, for nothing escapes God.[1]

An attentive reading of the Acts of the Apostles and the Letters of St. Paul demonstrates that the most original and primitive form of the ecclesial experience consisted in community meetings in the private homes of married couples. As early as the second chapter of Acts we find an outline of the elements of these meetings: the "teaching" (or memory) of the Apostles; mutual union, even and especially in the financial area; the breaking of bread; concern for the poor; and in a broader scope, communion with the other communities (Acts 4:32; 5:12ff.).

Sociologically these meetings appeared to be gatherings of "sects" or "heresies" ("the heresy of the Nazarenes," for example, as one expression of the time had it), especially after the split with the synagogue. It was the family home, the house (*oikos*, in Greek), that was the nucleus from which all Christian fellowship and support radiated. There was no building reserved for the purpose of Christian meetings alone. The earliest building serving exclusively for Christians' meetings, recently discovered in Dura-Europos in eastern Syria, dates from A.D. 232 — rather later than the practices presently under consideration.[2]

At that time the word "house" denoted not only the building in which a family lived but the family itself, including friends and relatives. It was from these family nuclei that Christianity spread throughout the Mediterranean Basin, and from there along the Nile, the Rhone, the Danube, the Tigris and Euphrates. This formula proved extremely dynamic, as we have seen, providing the ideal vehicle for the rapid expansion of Christianity in the first centuries.

St. Paul frequently employs the expression "church" (*ekklēsia*) to designate the group of "saints" who gather in the home of a Christian couple (1 Cor. 16:19; Col. 4:15; Phil. 2). In Romans 16 he mentions at least eight of these domestic communities by name — those of Prisca and Aquila, Epaenetus, Mary, Andronicus and Junias, Ampliatus, the "household of Aristobulus," the "household of Narcissus," and "Gaius, who is host to me and to the whole church."

The Apostles' letters are customarily addressed to these domestic communities, and they actually name the couples or individuals committed to the "Way" who open their homes for the meetings. "Aquila and Priscilla salute you in the Lord, as well as the church who meet at their house" (1 Cor. 16:19); "Nymphas and the church who meet at his house" (Col. 4:15). This seemingly so simple fact had profound repercussions. Christian morality now regarded the family no longer as a mere cell in the prevailing societal body — a classic theme of state religions — but as the leaven of a new society. This, then, is why the Apostles were so intensely, indeed so minutely, concerned with the development of these domestic churches, supporting them in every way they could and devoting to them the greater part of their time. They were seeking to avoid abuses, forestall disunion, and lay down rules for a life in common. They did not hesitate to go into detail, as shown in Romans 12:9–13, with all it has to say about respect, tenderness, fulfilling one's domestic duties, joy, patience, sharing one's goods with the needy, and hospitality toward visitors; or from chapters 10–15 of the First Letter of St. Paul to the Corinthians, which comes right down to the veiling of women, a synagogical usage highly recommended by the rabbis; or again from the third chapter of the Letter to the Colossians, which prescribes: "Wives, obey your husbands; slaves, obey your owners."

These recommendations were frequently interpreted in the perspective of the family as a building block of society. But this was the outlook neither of St. Paul nor of primitive Christianity, which was in the process of opening up to a new society and seeking to avoid, with very practical and timely logic, any obstacles to missionary penetration, as well as anything that the established authorities or the many other enemies of Christianity might use against the newborn church. Certain authors have erected St. Paul's practical recommendations for Christian practice into eternal principles, thereby completely disfiguring the perspective in which they were drawn up.

However clearly it may appear in the texts, the domestic character of primitive Christianity has been given short shrift by very many scholars of church history. Their attention, frequently motivated by an apologetical intent, has centered too exclusively on questions of church power. They have been preoccupied with the hierarchy, the episcopacy, the priesthood, the ministry of St. Peter and its relation to the city of Rome, and so on — to the wholesale neglect of those who actually preached the gospel in their homes and lodgings, their stalls and shops, without sermons but simply by the example of their lives. This basic model of evangelization, which predominated in Christianity's infancy, has always been the foundation of the imposing Christian edifice constructed over the course of time. Nor can it ever be otherwise, as long as the Reign of God is still under construction. But the model is such a humble, workaday one, and it clings so closely to the earth of life that we tread each day that many of us never manage to glimpse it. To observe what is transpiring beneath you, you must bow your head.

We have already alluded to the text of St. Paul that enjoins wives to obey their husbands and slaves their owners. There is another passage in which St. Paul appears to criticize the married state as well: In 1 Corinthians 7:25-31, the great apostle asserts that it is better to remain celibate than to marry. On the basis of these and other Pauline texts some authors have criticized the primitive Christian life as "encratistic"—imbued with the ideology of sexual continence as a Christian ideal—socially reactionary, and anti-feminist. I accept the criticisms themselves, and recall that St. Paul had been very heavily influenced by the rabbinical and Pharisaic ideology of the environment in which he had been reared. Thus for example married Jewish women were not permitted to go into the street without covering their heads according to the rabbinical tradition. St. Paul agreed and imposed this Jewish tradition on Christian women. But this does not mean that Christian women of all times and places must never enter a church without covering their head with a veil! St. Paul's recommendation is culturally conditioned. It cannot, therefore, be automatically valid for all times and places. Christian tradition preserves just as valid, just as weighty documents insisting on just the opposite of the Pauline position. For example, the letter written in the second half of the second century by an anonymous Christian to a certain pagan called Diognetus breathes a spirit utterly foreign to the encratistic atmosphere that marked other segments of Christianity, as well as some of the missionary cycles.[3] As this document shows, Christians are distinguished from others not by a rejection of marriage but by a life of total dedication to the building of the Reign of God. This is what makes "foreigners" of Christians. This is what marginalizes them in the eyes of those who make this earth their homeland.

THE COMMUNITIES AS BASIS
FOR THE NEW SOCIETY

There is every indication that the practice of the "little virtues" of hearth and home—actually very demanding virtues—indeed corresponds to the original intentions of Jesus of Nazareth, who sought to heal living interpersonal relationships from *within the community*. Jesus insisted we love one another as sisters and brothers. Christians did precisely this in the little things of every day, thus performing the most difficult of tasks, which consists in furnishing society with a leaven that works from the inside out—from the community of home and family to society at large. Hence the seemingly pietistic and fundamentalistic character presented by the first Christian communities in extant documents dealing with Christian origins. The larger society was not condemned across the board. Rather it was gradually leavened by the "ferment of the Christians" or illuminated by the "light of Christ." A life in community implied a communion of goods and certainly the communion of a common table, as the *Letter to Diognetus* proves. It was precisely this concept—that of a communion of goods and table—that moved the fourth-century church Fathers, especially St. Basil (330–79) and St. John Chrysostom (d. 407), to look upon the first Christian community at Jerusalem as the prototype of a new society from which private property and social exploitation would be absent. Here is how St. Basil understood the project of the first Christians at Jerusalem:

> We are misappropriating common property. We seize for ourselves what belongs to the community. We ought to be ashamed at the examples the pagans give: they have a most humane law among them that there be but one table, one meal, and that a most numerous people form, as it were, one family. But let us take leave of the pagans and appeal to the example of those three thousand persons [the first Christians]. Let us compare our life with that of the first community, where all property was held in common—life, soul, concord, table—forming a united community, a sincere love, making all individuals into one body, with the result that many hearts were now one, in one thinking.[4]

St. John Chrysostom went further. The primitive Christian community, he held, only re-established the observance of a law of nature: the law of common possession of the goods of this earth:

In the beginning God did not create one rich and another poor. God gave the same earth to all to cultivate, and distributed everything to everyone as if all had been brothers. He created for all the same eyes, the same body, the same soul, and a similar facial appearance. Everything has issued from the same earth, the same man, the same house. God made even other things common, as cities, squares, parks. But once covetousness is aroused, once folk have sought to grasp control of something, then the harmony is shattered. Confusion, disorder, and agitation reign. It is as if nature were protesting, recalling to us that God has joined us in a universal communion, while we seek to divide ourselves instead—to grasp control of property as if it were a personal possession, and we begin to call it by those impious words, "mine" and "yours." Then the situation becomes insupportable. In a society exempt from greed, there is no discord or power struggle. Nature provides for common ownership rather than private ownership.[5]

St. Basil and St. John Chrysostom are two examples of a vast current of Christian thought that finds in the community of the first Christians a model applicable to all human social life.

THE IMPORTANCE OF BAPTISM

How was the primitive church body constituted? Beyond a doubt, by the sign of baptism. To the eyes of those who shared one another's lives in the base community, baptism was a distinguishing mark of basic importance—a kind of surveyor's stake marking the boundary between Christian and non-Christian, and having manifold repercussions in the social sphere. Baptism was the decisive step in the life of a Christian (Rom. 6:3–5; John 3:5), the axis upon which everything else rotated and which was commemorated throughout the whole remainder of one's life, be it in the Easter liturgy with its renewal of the baptismal promises, or be it on the circumstantial occasions on which Christians were called to testify to their faith. Eusebius of Caesarea recounts the case of "a certain holy virgin who, whenever she was put to the test, defended herself with a simple appeal to her baptism: 'I am a Christian.' "[6] Christianity gave an altogether new meaning to a very ancient rite, and one encountered in many religions: the rite that appeals to the purifying power of water. Jewish proselytes were baptized. John the Baptist, who belonged to an especially fervent baptist sect, baptized. Jesus' innovative practice gave the baptismal rite a new meaning—that of rebirth through the Holy Spirit. To be baptized was to be born again. One began a new life, reorganizing the whole of one's existence in terms of a new project. The whole Christian social body took shape and form around the rite of baptism, articulating the whole of its community life in reference to it—its liturgy, the catechumenate and catechesis, its Eucharist, its penance, its fasting and prayers.

Rightly did the baptismal liturgy of the primitive church picture baptism as the last battle of a mythic struggle as old as human history itself, the battle between the primordial waters and Yahweh. This is the reason why that liturgy offered three prefigurations or prototypes of baptism: the Flood (Gen. 8:8), the passage through the Red Sea (Exod. 14:15–31), and the crossing of the Jordan into the land of promise (Josh. 3:9–17). The waters symbolized the maleficent powers from which Noah had rescued the elect; baptism or the passage through water "saved" persons from the powers of the waters (1 Cor. 10:1–2).[7] In later Christianity, especially after the abandonment of a rigorous and carefully planned catechumenate in preparation for baptism, this meaning was obscured in the eyes of most Christians. The age of infant or "sociological" baptism had dawned, with its gradual relaxation of the baptismal commitment and abandonment of the model of church whose vital substance had lain in that engagement. As I have said, the abandonment of the catechumenate is a historical fact of enormous consequence for the historical memory of the Christian people.

IMAGINATION AND WONDER

Various studies on Christian origins, especially those of the school of Rudolf Bultmann, have given us a cold, almost disagreeable image of the first Christians. These scholarly authors have fallen victim to the myths of the "scientificity" of the "modern" sciences practiced from the eighteenth century onward—myths so concerned to "purge" the world of all imagination and enthusiasm or any movement of the heart or the emotions. Bultmann himself, according to Rubem Alves, "capitulated to the scientific 'evidences' of our world, failing to realize that these very 'evidences' rest on an unconscious mythology of the structure of society."[8] But the first Christians experienced the "fascination of the splendor of the imagination" to a greater degree than we do today. They had not yet fallen under the spell of the rational culture that would one day come to characterize broad sectors of Western civilization and mark especially the clergy and their approach to the Christian life.

The fascination of the Christian life of the first generations was so intense a thing that it shone through in all the written documents, the iconography, the liturgy, the prayers of those generations—in all of the expressions of the community life. Hermas' *Shepherd,* for example, which is largely concerned with penance and the seriousness of the Christian commitment, is steeped in an atmosphere of wonder. Here the church is a marvelous tower under construction, and its builders are the Christians. Or it is compared to a woman who becomes ever more youthful instead of growing old. Or it addresses Christians with the authority of a "divine shepherdess." It is as if the documents of the first Christian communities were saying: Yes, it is hard to be a Christian, but it is worth the trouble—let us commence the journey together.

Penance, the rigorous fasts, the insistent prayers, the catechumenate—Christians embraced them all with an infectious enthusiasm. Enthusiasm was the mark of an authentic cultivation of the imagination on the part of Christians. The bright and radiant center of the universe was Jesus of Nazareth, the "Christ" of God and the universal Savior. The Apostles were the cosmic couriers of a message for the whole universe. Sacred scripture was the book containing the treasure of the human race.

The first Christians spoke of, and loved to hear of, apocalypses and secret revelations, "hidden" (apocryphal) stories and miracle cases, all very much to the taste of the time. They told their stories over their work tools (their looms, their plows, their millstones or cards), or by night in front of their houses. They cultivated their imagination. Nor was this any impediment to the seriousness of the Christian commitment. On the contrary, it sustained and nourished that commitment.

Certain marginal churches, such as that of Ethiopia, have preserved this climate of enthusiasm and imagination in their works of art down through the centuries. In the church at Goh, in Ethiopia, a fifteenth-century painting represents a group of nine apostles or African missionaries (as shown by their kinky hair), each with a book or a crucifix in his hand, moving out — in collegiality, without any hierarchical arrangement — from a central point occupied by Christ, to preach the gospel in all the corners of the universe, their eyes glistening with enthusiasm for the good news, their hands on their breast as if the better to safeguard that most precious of treasures (the sacred book of the memory of Jesus on the cross), their whole body prepared for mission. This painting is representative of so many testimonials to the extraordinary fascination exerted on Christian awareness by the experience of the base communities, not only in the first three centuries, but all through the history of Christianity.

CHAPTER XII

Service in the Base Church Communities

Perhaps the most important of the Christian innovations—indeed, it may be Christianity's greatest contribution to the history of humanity—can be formulated in the simple word "service" (in Greek, *diakonia*). Jesus was explicit:

> "You know how among the Gentiles those who seem to exercise authority lord it over them; their great ones make their importance felt. It cannot be like that with you. Anyone among you who aspires to greatness must serve the rest; whoever wants to rank first among you must serve the needs of all. The Son of Man has not come to be served but to serve—to give his life in ransom for the many." [Mark 10:42–45]

The word "service" comes from *servus*—the slave, the domestic who washes the clothes, the house, the dishes, and guests' feet. Jesus washed his disciples' feet, and then, in John's marvelous memorial, explained what he had done.

> "Do you understand what I just did for you?
> You address me as 'Teacher' and 'Lord,'
> and fittingly enough,

for that is what I am.
But if I washed your feet —
I who am Teacher and Lord —
then you must wash each other's feet." [John 13:12-14]

In the words of Sebastião Armando:

> Jesus means that there is only one gate through which his
> disciples may enter the Reign of God. To accept the Reign
> is not only to accept these "least ones" and be at their
> service; to accept the Reign is to become as these least,
> accepting the condition of the lost and sharing the condi-
> tion of the poor.[1]

SERVICE BY WOMEN

If we leaf through the documentation of the primitive church
with this in mind—the service of the least ones in little things,
and identification with these least—then we must acknowledge
that those who followed the memory and practice of Jesus most
faithfully were women. The first service in the history of the
church was performed by the women who anointed the body of
a "little one" indeed, the humiliated, tortured, crucified body of
Jesus, in such urgent need of attention in the days after his
death:

> The women who had come with him from Galilee followed
> along behind. They saw the tomb and how his body was
> buried. Then they went home to prepare spices and
> perfumes. They observed the sabbath [the day after Good
> Friday] as a day of rest, in accordance with the law.
> On the first day of the week, at dawn, the women came
> to the tomb bringing the spices they had prepared. [Luke
> 23:55-24:1]

In striking fidelity to the example of this first service,
Christian women have continued to care for bodies, food,
homes, and clothing throughout history, while men have only

plunged deeper and deeper into the struggle for power and prestige. Unless we rescue the memory of female service in the base communities, our vision of this important Christian novelty, the Christian "new way of being" by announcing the good news to the poor, the liberation of captives and the oppressed and the proclamation of the "Lord's year of grace" (Luke 4:18–19, citing Isa. 61:1; 58:6), will surely remain perverted and deformed. But this memory is beset from the outset with the problem of historical sources. The memory of woman in the history of the church has always been manipulated by men, and by men who were rarely without taint of the androcentric ideology: the man as center of all. In the 672 pages of the Altaner-Stuiber patrology—an excellent presentation of the Christian sources of the first six centuries—women are mentioned on only four pages. We have the passion (martyrdom) of Perpetua and her slave Felicity (p. 92); the legend of St. Thecla (p. 136); St. Mary of Egypt, surnamed the Penitent (p. 242); and Aetheria (or Eucheria or Egeria the fourth-century nun who went out to the Egyptian desert (p. 245).

Why such sparse information? Because the Fathers of the ancient church themselves simply failed to preserve memorials of women. Of the 240 letters of St. Augustine, fourteen are addressed to women, but he fails to record a single letter received *from* a woman. Of St. John Chrysostom's fifty-three letters to women, seventeen are addressed to his great friend Olympia. We have thirty-four letters of St. Jerome to women, and one written by a woman—a great historical rarity. Men did not usually keep the writings they received from women, doubtless because the male-female relationship was charged with such arrogant preconceptions in the societies in which Christianity, and the Christian social body itself, evolved. It becomes difficult, then, to know how women themselves experienced the important services they rendered in the constitution and propagation of Christianity. Truly it is they who, in large measure, have carried on the work of the church, and this to our very day. A major portion of the imposing edifice of the Christian institution rests on female shoulders, as the statistics on the relative membership of female and male religious congregations have consistently shown—to cite only a single aspect of this reality. Women emerge in the historical sources only when they somehow manage to be less manipulated. We have their records in the inscriptions found in Christian cemeteries (the so-called catacombs), for example, in the martyrologies, and in financial documents recording expenditures on behalf of widows, virgins, and orphans.[2]

Christian marginalization of women has its roots in the Old Testment. In the Book of Genesis Adam is presented as the image of the Creator (Gen. 1:26: in Greek, *doxa tou Theou*), and Eve as the image of Adam (*doxa tou andros*), Adama, the female reflection of the male. Man represents the divine side, woman the human side. Eve is the dependent wife, the virgin dependent on the male seed. The human couple stand for the love relationship between Yahweh (the man) and Israel (the woman): treacherous Israel is represented as Yahweh's unfaithful, even prostitute, spouse. Thus the notion of a covenant between Yahweh and Israel acquires an androcentric dimension. The same phenomenon is visible in the New Testament. In St. Paul, for example, woman is the image of man and must therefore submit to man (1 Cor. 11:7; 14:34). The New Testament does not speak explicitly of women's role in the service of directing the communities because Jewish tradition made no provision for female leadership ministries (Lev. 27; 6; Num. 3:4). Women fared no better in Roman imperial law, where they were totally dependent on men. At marriage they passed from the power of their fathers to that of their husbands. In other words they had value only to the extent that they bore healthy, vigorous sons to their husbands and to a society ruled by men. When all is said and done, women in Roman law were valued only because of the importance that law attributed to the family circle as the constitutive and perpetuating cell of society.

For Jewish and Greco-Roman traditions alike, Jesus' practice was an aberration and a scandal. His way of relating to Mary Magdalen or the Samaritan woman scandalized even the Apostles. But in the life of the base communities seeking to pursue and actualize Jesus' practice, women led the way. It was women who furnished practically the entire infrastructure of the first communities, offering their homes for meeting (Acts 12:12–16), lodging itinerant missioners (Acts 16:12–14), making clothing for widows (Acts 9:36–39), and even directing the communities (Acts 18:26–27) or prophesying (Acts 21:9). Women practiced "service" in a more genuinely Christian manner, and it was owing to them that the communities were a place of continual exchange of services among all (Phil. 2:3; Eph. 4:12), where no one gave commands but everyone sought to serve everyone else: "Obey one another in the fear of Christ" (Eph. 5:21). As Sebastião Armando, once more, is so concerned to stress:

> No relationship of servitude was admissible in the community—not between employer and employee, not between husband and wife, not between parents and children, not between church leaders and the faithful. All were called to bear one another's burdens.[3]

But this charismatic period of a vital experience of brotherly and sisterly service in the communities was not of long duration. Not only the surrounding culture but the mentality of male Christians themselves (see 1 Pet. 3:7; Tit. 2:9; Eph. 5:22–24) stocked a veritable arsenal of ideological weapons to be used against the freedom, leadership, and personality of women in the communities. The text best calculated to justify this assault was without a doubt the celebrated passage in the Book of Genesis in which woman had been the occasion of man's sin (Gen. 3:1–7), together with God's curse of woman (Gen. 3:16). Christians concluded from these texts that it is of the very nature of woman to be "mother"—limitlessly devoted, self-sacrificing, and self-effacing. We have the outburst of Tertullian: "O woman, thou door of Satan!"[4] St. Ambrose, for his part, regards things in the following light:

> The sublime condition of virginity is superior to that of marriage, for marriage entails labors and problems; virginity, on the other hand, is free and unencumbered.[5]

The great medieval doctor St. Thomas Aquinas repeats: "In man, more [than in woman], discernment and reason naturally abound."[6] Woman is "marked by frailty," he says.[7] Women, in the face of this discrimination and humiliation, began to react in various ways. The female culture in the male-controlled Christian social body was characterized by originality. Expelled from the decision-making center of the community and discriminated against in their sexual being, women always managed to organize. But only rarely did they manage to disturb the male hegemony.

SERVICE BY MEN

Moving on to a consideration of the services reserved to men in the first Christian communities, we are struck by the inescapable fact that all of them—designated with terms originating in the Jewish culture, such as diaconate, presbyterate, doctorate or ministry of teaching, the office of prophecy, episcopate, apostolate—were understood as consisting precisely in service (*diakonia*). Nothing could have been further from the mentality of primitive Christianity than the notion that some persons are superior to others. The memory of Jesus, of his insistence on a brotherly and sisterly relationship of service, was still very much alive in the minds of the apostles, and they in turn demanded of the "multitude of the disciples" that they should not abandon their Christian roots in this respect.

The controversies that raged in the first Christian communities over stable ministries or established hierarchies troubled the spirit of these base communities, just as did questions of the predominance of Jerusalem (or, later, Alexandria, Antioch, Rome, Constantinople) over the rest of the churches. Relations among the first communities were governed by the principle of love, not by "law" or prestige (Rom. 15:25–27; 1 Cor. 16:1–3; Cor. 8:9; Gal. 2:10; Acts 24:17). It is not that the first communities practiced some sort of enthusiastic anarchy. On the contrary, organizational forces were very much at work. Let us take a specific example. In the Jerusalem community, a language problem cropped up: in the daily assistance given to widows, those who spoke Greek were not well served, surely because they were unfamiliar with the language used in Jerusalem—Hebrew or Aramaic. "In those days, as the number of the disciples was growing, the Hellenists complained to the Hebrews that their widows were being neglected in the daily service" (in Greek, "in the day-to-day *diakonia*," Acts 6:1).

We have seen that these "widows" were often enough women who had abandoned husbands who had failed to respect them in the area of their sexual relations, so that the separated wife had come to depend on the charity of the community—on the "table," or right to daily sustenance. The service of "table" must have been of considerable proportions in the community in question, especially in view of the fact that the "number of disciples was increasing." The "Twelve" immediately adopted a pragmatic attitude:

> The Twelve assembled the community of the disciples and said, "It is not right for us to neglect the word of God in order to wait on tables. Look around among your own number, brothers, for seven men acknowledged [*marturoumenous*, "well attested"] to be deeply spiritual and prudent, and we shall appoint them to this task. This will permit us to concentrate on prayer and the ministry of the word." [Acts 6:2–4]

There is no implication here that the *diakonia* of the word is more important than the *diakonia* of table. But the former—the testimony to the resurrection and memory of Jesus—was non-transferable, inasmuch as it was constitutive of all of the communities and not just that of Jerusalem. The "Twelve" must preach the word, lest that word be lost over the course of time; and this *diakonia* might not be abandoned for the sake of other—equally important—services that others could perform equally well. And so the "Twelve" transferred to the "Seven" a task arising from the circumstances of this particular moment in the life of the community. In this fashion the primitive communities managed to avoid both extremes, charismatic chaos and legalistic juridicism. After all, they had been founded on love.

As Deacons

The First Letter to Timothy speaks of the qualities of deacons in the communities founded by St. Paul:

. . . deacons must be serious, straightforward, and truthful. They may not overindulge in drink or yield to greed.
They must hold fast to the divinely revealed faith with a
clear conscience. . . . Deacons may be married but once,
and must be able managers of their children and households. [1 Tim. 3:8–13]

Two deacons who surely met the requirements for this
ministry are Stephen (Acts 6:8 to the end of the long chapter 7)
and Philip (Acts 8:5, 38). Stephen's activity affords us the
wherewithal to understand the conflict between the synagogue
and the base community. It happened that the diaconate fell
victim to the same law that gradually came to govern all of the
services of the primitive church. In the course of time attention
was gradually concentrated on liturgical service, in an evolution
typical of the proto-Catholicism of the second and especially the
third century.

As Bishops

Another service answering to the daily needs of the communities
was that of bishop, or community inspector. The term "bishop"
(in Greek, *episkopos*), like everything else characterizing primitive Christianity, is Jewish in origin, and we do not know with
certitude what function the term originally denoted. Some texts,
such as Philippians 1:1, speak of "bishops and deacons." Others,
like the First Letter to Timothy, speak of a bishop for each
community. The function of bishop was certainly that of
organizing meetings, and there were various modalities in the
episcopal function, depending on the size of the community.
Thus Jewish Christianity (in Syria, for example) was predominantly presbyteral in character, while the Pauline communities —
gentile Christianity — were more episcopal. Both forms were
collegial, however. There was no monarchy in the first Christian
communities. The community tasks of organization were dis-
charged in collegiality, whether by a presbyterate or by the
bishops.[8] This collegiality in the organization of the primitive
communities is a product of the Jewish tradition. It was
expressed most especially in "presbyteral" collegiality (Acts

11:30; 15; 21:18, and passim)—the collegiality "of the older ones," the elders, especially in the Palestinian missionary cycle and the cycles deriving from it. Episcopal collegiality, typical of the Pauline communities, as we have noted, surely followed the same Jewish model—although Paul himself does not always mention bishops, speaking instead of those who "cooperate and toil" (1 Cor. 16:16), or "those who direct" or "preside" (1 Thess. 5:12; Rom. 12:8). His terminology is always plural. No concept of a defined ministry of direction is to be found in St. Paul. In his communities we find only tasks, positions, and functions.[9] These all lie along the lines of *diakonia*, daily service, in the organization of meetings in which Christians would lay out their concerns and attempt to solve their problems.

As Presbyters

We have already observed that the *diakonia* of the word was of special concern to the Twelve. This, after all, was the *diakonia* of Christian identity properly so-called—the *diakonia* of the remembrance and reiteration of the Jesus event, the specifically "apostolic" *diakonia* of those who had been personal witnesses of the life, passion, death, and resurrection of Jesus. The towering importance of this *diakonia* emerges from the writings of Papias, for example, who lived in the community of Hierapolis in Asia Minor around A.D. 130.[10] Papias, as we have seen, claimed to have been a "hearer" of the apostle John and wrote a five-book work under the title *Exegeses of the Words of the Lord* (*Logion Kuriakon Exēgeseis*), with recollections of the actions and words of Jesus and his disciples based on the oral communications of the oldest witnesses, the "presbyters" ("elders"), such as Aristion, John, and the daughters of Philip.

We have only a few certain fragments of Papias' work, but they are enough to give us a sense of the question facing the community with the death of the last of the Apostles. Who would continue the service of recalling the word of God and hence the roots of Christianity? The communities were anxious about this problem, and they solved it in the same direct, pragmatic spirit of popular realism with which they had addressed the question of the care of the Hellenistic widows in

Jerusalem. The solution was to reactivate one of the structures of the Jewish synagogue—the presbyteral structure. The presbyters or elders were held in great respect in the synagogues, and youthful Christianity enhanced this respect, entrusting the presbyters with the sacred service of preserving the memory of Jesus and transmitting it to new generations. Practically all of the documents recounting the life of the first communities—Papias, Clement, Ignatius, Pseudo-Barnabas in his letter, Irenaeus, Polycarp, Hermas—mention the importance of the presbyters. Some of these writings defend the presbyters against the insolence of the young, who hold these "elders" in contempt for their lack of culture. We have already heard the thundering of an Irenaeus, for example:

> Those who abandon the preaching of the church accuse the holy presbyters of ignorance. They are blind to the fact that it is of far more worth to be a simple but religious person than to be the subtlest of philosophers but an insolent blasphemer. [*Adv. Haer.*, V, 2, 20][11]

The letter written by Clement of Rome to the Christians of Corinth, examined earlier, is likewise motivated by indignation at the inability of certain young Christians (3:3) to respect the presbyters. The workers only detach themselves from apostolic tradition, which is what furnishes the Christian social body with its link to divine revelation. They turn their backs on that tradition and allow it to pass them by. "The church," says Tertullian, in his lapidary style, "proceeds from the apostles, the apostles from Christ, and Christ from God" (*De Praesc. Haer.*, 21, 4).[12] Clement of Rome applies to the presbyters a concept emerging from the actual experience of the base communities, then, when he refers to them as the ones "who precede us in the Way" (44:5).[13] Papias of Hierapolis tells us how he has managed to preserve the memory of Jesus and the Apostles:

> When anyone came who had visited the elders [the presbyters], I sought to learn the words of these elders—what had been said by Andrew or Peter or Philip or Thomas or James or John or Matthew or any other of the Lord's

disciples, and what Aristion and the presbyter John, disciples of the Lord, were saying. What appeared in books seemed to me to be less useful than what we hear *viva voce* and recited from [personal] memory.[14]

And again: "I did not hesitate to compare what I had learned with [what had been said by] the elders, and [thus with] what I had carefully preserved in my memory."[15] Availing himself of this method of investigation, Papias subjects the content of his memory to a detailed analysis in the light of the tradition handed down from Peter and Mark, pointing out that, although Mark had never heard or followed the Lord personally, he had heard St. Peter "do teachings." Mark had paid close attention to what he had heard from Peter and "strove for one end alone, not to lose anything of what he had heard and not to add anything to what he had heard."[16] What a precious service to render to the communities—to listen attentively and then to transmit what one has heard, simply and without commentary! This service of listening and transmitting is valued at its full worth in today's base communities in Latin America where, day after day, living experience projects a startling, vivid light on the first Christian communities, at a distance of nearly two thousand years.

Other authors who value and comment on the service performed by the presbyters are St. Ignatius of Antioch, Polycarp, Hermas, and Irenaeus. St. Ignatius repeatedly mentions both the presbyterate and the presbyters.[17] The famous passage from his letter to the Ephesians (4:1) "Their venerable presbyterate, worthy of God, is in harmony with the bishop, just as the strings of a lyre are in tune with the lyre itself"[18] is to be understood in the perspective in which I have already analyzed it in these pages. The letters of St. Ignatius of Antioch are written in a tone of alarm. Their author fears a loss of Christian identity and the dismemberment of the authentic Christian movement, leaving it helpless against the onslaughts of heresies and gnostic doctrines. This is why Ignatius is so emphatic on the importance of the union of all Christians around their bishop and their presbyterate. He insists, in his letter to the Christian of Thrales (6, 1): "I beseech you, consume Christian victuals alone. Abstain from other foods. I am speaking of heresy."[19] This is the prime concern of Ignatius' generation, the third Christian generation. The last of the Apostles has died. The genuine Christian tradition must not be lost. The various communities, scattered over such immense distances but grafted onto the living tree of this tradition through the service of the bishops, presbyters, and deacons, must stay attached to that tree.

As for Polycarp, the recommendations he makes to the presbyters can well be taken to heart by the bishops and deacons. There are no specialized, "privatized" ministries at this time. There are only tasks, services, and functions assumed in collegiality, constituting a means of confronting the challenges of concrete community life. He says: "And let the presbyters be sensitive, and merciful with all. Let them set deviations aright, visit the sick, not neglect the widow, the orphan, the poor."[20]

The *Shepherd* of Hermas, for its part, furnishes some precious indications as to what were regarded as the tasks of presbyters in the church of Rome. The presbyters are directed to read and safeguard books and preserve the traditions, and thereby give the church its proper orientation.[21] Finally, Irenaeus of Lyon refers so often and so emphatically to the presbyteral tradition in the church and its capital importance ("I have heard from a presbyter. . . . As the presbyter said . . . As the presbyters recall . . ."—and so on) that we may call him the veritable archivist of this tradition, from whose arsenal he is so sure of being able to draw the wherewithal to combat the heresies of his time.[22]

As Apostles, Prophets, Teachers

The ancient base church communities also carried out other "sacred missions" or "liturgies"—in the original sense of the word *leitourgiai* before it acquired its liturgical meaning. The Letters of St. Paul (Rom. 12:7), like the Acts of the Apostles (13:1–3), refer to the tasks of "teachers and prophets" as "liturgies." These teachers and prophets saw to the spiritual nourishment of the communities, and the *Didache* makes it clear that bishops and deacons were deserving of the same affection as was shown the prophets and teachers, who were usually itinerants and visited the community only occasionally. As the *Didache* is treating of "prophets, apostles, and teachers" (in

Greek, *didaskoloi*), we must obviously see in these offices a "sacred mission" highly esteemed and respected in the first Christian communities — surely because it corresponded more explicitly to a specifically Christian intuition than did the service of the "deacons, bishops, and presbyters." How are we to understand this?

Both the *Didache,* a Syrian composition, and the New Testament lead us to believe that there were two ways of serving the word of God in primitive Christianity — one more fixed and stable, corresponding to certain models existing in Judaism (deacons, bishops, presbyters), and another series of ministries, those of the itinerants, which better translated the novelty of Christianity (apostles, prophets, teachers). It is perfectly understandable that Christians in the communities would be inclined to show greater respect for this second series. They were more stimulating! With all the impact of a life of testimony lived before Christians' very eyes, these ministries recalled one of Jesus' most important lessons: that his disciples must leave all things and follow him and his gospel.

Now, the Apostles, prophets, and teachers were poor by option. They had abandoned their stability and security, their work at home or workplace, in the fields or in commerce, in order to travel about preaching the word. Jesus had given all his attention to the training of these itinerants, these "poor in spirit" (Matt. 5:3), and had presented them to the multitude with the words, "Blessed are the poor, for theirs is the Reign of God" (Luke 6:20). In another passage from St. Luke's Gospel, Zacchaeus is held forth as an example to follow, since he had given half of his possessions to the poor (Luke 19:8). Those who had given all, like the one who gave half (Zacchaeus), were the very foundations on which Jesus planned to build his church. They were the figures that gave this church its orientation.[23] And the apostles, prophets, and teachers perpetuated these orientating figures. They had had the courage to take up voluntary poverty with a view to the sacred mission and everywhere founded communities in which everything was shared. But it was through these communities, in virtue of this very sharing, that the Reign of God in this world was inaugurated. The service rendered by the apostles, prophets, and teachers, or by any itinerant minister, presupposed voluntary poverty, availability, detachment from money (2 Pet. 2:3), flight from heresy (2 Pet. 2), an exemplary life, and a readiness to support the many inconveniences of a life on the road.

The letters of St. James, St. Peter, St. Jude, and St. John, along with the *Didache* and *Shepherd* as well as certain other writings, constitute the best introduction to a study of the life and activity of these itinerant ministers. The model of a church founded on the service rendered by the itinerants was so basic for the first age of Christianity that everything seemed to be governed by it. A religious vocation, for example, was conceived in terms not of entry into the ecclesiastical state but, on the contrary, of a readiness to go about without any definite place of residence, "without money, or sandals, or pouch, or stick," from village to village, accepting lodging for two or three days at most in each village (*Didache*), and receiving room and board but never money or honors.

It is interesting to observe the ubiquitous appearance, in the third and fourth centuries, when the practice of the apostolic life was gradually abandoned, of the apostolic myth that comes to expression in the *Didascalia Apostolorum,* the *Constitutiones Apostolicae,* and the *Traditiones Apostolicae.* The moment the church abandons the apostolic life it appeals to the apostolic name in order to legitimate its projects and organizational structures. The authentic apostolic tradition—the tradition of going about preaching and living the promises of the gospel in poverty and humility—has never been completely abandoned, however, and the history of the church retains the memory of great apostles: Ephrem in Syria, Frumentius in Ethiopia, Patrick in Ireland, Boniface in Germany, Columbanus in Gaul; later, Bartolomé de las Casas in Latin America, Robert de Nobili in India, Matteo Ricci in China, and recently Charles de Foucauld and others. The apostolic model was so vividly present to the Christian mind that Christians actually divided the world into apostolic regions, as we saw in the introduction.

The most famous apostle of the Christian tradition is St. Peter. The Christian memory has attributed to him the most varied roles: fisher, missionary, pastor, martyr, the recipient of private revelations, confessor, defender of the faith, repentant sinner, pope, and very gatekeeper of heaven. This wealth of attributions eminently demonstrates the fondness that the Christian tradition has always had for this humble fisher who left his nets to "fish human beings" (Matt. 4:19), embracing the itinerant life in the following of Jesus. And yet, when Christianity had become a mighty organization and attained the position of an official religion, the image of St. Peter, like that of St. Paul, came to be invested with the interests of the historical moment. In a representation of Saints Peter and Paul dating from the time of Pope Sylvester II (999–1003), the pair of apostles are shown as presenting the terrestrial emperor and empress before the throne of Christ the Supreme Emperor. This would be a response to demands of the interests of the age, when the church (projected in Saints Peter and Paul) needed official support (represented by the imperial couple) if it were to have the power to establish the Peace of God, whereby clerics, rural folk, travelers, tradespeople, and women, as well as mills, beasts of burden, and finally the entire trade and commercial movement could be protected from the violence of the armed lords.

Saints Peter and Paul were manipulated, then, by those who had interests to defend (very important and worthy interests, to be sure) in the eleventh century. Another representation, this time from the fourteenth century, shows St. Peter crowning the church, with the historical papacy and its interests providing the background—symbolizing the struggle of Pope Boniface VIII (1294–1303) with King Philip the Fair of France, who threatened to appropriate the possessions of the ecclesiastical institution in keeping with the feudalism of the age. Today we understand that these historical images have no connection with the actual life of St. Peter or with his *leitourgia*—his sacred mission of abandoning the security of living, home, and stability to undertake an itinerant life filled with insecurities and dangers. They are only projections into the past of the conflictual situations of later power struggles in society.

The second most outstanding apostle in the Christian memory is St. Paul. The very fact of his calling himself an apostle, when he was not one of the Twelve, clearly demonstrates that Christianity in its infancy did not pose institutional questions in the same spirit of legalism with which it would address them later.

But Paul does not allow the name of apostle to be the occasion of pride on his part. He also styles himself father (1 Cor. 4:15), doctor of the gentiles, and prophet. And indeed St. Paul was the greatest itinerant of the primitive church, the missionary who forms the link among the mission cycles of Syria, Asia Minor, and Europe, by way of Greece. He is also the only person in primitive Christianity about whom we possess enough precise information to construct a biography in the strict sense of the word.[24] In the case of the other "servants" of earliest times — such as Peter himself, John the son of Zebedee, James the Just, Barnabas, Apollo, the evangelists Matthew, Mark, and Luke — the information we possess is sparse indeed and frequently entangled in legend, as with Peter and especially John.[25] St. John was so discreet that, in the Gospel attributed to him, he never so much as mentions his own name or for that matter that of his brother James.

This sort of thing occurred with many of the first apostles of the gospel and their collaborators. In this modesty we discover one more trait of the Christian memory of earliest times. It is made up not of heroes and great personages, nor of the religious experiences of exceptional persons, but simply of faith in Jesus. We cannot escape the impression that what was considered important was faith lived in community — not the biographies of the first followers of Jesus. When, in the second century, the communities came to define a canon of sacred books (the New Testament), they deliberately rejected writings that they thought insisted too much on great deeds and great figures or extolled miracles and marvels too highly. A fine sense of humility and simplicity is surely a characteristic of original Christianity.

We perceive the same phenomenon in St. Paul, with his astounding activity as he went about organizing so many communities, or with his development of a theology of universal validity — a theology originating not in an exceptional religious experience but in a profession of faith in Jesus. What mattered to Paul was not the propagation of his personal manner of experiencing the Christian religion but the objective foundation of faith: Jesus Christ crucified and raised again. It was this objectivity that won Paul the crowd of enthusiastic collaborators found at his side — Barnabas, Silas, Silvanus, Titus, Timothy,

Priscilla and Aquila, and all the rest—who propagated the model of the base communities over such a wide geographical area.

FROM CHARISM TO INSTITUTIONALIZATION

The authors define this character of service to the community, modest and free, enthusiastic and specific, as "charism." Primitive Christianity was "charismatic." What is meant by this term? Hans Küng explains: "Charism is the calling addressed by God to each person for a particular service in the community and simultaneously rendering him or her apt for this service."[26] As for St. Paul: "The wealth of the gifts of the Holy Spirit has been manifested to us by the abundance of the graces of Jesus Christ" (1 Cor. 12:4–6). The charisms were most varied—charisms of sisterly and brotherly aid, assistance to the sick, financial aid for the poor, the *diakonia* of tables—but especially of the service of the word of God and its preaching by the apostles, prophets, teachers, bishops, presbyters, and deacons.

In the beginning, when community membership was smaller, the charisms of government and organization obviously did not have the importance they would acquire later with the proliferation of the communities and an increase in the number of Christians. In the first communities the charisms of the word came first. Those of organization "served" and supported them. All of the charisms had been bestowed for the proclamation of the Reign of God to the "ends of the earth," and it mattered little whether the one who preached or prophesied was called deacon or prophet or bishop or presbyter or teacher or apostle. The important thing was to live the new Christian life and to win new disciples who would be willing to come along on the journey. From a strictly sociological viewpoint, charism constituted an irregularity, a deviation vis-à-vis the "normal" way of organizing into groups and communities. Jesus had once said, "As you know, those who govern the nations tend to dominate them. . . . Among you it must be different" (Mark 10:41–45). And:

"As for you, avoid the title 'Rabbi.' One among you is your teacher, the rest are learners. Do not call anyone on earth your father. Only one is your father, the One in heaven. Avoid being called teachers [leaders]. Only one is your teacher, the Messiah." [Matt. 23:8–10]

This last phrase constitutes a precious memorial of Jesus' own way of acting and reacting, and it was preserved in the communities, where no one was called "rabbi" or "father" or "teacher," as all felt co-responsible for the great task of service to the lowly as the proclamation of the Reign of God on earth. St. Peter, meditating on the grandeur of this "sociological irregularity," exclaims:

"You, however, are a chosen race, a royal priesthood, a holy nation, a people he claims for his own to proclaim the glorious works." [1 Pet. 2:9, citing Exod. 19:6]

Sociological regularity would have consisted in the obedience of "subjects" to their "superiors," in institutional establishment, and in the "peace of order." Primitive Christianity, as it happens, did not observe this regularity but found new ways of gathering and organizing.

Charism, as expounded above, must be understood as an attempt on the part of the communities to remain faithful to the memory of Jesus, and not as a once-and-for-all acquisition and accomplishment. In daily practice the experience of the marvelous freedom and autonomy of the gospel entailed division and discord, both within and among the various communities. In his First Letter to the Corinthians, St. Paul writes:

I have been informed, my brothers, by certain members of Chloe's household that you are quarreling among yourselves. This is what I mean: One of you will say, "I belong to Paul," another, "I belong to Apollos," still another, "Cephas has my allegiance," and the fourth, "I belong to Christ." . . . Who is Apollos? And who is Paul? Simply ministers. . . . I planted the seed and Apollos watered it, but God made it grow. [1 Cor. 11–12; 3:5–6]

And in St. Mark's Gospel we hear of the ten apostles' jealousy of James and John, who appeared to have been granted certain privileges by Jesus and who now besought him that they might "sit, one at your right and the other at your left, when you come into your glory" (Mark 10:37). From the year 100 a clear anti-charismatic tendency emerges in the documents of the base communities, as in the Letter of Clement of Rome to the Corinthians, in the seven letters of St. Ignatius of Antioch, in certain passages in the *Shepherd* of Hermas, and even in chapter 15 of the *Didache*.[27] It is as if church organization suddenly spoke out against free and independent charismatic practices in the name of the survival of the experiment as a whole. The organizational texts spoke, then, in the name of life, and in this sense they were necessary. But at the same time they were dangerous. They threatened to conceal the authentic memory of Jesus, from whose freedom and autonomy ("It was said of old . . . but I say to you. . . .") the Christian practices characterized by deviation from the norm of laws and regulations had come into being.

This is a matter of paramount importance. What was impressive about Jesus in Jewish eyes, and what essentially distinguished him from the prophets before him, was precisely the autonomy of his action and speech — an autonomy that made no attempt to justify a deed or an utterance by recourse to the Law of Moses, but that, on the contrary, assumed an explicit posture of deviation from that Law. Jesus moved within the Jewish institution and yet created new meaning and a new conversion. For the Jewish establishment, such behavior could only be qualified as deviation and aberration. But for Christians it came to be the rule of conduct and was expressed in the charisms and other manifestations. And all down the centuries since, a practice of deviation, inspired in the active memory of Jesus, found a thousand and one ways in which to protect the vast majority of the faithful by silence and yet preserve and protect the practice of anonymous Christians — the laborers, the homemakers, all the humble folk. Only from time to time, in some figure upon whom historiography managed to focus — a St. Francis of Assisi or a Meister Eckhart in the Middle Ages, a

St. Vincent de Paul or a Bartolomé de las Casas in modern times — was that anonymity unveiled.

Charism, then, was one of the practices generated by Christianity in the following of Jesus, just as other forms of this discipleship were generated later: monasticism in the fourth century, mysticism, the popular movements of the second millenium of Christian history, today's political militancy. Thus the Jesus event has diversified, over the course of time, into a multiplicity of practices that, more often than not, are anonymous. None of these practices can be called "authentic" in any essential sense. None exhausts the richness of the foundational event. They are all transitory, relative, and historical.[28] Christianity cannot, then, be seen as a doctrine preserved intact down through the centuries. It must be thought of as a generative source of repeated embodiments, each stemming from fidelity to the foundational event that is Jesus and his practice.

Far from exhausting the wealth of that event, these experiences, these experiments, realized in time and space, simply demonstrate the fidelity of the Christian communities to Jesus and his message. No one owns Christian truth. But many speak that truth in the truthfulness of their lives — in the vestiges of the Jesus event to be found in those lives. Each of us speaks of Jesus and his gospel in his or her own fashion, in practices that have always been and always will be "aberrations" with respect to "laws" — laws that, to be sure, are necessary for the societal survival both of institutions and of the Christian life that depends on these institutions for its security. Thus Christians find themselves to be at one and the same time members of institutions with their own sociological *raisons d'être* and engaged in practices of deviation from the norms of these institutions, which seem ever beset with the risk of yielding to the dead weight of immobility and social conformism. By this very fact, as the *Letter to Diognetus* told us long ago: "Christians live in their countries as foreigners. . . . Any foreign land is home to them, and every homeland foreign."

The aim of this somewhat theoretical consideration is to explain the replacement, in the ecclesial *diakoniai*, of the autonomous charism with more strictly legalized and stabilized forms of the service of governing the communities. There are various ways of explaining this substitution. One of the most interesting is that of Professor R. Gryson, a scholar of the history of the ancient church, who speaks of it in terms of a victory of the pastoral services (episcopacy, presbyterate, diaconate) over the more autonomous itinerant or prophetical, and even teaching, services (apostles, teachers, prophets).[29] Gryson begins with the fact recorded in chapter 15 of the *Didache*: that the authority of the teachers was enormous in the primitive communities, and that it outweighed that of the established ministers. To maintain a balance of forces, the *Didache*, like St. Paul in his Letters to the Corinthians, appeals to the principle of charity. But the teachers or charismatics had always said that their authority came directly from the Holy Spirit, while the "establishment" now insisted on the special sign of its own authority, the laying-on of hands — acceptance by the community, "ordination."

Later, around A.D. 200, Tertullian let it be known that he was not at ease with this controversy between the two groups, the charismatics and the ordained (*De Praescr. Haer*, 3, 5). In the course of the third century the pastors definitively established their supremacy over the teachers, relegating the latter to the framework of a catechetical preparation for baptism in a catechumenate supervised by the pastors themselves. Later the teacher would be confined to schools of theology (see *Apostolic Tradition*, 19). A typical case is that of Origen, a Christian with a genuine teaching vocation who was all but forced to accept priestly ordination if he hoped to have the authority to confront his bishop, Demetrius of Alexandria.[30] In this way the teaching function was gradually appropriated by the pastoral hierarchy. This development would be complete by mid-third century, as can be seen in the case of Cyprian in Africa (Carthage). Later Christian antiquity would make little more than a verbal distinction between pastor and teacher, as we gather from the biographies of the fourth-century church Fathers. Another typical case of a Christian called to be a teacher, if anyone ever was, is that of Augustine of Hippo. If the great African hoped to have his voice heard and respected, he had to become a pastor.

This entire development culminated, at all events for Christian antiquity, with the decree of Pope Leo the Great (440–61):

"Let no one dare to preach but he be a priest, either monastic or lay, however much he may glory in the name of learning" (*Letters,* 210, 6).[31] The situation eventually became insupportable. The aspects of Christian memory that failed to fall into place in the framework of pastors' interests were no longer recorded and could easily meet with oblivion, while other aspects would be presented in exclusivity. Conzelmann dates the transition from charism to the more legalized ministerial forms circa A.D. 100, especially in the light of the letters of Clement of Rome and Ignatius of Antioch, with their markedly anticharismatic tenor as early as the third Christian generation,[32] while Brox prefers a date around 150.[33]

A general study like this one cannot examine the question at greater depth, but the importance of this historical transition cannot be minimized as the mere upshot of certain general laws of religious sociology. Any religious movement, we are told, begins in the charismatic or "enthusiastic" phase, which is followed by periods of stabilization and "normalization"—a kind of shaking together and balancing out. In my view this is an oversimplifcation, especially where the religious movement concerned is based on such innovative practices of predilection for the marginalized, humility and modesty, and faith to the very death—the death of a martyr—or at least to the point of a generalized social rejection. No, surely the fascination exerted on Christians by the Roman organizational system, as well as by Platonic and Stoic ideas, played a relevant role in the second-century diaconic reversal. But as a result the Christian memory must "dig for its roots." It must look beneath these societal influences or suffer the total confusion of its key concepts with their extraneous correlates: Christian morality with Stoic morality, Christian spirituality with Neo-Platonic spirituality, Christian hierarchy with the hierarchy of the Greco-Roman world. This is precisely why the charismatic period has always guided the Christian memory at every time of crisis, or any time when Christianity has taken fresh stock of the original Christian truth—and not on account of any "myth of origins" (Mircea Eliade) or devotion to "founding heroes," but as the outgrowth of a quest for the origins of a complex historical movement now nearly two thousand years old.

A "CATHOLIC" CHURCH

In order to move toward reaching some conclusions to part 3, certain observations are needed with regard to the adjective "catholic" (in Greek, *katholikos*). We meet the expression "catholic church" for the first time in the letter of St. Ignatius of Antioch to the Christians of Smyrna, around A.D. 110.[34] "Where the bishop is, there the multitude gathers, just as where Christ Jesus is, there is the catholic church."

The patrologist de Halleux, who has studied the use of the adjective "catholic" in the language of early Christianity, has concluded that St. Ignatius' readers understood perfectly well that by "catholic" he meant "entire," "general," or "total," since the word was in common use in this sense:

> The "catholic church" was simply the church, but the church taken precisely in its entirety, taken generally, considered as a whole, regarded in its totality. This meaning of *katholikos*, unencumbered with any etymological connotation of conformity with a whole, was common in the profane literature of the imperial era.[35]

The expression "catholic church," de Halleux concludes, had nothing to do with the development of a theology of catholicity, and it cannot be given this interpretation in St. Ignatius' letter. The homonymity between the use of the adjective "catholic" to modify "church" in St. Ignatius' letter and its use to denote the historically defined Catholic Church is purely coincidental.

On the other hand, of course, when authors like Conzelmann or Brox speak of a "proto-Catholicism" they are referring to the first signs of what will later come to be called Catholicism—a specific, historically determinate ecclesial model. Here "proto-Catholicism" denotes the earliest stirrings of the movement that will culminate, one day, in communities with only one bishop each instead of with various *episcopoi* or organizers who are so frequently confused with the presbyters; communities whose ministers will function first and foremost in a context of ritual worship; communities maintaining a new relationship between the Christian religion and its environment; communities in which the administration of the sacraments and the official preaching of the gospel will have been entirely pre-empted by the clergy; communities organized on the principle of territoriality, according to which the church will no longer be that "of the Corinthians," but that "of Corinth." All of this will develop in the course of the second and third centuries and attain a certain degree of maturity at the Council of Nicaea (A.D. 325).

CONCLUSIONS

By way of concluding part 3, then, and more specifically the present chapter on the services or *diakoniai* in the base communities of early Christianity, I offer the following summary:

1. Nothing could have been further from the spirit of primitive Christianity than the notion of a power or authority that would not be one of sisterly and brotherly service. The principle of a community of brothers and sisters forbade any arrogance of power and held up before the eyes of all the example of Christ:

> Though he was in the form of God,
>   he did not deem equality with God
>   something to be grasped at.
> Rather, he emptied himself
>   and took the form of a slave. . . . [Phil. 2:6–7]

2. The first Christians had a keen sense of the provisional. They tried not to organize things too much. They had no wish to hamper the free movement of the Holy Spirit, who "breathes where he will." To seek the first traces of the ponderous hierarchical structures of a later church evolution in the documents of primitive Christianity is to lack a historical sense, which is always careful to situate everything in time and space.

3. The first Christians maintained an altogether special sense of moderation—modesty, good sense, realism. They truly lived the "little virtues" of which we read in the texts setting forth the qualities of presbyters, bishops, and deacons: temperance, mar-

ital fidelity, responsibility in the upbringing of one's children, monogamy, abstention from rebellion or pride or "bad temper," honesty in the acquisition of money, hospitality, "good judgment," justice, piety, self-control, the capacity to "lead [others] along the path of sound teaching and refute those who attack it," "seriousness," detachment from money, and respectability in the eyes of one's own children (Tit. 1:5-9, 1 Tim. 3:1-7). Even in and of themselves, these texts breathe the climate that reigned in the primitive Christian communities — an atmosphere far removed from anything like sheer formalism or social "etiquette."

PART FOUR

THE CHRISTIAN NOVELTY

Introduction to
Part Four

Christianity manifested itself to the eyes of its contemporaries
through a multiplicity of new and occasionally strange practices
that non-Christians frequently failed to understand. For example, the philosopher Celsus (A.D. 170) did not understand why
Christians refused military service. In his dialogue *Octavius*, the
African writer Minucius Felix, a contemporary of Tertullian,
asserted that Christians worshiped the head of an ass, sacrificed
the flesh of an infant in their celebrations, and gave themselves
over to the most terrible sexual orgies. Few understood why
Christians refused to attend the gladiators' games in the circus or
the public baths in the *Thermae*. Many were puzzled by Christians rejoicing when a "brother" or "sister" died. Even more
strange were the exhortations of one of their number, a certain
Ignatius of Antioch, that they do nothing to avoid death as
Christ's "martyrs." Others felt that Christians went too far when
they forbade abortion or the exposure of a newborn child who in
one way or another would not have the wherewithal to survive.
Clement of Alexandria (A.D. 200) forbade women to dye their
hair or use lipstick. And so the list of Christian "novelties" could
be extended.

In their daily doings, in their particular attitudes, Christians
were a leaven in the dough that was Greco-Roman society. But
as we know, the everyday is multiple, all-embracing, diverse,
and irreducible to a common denominator. When theology
began to develop concepts of salvation, redemption, faith, hope,
charity, and grace, as well as those of sacrament, liturgy,
penance, and so on, it developed a theorization whose point of
departure was a multiplicity of specific actions, and it ran the

constant risk attendant upon all theorizing: that of failing to correspond to actual experience. For example, the "soteriology" of the theologians was frequently anything but a theorization of people's actual aspirations for salvation, as we shall see in the first chapter of this part. It is astounding how long theology can remain deaf to the appeals of the people in whose midst theologians themselves live. In this final part, then, I propose to assemble a series of texts springing from the actual Christian practice of the first three centuries and range them under four successive themes: salvation, the holding of goods and possessions in common, a new relationship between women and men, and martyrdom. This certainly does not exhaust the wealth of the Christian novelty as it was lived in people's daily lives in these centuries. But at least it begins to tap this magnificent treasure.

CHAPTER XIII

The Practice of Salvation

Paradoxically, the question that fairly exuded from the pores of the first Christian writings has left little or no impression on many scholars of Christian origins. As early as the time of the composition of the Johannine writings, a long, difficult struggle arose that did not end until the fourth century, when it finally disappeared from the center of Christian writers' attention.[1] The controversy left its mark on the New Testament, the *Didache*, the *Letter* of Pseudo-Barnabas, the letters of Ignatius of Antioch, the *Shepherd* of Hermas, and especially the writings of Justin and Tertullian. The pagan philosopher Celsus criticizes Christianity for its understanding of the matter and the majority of the apocryphal texts deal with it at great length and in profuse detail. Nor is it absent from the reflection of the authors of the Alexandrinian school, such as Clement and Origen.

It is a controversy couched in a variety of key terms: "magic" and "miracle," the "wisdom of the Persians and Chaldeans," "trickery" and "witchcraft" (or "pharmacies"—in Greek, *pharmakiai*), "idolatry," "salvation" and "prodigy," "forces" (*dunameis*) and "signs" (*semeia*), "principalities" and "powers." Around these and other watchwords, a relentless struggle was mounted—between "us" and "them," between the Christians and those who, like Simon Magus, were regarded as false prophets and impostors. This resistance to a magical interpretation of Christianity on the part of the dominant culture—as the writings of Justin and Tertullian, and even Irenaeus and Origen, clearly attest — gradually created a powerful sense of Christian identity.

Christians defended themselves tooth and nail against the allegation that they practiced magic and gradually formulated a clear distinction between magic and miracle. Hermas' Shepherd sallies forth to battle with the false prophets who present themselves as magicians and who speak by the devil rather than by the Spirit of God, whereby they "destroy the sense of God's servants" (Comm., 11, 2). After all, their utterance is according to "desires of malice, and they fill souls with vanities." The *Shepherd* of Hermas is one more testimonial of the sustained struggle in primitive Christianity between miracle and magic, the true and the false prophet, the true and the false saviors of the people. Our best access to an appreciation of the dimensions of the conflict will be in a comparative reading of Justin and Celsus. Here are two Middle Platonists, of comparable intellectual formation, who arrive at completely opposite conclusions in the matter. For Celsus, Jesus Christ is no more than a magician and "charlatan" (in Greek, *goes*), while for Justin, Jesus is a miracle worker, and his miracle is salvation (*sōtēria*; cf. *sōter*, "savior").[2]

How does this literary conflict reflect the daily life of Christians? What actual occurrences were giving rise to the texts to which we refer? Lamentably, the mixture of philosophy and superstition that pervades the ancient texts discourages modern minds, and most scholars simply ignore the large body of literature that deals with magic, miracle, astrology, and sorcery. Adolf von Harnack himself expressed wonder that writers as enlightened as Origen and Celsus could have presented Christ and Asclepius (the Greek god of medicine, son of Apollo) as rival divinities. But he investigates the matter no further. Many scholars since Harnack's time have been struck by the persistence of "saviors" in the Greco-Roman world of the age of infant Christianity and the insistence of ancient authors on miracle and magic. Most, however, ignore the subject. Of the three contemporary histories of the church now considered classic — *A New History of the Church*, edited by Roger Aubert, L. J. Rogier, and M. D. Knowles; *History of the Church,* edited by H. Jedin; and *History of the Church*, by K. Bihlmeyer and H. Tuechle —

only Jedin's so much as mentions Asclepius, and only very summarily. The other two fail even to cite the great controversy agitating the Christian milieus of the first centuries.[3]

A study such as this, of a type that seeks to grasp the history of the primitive church from the viewpoint of the people, cannot afford to ignore a subject so close to people's ordinary lives and so important for their way of understanding and living Christianity. To leave it out for the sake of a "scientific" approach would be forgetting what makes up the actual life of ordinary Christians. I prefer to abide by what Justin himself wrote: "I have no need of sophistication. I need only be frank and candid" (*Dialogue*, 80, 2). Justin would rather deal with the questions that torment simple persons' lives than rise to the heights of theoretical thought.[4]

SALVATION, MIRACLES, AND MAGIC

Before addressing so typically popular a subject, however, we must clear the way, explaining the sense of the words "miracle" and "salvation" respectively, lest any misunderstanding disturb the meaning of what this chapter intends to convey. By way of an explanation of miracle, let us briefly glance at only two studies among many on the subject. A. Suhl has recently collected and reprinted a number of articles on the New Testament miracles published in Germany between 1895 and 1970.[5] These essays evince the tendency among New Testament scholars, over those seventy-five years, to avoid a certain "illuministic" conceptualization of the miracle as an instance of the "suspension of the laws of nature." In biblical studies today, miracles are understood rather as religious phenomena that point to a new world, signs of God's activity in Jesus and the Apostles by which Jesus is shown to be stronger than the devil. The New Testament miracles are not purely fictitious. They simply call for a reading of the facts from the standpoint of faith in Jesus. We can no longer recover the exact nature of the physical occurrence reported in an ancient miracle account. But this does not give us the right to relegate the miracle to the status of myth and fiction. The second study is that of Francisco C.

Rolim.[6] Rolim characterizes miracle, most felicitously, as the "oxygen" of popular religion: "The piety of the poor feeds on the daily miracle. [The miracle] is not the extraordinary event. It is the daily one."[7] Miracles spring from the precarious nature of the life of the poor. The poor see the saint as the mighty wonder-worker and thus their protector in the hour of danger and frailty. The poor "live by miracle alone," and the greatest miracle of all is that they manage to stay alive. According to Rolim, the distance between the "official" and the "popular" view of miracles shows the distance between authority and the people: the miracle discourse is an essentially popular discourse, inaccessible to the bourgeois class. In this way the people safeguard a space for communication, and within this space "miracle continues to be the daily proclamation of the presence of an extra-terrestrial power in confrontation with the power, installed in the social body, that creates and shapes that body and the face of the poor."[8]

Miracle, like promise or any other expression of popular religion, is the victim of certain old, deep-rooted prejudices. It is said that religious expressions of this kind are more self-seeking than other, more spiritual and "disinterested" ones. But is this actually the case? Does not a spiritualization, precisely, of religious discourse correspond to particular interests as well— interests that usually lie concealed? It is worth considering this question from the viewpoint of the poor.

As for the concept of salvation, B. A. Willems has demonstrated that its theorization in Christianity came about only gradually. Irenaeus of Lyon, Anselm of Canterbury, and Thomas Aquinas mark the successive steps in this process of theorization.[9] The Greco-Roman world, as we have said, hailed numerous "saviors," depending on the precise expectations of the various social groups and classes. In Egypt, Isis and Osiris were venerated as the guarantors of eternal life, while in Asia Minor it was Cybele who fulfilled such expectations. In Syria, Atargatis and Adonis promised eternal youth and everlasting beauty. Later would come Serapis, also of Egyptian origin, as the "savior" of persons from all needs of body and soul. And the god Mitra of Syria would in his turn represent, for important sectors of the populations of the Roman Empire, the fulfillment of their desires for eternity, felicity, and peace. These saviors, as it happens, and their cults corresponded basically to the aspirations of the middle class, while the poor placed their hope especially in the god Asclepius, and the upper class pursued "salvation" in philosophy and the contemplation of the eternal verities.[10] Thus were various means of securing salvation in the cultural environments of the Roman Empire. Everything depended on the nature of the aspirations of the social class in question. There was no general concept of, simply, "salvation." What is of interest to us is the popular concept of salvation. And so we must address the question of the popular devotion to the god Asclepius.

If we are to understand devotion to Asclepius, that most venerated of all the divinities of the Greco-Roman pantheon in the era of Christian origins, we must keep in mind the situation of the poor in the Roman Empire before the arrival of Christianity. As L. Prunel demonstrated long ago, in his still authoritative study, the poor of that time lived in utter dereliction, reduced to slavery or other forms of dependence in their work relations.[11] Their poverty made itself felt more acutely in moments of illness. The near universality of poverty provoked an enormous new wave of religious devotion throughout the Mediterranean region: that of the cult of Asclepius. Temples dedicated to the healing god sprang up like weeds. The social matrix of Asclepian devotion, then, was the one we find in popular worship throughout history: the absence of hygienic conditions or health care, a situation of misery and social dereliction, the indifference of the constituted authorities, and the absence of any charity. Nothing is more stable, down through the course of history, than popular religion and its roots.

From the end of the fifth century B.C. to the third century A.D., Asclepius was the great saving god of the ancient world. Son of the Olympian god Apollo, Asclepius gradually replaced not only his sire but all the gods of Olympus as the object of popular worship. The great divinities were very distant from the people and their problems. But the devotion to Asclepius was based on miracles. In the small locale of Epidauros, in Peloponnesus in the north of Greece, in the sixth century B.C., the series of miracles occurred on which the prestige of the new god would be based. We still find his ex votos scattered throughout the Mediterranean Basin, since his devotion spread by way of the *Asclepieia*, his temples, in numerous cities and regions. In 420 B.C. Asclepius conquered Athens. In 293 B.C. he entered Rome, now with the title of "Savior" (*Sōter*). Beginning very early in the fourth century B.C., the priests of Epidauros began to record "salvation stories" on great stone tablets. Seventy of these tablets are still in existence. The salvation stories reveal that the ultimate remedy for disease consisted in a "dormition" (*incubatio*) in the temple. A dream in the course of this temple sleep meant that the dreamer had encountered the god and was guaranteed a cure. The *Asclepieia* also had pools of saving water in which the sick bathed in the hope of a cure. Thus the god Asclepius did what the physicians failed to do: care for the sick who were not a privileged clientele.

Actually the phenomenon of the physician god was not restricted to the case of Asclepius, as shown in the old but still definitive study by W. A. Jayne, who researched the subject of the physician gods of the Iranians, Egyptians, Assyrians, Sumerians, Semites, Greeks, Romans, and Celts.[12] In the Hellenistic age the temple of Asclepius in Epidauros was overshadowed by the one in Pergamum, where some dozens of Asclepian societies were founded. It was Asclepius who restored sight to the blind, speech to the mute, and health to all. The devotion to Asclepius was so important and so tenacious that, as late as the fourth century A.D., the Emperor Julian (surnamed by the Christians "the Apostate") sought to re-establish his cult as savior of all humanity and thereby counter the Christians' new savior, Jesus of Nazareth.

This fact alone demonstrates that faith in Jesus Christ must have arisen in the consciousness of many persons of Mediterranean culture in terms of an alternative to faith in Asclepius. And a mighty conflict of interpretations arose, as the religious elements of the Asclepian cult included magic, oracles, and prophecy. The magical element had originated in the Babylonian-Assyrian world, penetrating Hellenism in the period of the Persian wars. The magicians reached the apogee of their popularity in the time of the Roman Empire, during the first two

Christian centuries. Now the people placed more trust in their magicians than in the old deities. Everywhere appeared manuals of magical recipes, among which the people preferred the ones from Egypt.

Belief in magic rested on belief in the devil and his influence on human life. The art of magic consisted in repelling the evil *daimones* and conjuring up the good ones, the "demons" with a "sympathy" for the stars, the fauna, the flora, and yes, humanity. The magician was someone capable of grasping hold of this cosmic "sympathy" somehow and of repelling the antipathies that likewise emanated from the cosmos. Hence the importance of the magical properties of plants, rocks, and metals, or to formulations and prayers to be pronounced at the moment of the magical practice.

Side by side with the magicians were the "divine men" (in Greek, *theioi andres*), who worked miracles and pronounced oracles. The prototype of the divine man was Pythagoras, who had likewise been fathered by the god Apollo and who had lived a holy life. By way of devotion to Pythagoras, encratism—the doctrine that perfect virtue was incompatible with marriage— penetrated Hellenistic culture in depth. Pythagoras' disciple, the great Empedocles, had ended his life by casting himself headlong into the crater of Mt. Etna. Other "divine men" were Menecrates of Syracuse and Apollonius of Tyane, the contemporary of St. Paul who had lived such a harsh, encratic asceticism and had been a prophet and magician who could predict the future, expel demons, and raise the dead.

In the latter half of the second century A.D., in the little town of Abonoteichos in Paphlagonia (in Asia Minor, near the Black Sea), a new manifestation of Asclepius occurred under the auspices of a certain Alexander. Alexander claimed to be the new Asclepius. He had pronounced oracles and now called forth a new apparition of Asclepius in the form of a serpent hatched from a goose egg. The fame of Alexander of Abonoteichos spread throughout the empire, creating great difficulties for the Christian prophets, since the oracles of Abonoteichos rivaled the Christian prophecies and thereby created confusion in many minds. It is in a context of this confrontation that Commandment 11 of the *Shepherd* of Hermas is to be situated. Hermas insists on the *toto caelo* difference of the Christian prophecies from the oracles of Alexander, as the latter sought only to satisfy the curiosity of the "vain," while Christian prophecies were addressed to the defenseless little Christian communities awash in the heterogeneous mass. As the sky was unreachable, so was Christian prophecy utterly above the things of earth. Christian prophecy was the very might of God, and the guarantee of a salvation that was impossible only in the eyes of the world as it was possible for God (Commandment 11, 18–21). Hermas' startling reaction to the presence of these oracles proves that their use had penetrated the Christian communities in the second part of the second century and now constituted a danger to the faith.

I have offered this rather lengthy explanation of the cult of Asclepius, magic, oracles, and miracles because Christianity came on the scene as a rival to the other salvation cults. The thinking was as follows: Confronted with the ills that afflict the poor, the sick, and all the other marginalized, people had two "ways out," two salvation practices. But they must choose between them. On one side was salvation through Asclepius, the magicians, the astrologers, and the oracles pronounced by the "divine men." On the other side was salvation through faith in Jesus Christ, in the prophecies, and in the daily miracles and wonders wrought by Christians.

There can be no doubt: for the converts of the first two centuries Christianity was propagated by "signs" and "prodigies." It was by a "sign" or miracle that the Christian movement achieved its first publicity—the sign of the cure of an invalid lying at the Beautiful Gate of the temple in Jerusalem, the miracle wrought by Peter "in the name of Jesus of Nazareth" (Acts 3:1–10). And so it continued; Christianity was propagated by signs and prodigies that "astonished" the people (Acts 2:43). When the second century prophetess Philomena wrought "signs and prodigies" (Tertullian's words), she caused the same astonishment among the people.[13]

Now, magicians and "divine men" likewise practiced the art of the miracle and uttered oracles. So did rabbis.[14] The people therefore failed to perceive just what was so new about Christianity. Suetonius spoke of Christianity merely as a *nova superstitio*, a "new superstition." Celsus presented Jesus as a disciple of the magicians of Egypt. A respectable theory analyzed be E. Trocmé maintains that it was fear of this magical interpretation that motivated the Gospel of St. Matthew to avoid any emphasis on miracles, preferring to picture Jesus as a teacher, a "master."[15] St. Mark, the theory goes on, attempted to correct this image by seeking out persons in Galilee who had seen Jesus with their own eyes and who preserved the clear recollection of his healing the sick and working miracles. It was by way of the miracle accounts that the Good News was first propagated from mouth to mouth before being consigned to writing. Now, to maintain the memory of a Jesus concerned with the sick and suffering, a Jesus who based his life on the practice of salvation and not on mere words and teachings, Christians had to begin to defend their miracles against the allegation that they were mere magic. They had to defend true salvation practice against that of the false saviors. This was the primary concern of the second-century apologists, especially Justin and Tertullian.

Justin, Tertullian, and Celsus

Justin was particularly doughty in the battle with a magical interpretation of Christianity, vigorously advancing the thesis of a demonic imitation of the scriptures and the whole treasury of revelation. In accordance with a thesis current in the first centuries, Justin excoriated the deities of paganism as demons who sought to manipulate the sacred scriptures, and who had inspired the poets to create the "myths"—monstrous adventure stories resembling the biblical narratives—for the purpose of reducing biblical history to sheer adventure and fable.

Justin developed his thesis by way of abundant examples. He claimed, for instance, that Moses worked real miracles before Pharaoh, while the magicians only imitated Moses by working false miracles (*Dialogue*, 79, 4). Tertullian resumed the theme, writing in his customary lapidary style: "The truth of Moses devoured the lie of the magicians of Pharaoh" (*De Anima*, 57, 7). According to Justin, one element of revelation always escaped the imitators, the magicians who manipulated the truth:

salvation by the cross (*Apol.*, I, 55, 1). It was simply unthinkable
to the demons that a son of Zeus could die on a cross. Thus the
true imitators of Christ could be recognized by the sign of the
cross, which the demons would never succeed in corrupting or
imitating.[16] Justin goes further still, asserting that Jesus had
converted the magicians (also called Chaldeans or astrologers)
and moved them to place their science at the service of the
gospel. This is Justin's reading of Matthew 2:1–12, the story of
the journey of the magicians of the East to see the child of
Bethlehem (*Dial.*, 77, 4; cf. Irenaeus, *Adversus Haereses*, III, 9,
2; Tertullian, *De Idolatria,* IX; Ignatius of Antioch, *Letter to the
Ephesians*, 19, 3).

Taking up the same theme, then, Tertullian insists that
Christians must exorcise the demons who present themselves as
deities, and thus reveal their inauthenticity (*De Anima*, 57, 2).
The consummate example of a false, deceitful magician, to the
eyes of the second-century apologists, was Simon Magus. In the
apocryphal Acts of St. Peter, Peter is presented as defeating
Simon Magus in a contest of miraculous powers and thus
unmasking the false magician (*Acts of Peter*, 5). Justin asserts
that Simon's powers (in Greek, *dunameis*) are magical (*Apol.* I,
26, 2), while Irenaeus writes that Simon performed "illusory
works" (*Adv. Haer.*, 1, 13). The Acts of the Apostles (8:9–11),
like Clement of Alexandria, Origen, and Hippolytus, are concerned to make the same point, thereby demonstrating that the
figure of Simon the Magician and related concerns were very
much at the center of popular discussion in earliest Christian
times.[17]

For all their denial of Christianity's magical nature, the
apologists never ceased to insist that it was miraculous. But
precisely, Christianity proceeds by miracles, not magic. Both
Justin and Tertullian wrote at great length to establish that Jesus
was not a magician but an authentic wonder-worker, since his
miracles proved his divine power (Justin, *Apol.,* I, 30). The
principal object of most of the writings today called apocryphal
was to distinguish between miracle and magic and thereby to
establish the miraculous nature of Christianity. The difference
between miracle and magic seems to be that magic is manipulated by demonic powers, while miracle comes about through the

power of the Holy Spirit. In order to establish a clear distinction between a false miracle and a true one, Christian authors avoided words like "magic" or related verbs like *mageuein* (Greek, "to practice magic") in their descriptions of Christianity. They preferred words like "sign" (*sēmeion*) or "wonder, prodigy" (*teras*).[18] Responding to Celsus' allegation that Jesus had been a magician, Origen demonstrates, in lengthy considerations, that magic is performed for the purpose of exalting the magician himself, while the miracles of Jesus and his disciples had been at the service of persons, for their health and well-being.[19]

To appreciate the novel effect of Christianity on the prevailing mentality, suffice to compare the devotion (*pietas*) of someone like Celsus for Asclepius with the devotion of Christians for Jesus Christ. For Celsus, "piety" falls within the framework of societal "law" (in Greek, *nomos*). Piety assists the individual in adjusting to society by demonstrating the "logic" (in Greek, *logos*) of that society. But in Celsus' opinion Christians had no "law." Christianity had arisen out of a revolt against the Jewish Law and consequently failed to follow the "logic" of society. Therefore Christians could have no true piety. The Christian outlook on piety was altogether different. In Jesus, Christians venerated the physician who had always linked his salvific activity (his practice of saving persons from disease or suffering) to the eschatological coming of the Reign of God (Matt. 12:28). In current salvation practice Christians perceived signs of the coming of another world. Miracles actualized, in daily life, in the concrete healing of bodies and the concrete practice of charity, God's ultimate purpose for the universe. Christian piety had perceived God's manifestation in Jesus and the coming of the Reign of God in this world of misery by way of the salvation of bodies (Matt. 11:4–6; Luke 7:22–23). The piety of the earliest Christians must be seen as a unique phenomenon in the history of religions. It associated the humblest bodily service to the humiliated and marginalized with the sublime coming of the Reign of God. This is the great novelty that the second-century writers, if in a babbling and stuttering way, attempted to express. Writings like the *Shepherd* of Hermas and the *First Apology* of Justin interpret everything in terms of the concept, "impossible (in Greek, *adunaton*) for human beings but possible for God." "All things become possible in God," Justin states (*Apol.*, I, 19, 6), and Hermas repeats: "Nothing is impossible for God. . . . Just as the sky is unreachable, so is true prophecy, which comes to us with the power of God" (Comm. 11, 20–21). Celsus, who has had the same philosophical training as Justin, objects that the body is "the hope of worms" (*skolekōn hē elpis*), and that the Christian theme of the holiness of the body and of all matter is philosophically repulsive and detestable. But Justin replies, very simply: Nothing is impossible for God. It must have been very difficult for Justin to move from the ideology of Middle Platonism, with its contempt for the material, to the Christian faith, which generated the new world of the salvation of matter, precisely, the world of the "resurrection of the flesh." But Justin overcame all his difficulties by relying on the axiom of the primitive church: nothing is impossible for God (see also Irenaeus, *Adv. Haer.*, II, 31, 2).

MIRACLE OR DOMINATION

When all is said and done, the most characteristic trait of the Christian miracle is the absence of any kind of sensationalism. There is nothing sensational in the miracles of Jesus and his disciples, and this for a very simple reason. Christian miracles are wrought not for the purpose of justifying institutions or exalting power and authority, but for the purpose of meeting the needs of persons. There is a sentiment pervading all of the accounts of the Jesus event, a sentiment that trembles with Jesus' own heart and entrails, and which can be called compassion. But even the word "compassion," as A. Nolan reminds us, is too weak to express the profound emotion Jesus experiences when confronted with human misery, and which the Greek word *splanchnon* identifies as a throbbing of the innards or the heart: "His heart was moved," or "he was touched with tenderness and compassion," or "he wept," and so on.[20] The primitive Christian memory could not abide untouched by this compassion of Jesus for the "people of the earth," for the rejected and despoiled of this world, and it imitated this compassion by working miracles of healing in the daily life of the people. Very simply: Christianity is propagated in only one of two ways, and there is no slipping between the horns of the dilemma. Either Christianity is propagated by miracle—that is, by the concrete witness of the life of Christians—or it is propagated by domination. It is with profound sadness that the historian must record that the church that sprang into being working miracles of compassion and charity later abandoned this route, so clearly mapped out by Jesus, and followed the way of domination instead. The route of "miracle" was the route along which Christianity, through the course of history, created hospitals, orphanages, and lepro-saria—houses of charity and compassion for the sufferings of the world. But the same Christianity also embarked upon the paths of power, of the idolatry of domination, and of the demon of lucre, ill-gotten and ill-spent.

CHAPTER XIV

A Communion in Goods

In the years 253–54 a terrible pestilence swept through Roman Africa, sowing death on every side. The bishop of Carthage, St. Cyprian (200–58), was not aloof from the problem of the mass of sufferers and organized services of assistance to the plague-stricken.[1] With a view to stimulating even greater assistance to the plague victims, he wrote his treatise *On Good Works and Alms* (*De Opere et Eleemosynis*), where we read the following:[2]

> Let us consider, dear brothers, the actions of the faithful in the time of the apostles, when the faith of converts was vivid, fired with a burning charity. They sold their houses and inheritances and gave the price to the apostles to distribute to the poor. Thus they gained eternal riches. Many were their good works, and great was their unity. . . . This is what it means to become a child of God and to imitate his justice. For everything that is God's is also common to all, and no one is deprived of his graces and benefits. The light of day shines on all equally, and the sun's rays stream to every corner of the earth. The rain soaks every field, and the wind wafts over the entire land. The same night wraps men in the same sleep, and the same light of the moon and stars shines for all. Whoever, in accordance with this natural model of equality, shares his goods with his brothers, imitates God himself.[3]

Clearly, then, as early as the middle of the third century, the primitive community of Jerusalem was regarded as the model of a Christian experience that was now almost beyond realization in its radical demand for poverty and a sharing of goods. During the whole later history of the church, the theme of the "primitive church," a "communion of goods," and "perfect fellowship" rings like a refrain, while the familiar passage of Acts 2:44–45 is regarded by some as an idealization, by others as an actual phenomenon but of brief duration, and by still others simply as an exaggeration.

CHARACTERISTICS OF THE COMMUNITY OF GOODS

What can the historian say to all this? Was there really a community of goods among the first Christians? If so, what were the characteristics of such a phenomenon? Let us attempt to answer these questions.

Judaic Roots

First of all, a community of goods in the primitive church did not fall from the sky but was founded on a solid Jewish tradition codified in the scriptures. L. Prunel, in the article already cited, lists a number of elements in what he calls the "economic legislation" of the Old Testament.[4] I shall cite only those which bear on a community of goods.

1. The earth is the Lord's. We are but his colonists and tenants (Lev. 25:23).

2. A tenant may not sell land, since, every fifty years, in the year of jubilee, land reverts to its original holder or his descendants (Lev. 25:18).

3. The fruits of the earth are subject to the tithe, of which one part goes to the tribe of Levi, the priestly caste, which has no possessions, "for the Lord himself is its possession" (Deut. 10:9).

4. Another part of the tithe goes to the poor, as likewise the leavings of the harvest and the festivals. Feasts are arranged to which widows, orphans, and the poor are invited (Deut. 16).

5. The corners of the plantations, as well as any grain falling to earth in the course of the harvest, belong to the poor.

6. Every seven years is a sabbatical year. The land lies fallow, and all may reap its fruits (Exod. 23:11).

7. The laborer must be paid his wages before sundown on the day he earns them (Deut. 24:14).

8. Interest-free loans must be made to those in need (Deut. 15:9).

9. There must be no beggars, since the "haves" must succor the "have-nots" (Deut. 15:4–11).

10. The poor may appropriate the possessions of others in order to keep from starving (Deut. 23:24–25).

As we see, the purpose of this economic legislation is to prevent an accumulation of goods in the hands of a few. Goods are to be distributed among the greatest possible number of persons. Israel's later development, especially after the Babylonian Captivity and the excoriations of the prophets, was not always in accordance with this legislation. Even so, the social and economic organization of Israel contrasted with that of neighboring peoples by reason of its relative tendency to distribute goods among all.

The Practice of Jesus

Jesus' activity was calculated to radicalize the social and economic organization of the Jewish people that had been handed down in the scriptures. That activity raised eyebrows in Palestinian milieus, since Jesus was the son of a carpenter and a laboring-class person himself (Matt. 13:55) — a socio-economic matrix scarcely corresponding to that of a typical religious leader, who was expected to operate on a higher plane than the world of work. It was difficult to imagine, at the time, a relationship between the "condition of God" and the "condition of a slave" or worker (Phil. 2:5–11). St. Paul had to explain that the one who was "in the condition of God . . . emptied himself and took the condition of a slave" precisely that his audience might better understand this new and unaccustomed relation. It was surely owing to his existence in the world of work that Jesus gathered the impressive realism he projected into his communities. Those communities would practice the spirit of sisters and brothers even where financial matters were concerned. They would succeed in being the germ of a new society only if they actually practiced, and not merely mouthed, the new law of universal participation in material goods. Jesus avoided the danger that threatens so many generous projects, that of becoming lost in nice theoretical proposals. And so he began with the financial basis: "Go, sell all you have, give to the poor and you will have treasure in heaven. Then come and follow me" (Mark 10:21). "If you wish to be perfect, go, sell your possessions . . ." (Matt. 19:16–30). Besides being radical, this behavior is profoundly religious. It adopts the ancient inspiration of the scriptures according to which all things are the Lord's and the Lord distributes them equally among all. "The earth cannot be sold forever, for the land is mine, says the Lord, and you are but strangers and guests" (Lev. 25:23).

The Practice of the Primitive Church

The Acts of the Apostles recount how Barnabas complied with the Lord's command. He sold his land and gave the proceeds to the Apostles (Acts 4:36–37). Many did the same, as Acts, again, attests: "They sold their property and fields and distributed the income among all according to the needs of each" (2:45). Unless they abandoned their wealth, the first converts to Christianity were not allowed to become members of the community, as the *Shepherd* of Hermas shows in the Third Vision:

> "The white, round stones, unsuitable for building [the tower, i.e., the church], are those who have faith, but who have the wealth of this world, as well. When affliction comes they deny the Lord, on account of their wealth and their business.
> "When will they become suitable for building?
> "When wealth, which today is their gladness, is trimmed from them, then will they become apt for God. For, just as a round stone cannot become square without being trimmed, so neither can the rich of this world become

suitable for God unless their wealth be trimmed from them." [Third Vision, 6, 5–7].

In the Ninth Comparison, the *Shepherd* of Hermas returns to the same theme:

Those who live in concern for many things do not join the servants of God. They flee, suffocated by their business. It is hard for the rich to join the servants of God. After all, something might be asked of them! It will be difficult, then, for them to enter the Reign of God. . . . Just as it is difficult to walk barefoot on thistles, so for this sort of person it is difficult to enter the Reign of God. [Ninth Comparison, 20, 2–3]

Even so, Hermas is not disheartened. The rich can be converted, of this he is certain. St. James, of the Jerusalem community, insists on these same points, recounting the most painful experiences of the communities with regard to wealthy persons (James 2:6–7) and declaring: "The rich will wither like the flower of the field" (James 1:10). Jesus' realism in recommending to the communities a community of goods finds an echo in the following words of St. James:

If a brother or sister has nothing to wear and no food for the day, and you say to them, "Good-bye and good luck! Keep warm and well fed," but do not meet their bodily needs, what good is that? [James 2:15–16]

The entire fifth chapter of the *Didache*, the first Christian catechism, is devoted to a description of the "road to death"—the path trodden by those who "oppress the afflicted, defend the rich, judge the poor with injustice, and are full of sin" (*Didache*, 5, 2). The good disciple, by contrast, "places all things in common with his brother, since if we enter into communion in immortal goods, so much the more do we do so in respect of goods that are perishable" (ibid., 4, 8). The same teaching is found in chapter 20 of the *Letter* of Pseudo-Barnabas: "Those who attend not to the needs of widows and orphans, who have no compassion for the small, who are against the poor, who oppress the needy, who are advocates of the rich and unjust judges of the poor"—these walk the way of darkness (Pseudo-Barnabas, *Letter*, 20:1–2). We find the same testimony in Justin's writings: "Before all else we sought money, and goods of all kinds. Today we share what we have, and we distribute it to the poor" (*Apol.*, I, 14, 2). Nor is Tertullian's language any different:

Money plays no role in our religion. We do have a treasury, but not because we sell our faith. Everyone simply contributes a small monthly amount, if he wishes, when he wishes, and if he can. No one is constrained to do so. The contribution is entirely free. But if it is made, it is a deposit of piety, and is not squandered on banquets and drinking-bouts. [Tertullian, *Apol.,* 39, 6–8]

And further on:

We are brothers because we live from the same inheritance. We who live united in spirit and soul have no hesitation in placing our goods at the common disposition. [Ibid., 11]

Thus the title "brother," with which Christians addressed one another, was not an empty formula but expressed their actual attitude toward one another. A community of sisters and brothers was a reality, based on common ownership of goods.

Tertullian's observation regarding the financial basis of Christian fellowship affords us a glimpse into the deep seriousness with which common ownership was taken. The Christian community functioned like a natural family having a common patrimony. The monthly contributions of the faithful were like loans, or deposits in the "bank" of piety, a word meaning charity. Tertullian speaks of these "deposits of piety" (*deposita pietatis*) as deposits benefiting the depositors themselves, since it was money spent within the community. And who were the community? Tertullian explains:

[These deposits] are expenditures for the maintenance and burial of the poor, for boys and girls who have no money and have lost their parents, for elderly slaves, for the victims of shipwrecks, or for those who toil at hard labor deep within the mountains, on the islands, or in the prisons. [Tertullian, *Apol.*, 39, 6]

THE CHURCH AS A COMMUNITY OF GOODS

Thus the church is not only the community of those who profess the same faith but also, and especially, the community of those who live sharing goods in common. The church jealously guards not only the "deposit of faith" (*depositum fidei*) but the "deposit of piety" or charity (*depositum pietatis*) as well. In the early church, giving to the poor was not only lending to God but especially lending to the community, which was fortified by the contributions made by all for the benefit of poor and needy who did not live *ad extra,* outside the church, but *ad intra*, inside the community. In the early church, to succor the needy, and to assist widows, orphans, and the poor generally, was in no wise a sporadic, transitory activity. It was part of the very life and being of the church. The church cannot be understood apart from some form of holding goods in common, whether through a community chest, a "college" or association of mutual assistance, or a monthly collection.

The Christian sources of the first centuries are unanimous on this point. To begin with St. Paul: recent research has uncovered the fact that the collection taken up by St. Paul for the poor of the Jerusalem community was not a one-time occurrence. On the contrary, it was essential to St. Paul's understanding of church and mission (Rom. 15:25–28).[5] St. Justin, for his part, insists that the Sunday collections taken up among Christians are demonstrations precisely of the Christian self-concept and not simply manifestations of Christian charity devoid of any further meaning for the church as such. They constitute, as it were, membership in the church by way of a concrete deed (*Apol.*, I, 67, 6). St. Irenaeus refers to a practice of placing a money offering on the Eucharistic table for the benefit of the needy.

Over the course of time, the custom of placing offerings on the altar gave rise to the Offertory of the Eucharistic celebration. But what a difference between the offerings of the primitive church, which actually molded the community by way of providing goods in common, and the solemn offertories of, for example, Byzantine Christendom! The only common element in the offerings of the first Christian generations and the symbolic offerings of the majestic Eucharists of later Christendom is their external formality as gift. The realities are altogether different. In the primitive church, offerings constituted the community, perfected the church, and formed the basis on which the church was maintained. This was no longer the case in the era of Christendoms, when church monies fell into the hands of the clergy.

The *Didache* prescribes the ancient Jewish tithe as constitutive of the community:

You shall take the first-fruits of the wine press and the threshing floor, of the oxen and ewes, and give them to the prophets, for they are our high priests. If there be no prophet with you, make a gift of these first-fruits to the poor. When you make bread, take the first loaves and bestow them according to this same precept. Likewise if you open a cask of wine, take the first draught and offer it to the prophets. Of money, vesture, or anything else, take the first of it and bestow it according to this precept. [*Didache*, 13, 3–7]

A further result of the adaptation of the principle of sharing—of placing goods at the common disposition—was that certain churches, such as that of Rome, began to share their possessions with communities scattered throughout the empire. The Roman community surely gained some benefit from the prosperity of the life of the capital of the empire. And so it undertook to assist its far-flung brothers and sisters. Eusebius of Caesarea, in his *Historia Ecclesiastica,* reports a letter from the bishop of Corinth, Denis, to the bishop of Rome, Soter, in which we see that the Christians of Rome gave financial assistance to those of Corinth. The letter dates from A.D. 170.

Nearly a century later, in 255, a letter from Bishop Denis of Alexandria to Bishop Stephen of Rome shows that the help afforded by the Roman Christians had spread as far as Mesopotamia, Pontus, and Bithynia, the farthest reaches of the empire (*Hist. Eccl.*, 4, 23, 10). The history of Marcion of Sinope, which we examined in part 2, is a case in point. Marcion made a gift of no less than 200,000 sesterces — about $100,000 — to the Christian community at Rome in the year when he became a member, A.D. 140. When he left Rome, some years later, to found the Marcionite Church, the Roman presbyters promptly returned his money to him (Tertullian, *Adv. Marcionem*, 4, 4, 3).

By the 250s the financial power of the Roman community had become so great that, under Bishop Cornelius, the list of those for whom it provided included its bishop, 46 presbyters, 7 deacons, 7 subdeacons, 42 acolytes, 52 exorcists, lectors, and doorkeepers, and finally, the considerable number of 1500 widows and other needy. And Cornelius, our source for these figures, adds significantly: "All of these persons are benefited by the grace and bounty of the Lord" (Eusebius, *Hist. Eccl.*, 6, 43, 11).[6] As we see, then, the Christian church in the third century had become such a powerful financial organism, operating in the service of the poor, that it aroused the envy and greed of authorities and functionaries of the Roman Empire itself. We have an eloquent example in the church of Carthage in Roman Africa. The Carthaginian church had sufficient financial power to ransom a group of Christian slaves who had fallen into the hands of Numidian marauders for the sum of 100,000 sesterces — corresponding to $50,000 — in the time of Bishop St. Cyprian, around the 250s.[7] Eight years later a violent persecution, the so-called Valerian persecution, one of whose victims was Bishop St. Cyprian, fell on the Carthaginian church. Historical research has demonstrated that the basic intent of this persecution was to fill the state coffers, which were suffering from the crisis known to have affected the finances of the empire in the third century, with Christians' money.[8]

It is understandable that, under these conditions, the question of the able and honest administration of community money would be a basic one. Primitive Christianity developed powerful images to demonstrate its rejection of such administrators of the "community purse" as might turn out to be thieves. The thieving administrator par excellence was Judas, who polarized all the hatred the Christians had for those who misappropriated community property for personal ends. How well the Gospel of John describes Judas: "He was not really interested in the poor. He was a thief, and being in charge of the community purse, made off with what he found therein" (John 12:6). Here is a document precious for the Christian memory: how Judas made off with the community money, not even hesitating to betray Jesus himself in exchange for silver. He was a traitor because he was a thief. Hatred of the thief, so typical of the popular culture of all times and all regions of the world, made Judas the prototype of all who keep their possessions to themselves instead of sharing them. There are medieval engravings in which Judas is represented as the prince of heretics. Anyone capable of draining off the money of the poor is capable of anything, as that person lacks the most elementary humanity. Later, monks would frequently teach that the Christian ought to abstain from all possession or use of money as from a thing vile and worldly in itself. But this was neither the teaching of Jesus nor that of the first Christian generations. Jesus taught, in the famous parable of the wily manager (Luke 16:1–12), how to make money benefit the poor and abandoned: "Make use of the mammon of iniquity to make friends . . . (v. 9). And in verses 10 and 11 of the same passage we catch a glimpse of the vibrancy of the palpitating life of the first communities:

If you can trust a man in little things, you can also trust him in greater. . . . If you cannot be trusted with elusive wealth, who will trust you with lasting? And if you have not been trustworthy with someone else's money [in the administration of the community goods], who will give you what is your own? [Luke 16:10–12]

Trustworthiness in financial matters, then, was a vital subject in the first Christian communities. We have proof of this in the letter written by St. Polycarp, the bishop of Smyrna, to the Philippians. The entire letter can be summed up in St. Paul's warning to Timothy: "Greed is the root of all evil" (1 Tim. 6:10). Paradoxically, St. Polycarp warns widows especially of the danger of greed and the misappropriation of money. Widows— the prime beneficiaries of the common holding of goods in the communities, as we have seen in part 3—often thereby attained an enviable status in the communities and began lending money at interest to persons more needy than themselves (*Didascalia Apostolica*, 15). Accordingly, St. Polycarp warns them, ominously:

> Knowing that we have brought nothing into this world and shall be taking nothing with us when we leave it, let us arm ourselves with the weapons of justice, and let us teach ourselves, first of all ourselves, to walk in the commandment of the Lord. Next . . . widows, to be wise in the things of faith in the Lord, to intercede uninterruptedly for all, to live far from calumny, backbiting, false witness, greed, and every evil, knowing that they are the altar of God, where all offerings are inspected with care, for nothing escapes God, in intentions, in thoughts, in the secrets of the heart.[9]

The *Didascalia*, a Syrian document dating from the early third century, defines bishops as "God's stewards" in the spirit of Luke 16:1-12. After all, they receive tithes, first-fruits, and other gifts from the hands of the faithful, but they receive them for the benefit of the community. Of the bishops scripture says, "Let them be good administrators of the things of God" (literally, "good moneychangers," *kollubistoi*, in Greek), surely an allusion to Matthew 21:12, which speaks of the wicked moneychangers Jesus expelled from the temple. Let the bishops not imitate the Pharisees, who "put on an appearance of perfect folk, but God knows hearts" and knows that in reality these are persons "attached to money and that this is why they mock [Jesus]" (Luke 16:14-15). Let them be discreet about the amount of money the community has, let them not accept the offerings of persons outside the community, or ill-behaved individuals who "keep persons in chains, maltreat their slaves, act without piety in the cities, or oppress the poor" (*Didascalia* 9: 10, 15,

18).[10] At about the same time, Origen compares certain bishops, presbyters, and deacons with the moneychangers and vendors of the temple of Jerusalem (Matt. 21:12): "For they seek only their own profit" (*On Matthew*, 16, 21-22).

Here, as in the question of the practice of salvation, Christian consciousness gradually developed important criteria for distinguishing between the true and the false. The purpose of the true miracle is the good of another, while that of the false miracle, called magic, is merely the prestige of the quack healer or the power of the institution. Just so, the true "moneychanger," praised in Luke 16:1-12, changes money to his employer's advantage, who in the parable represents God as the "master" of the communities, while the false moneychanger of Matthew 21:12 changes money to his own advantage.

Christians were realistic. They did not condemn the use of "the mammon of iniquity" (Luke 16:9) across the board, since money made possible an exchange within the community and thereby the establishment of a communion of goods among Christians. The first Christians, then, formed an exceedingly close-knit social body. That was the secret of their rapid penetration of the tissues of society, as well as of their extraordinary strength when it came to resisting the dominant ideologies. The nameless Christians who bore Christianity to the farthest reaches of the Roman Empire, and even beyond, were not freelance individualists. They were members of vigorous social bodies. A reading of the *Didache* convinces us: the prophets, teachers, and apostles were not without their community commission. They had been sent, and sent for a purpose.

FROM A COMMUNITY OF GOODS
TO INDIVIDUALIZATION

So there is no reason to be surprised at the great change produced in the socio-cultural postulates at the basis of the Christian life the moment the unit of reference ceased to be the community and became the group of the organizers, that is, the clergy. With this fundamental process of change in Christianity's organization, morality as well as doctrine gradually began to be addressed to individuals, leaving social interconnections out of the picture and so creating the familiar pastoral approach to the masses in which sin, salvation, morality, poverty, and finally the whole series of Christian themes are individualized. Never in the course of church history were Christians to abandon the struggle to reorganize their social bodies, never were they to abandon the quest for community life. But the hegemony of church officialdom never permitted the emergence of lay organizations that might threaten official stability. Today our sensitivity to questions of justice and charity is marked by a centuries-long individualization of charity. It is difficult for us to grasp the scope of words like those of Gregory of Nazianzen (330–90):

> Reverently I recall to your minds the memory of Christ's purse, which invites us to support the poor; of the concord between Peter and Paul, who go their separate ways in the preaching of the gospel but not in their care for the poor (Gal. 2:10); and of the perfection of the rich young man, which would have consisted in his bestowal of all his possessions on the poor. [*Oration* 14, *PG* 35:909]

The economic unity prevailing between the "haves" and the "have nots" in the Christian communities molded these communities into the powerful financial and social cells that aroused such admiration and even jealousy on the part of pagans, and surely contributed to making Christianity a living and transforming force of society in late antiquity.

But the Christian practice of holding goods in common proved not impervious to the effects of time, at least as a form of church organization. Holding goods in common was replaced by the practice of almsgiving (*eleēmosunē*—literally, "compassion"). The transition to the practice of almsgiving can be observed in the single extant homily of Clement of Alexandria, *What Rich Man May Be Saved? (Quis Dives Salvetur? Tis ho sozomenos plousios;*), a commentary on Mark 10:17–31—the passage containing Jesus' "terrible" words: "It is easier for a camel to pass through the eye of a needle than for a rich man to enter the Reign of God" (Mark 10:25). Let us see Clement's commentary:[11]

These words are not to be taken literally, as holding no hope. . . . The terror felt by the rich [at hearing them] is without foundation. The Lord will accept these [persons] if they so desire . . .

Commenting on the passage in which the rich youth departs in sorrow after Jesus has told him that he must abandon his possessions if he wishes to become a disciple, Clement says:

What do these words signify? Some, taking them literally, imagine that the Master orders us to abandon all of our goods and renounce them definitively—whereas in reality he wishes only to uproot our preconceptions concerning wealth, passion, unbridled greed, and avarice—the thorns that rend our existence. It is not a matter of the highest ideal—this poverty that takes no heed of eternal life. If it were, then the poor who beg, and those who are scattered along the streets, knowing nothing of God or his justice, would be the happiest and most Christian of men, by sole reason of their misery, their indigence, and would merit, they alone, eternal life. Furthermore, a renunciation of one's wealth and its distribution among the poor and needy is nothing new. Many had already done this before the Lord's coming. . . . What, then, is the new precept that comes from God alone and bestows life and newness? This precept does not command doing anything superficial, or what others have done before, but something greater, a thing more divine and more perfect: it commands us to strip our soul of its passions, to uproot and cast far from us whatever is alien to the spirit. This is the doctrine worthy of the Lord. If no one possessed anything, who would give sustenance to the poor, who would give the thirsty to drink, clothe the naked, lodge the wanderer—if we sought to be poorer than the poor? Therefore the goods that can assist the poor are not to be rejected. The nature of possessions is to be possessed. The nature of goods is to spread out. The possessions in our hands are instruments by which we may surely profit if we but know how to use them.[12]

Clement's homily echoes the inumerable discussions, down through the centuries, over the thorny question of Christianity and poverty.[13] Its author, Clement of Alexandria, is a practitioner of the celebrated allegorical reading of scripture, on which I have commented in chapter 8. He shifts the burden of Jesus' discourse in the passage about the rich youth from the relationship between rich and poor to that between vice and virtue. The practice of Christian poverty suddenly hinges on the practice of a spiritual gnosis having no effect on concrete reality. The effects are internal and "spiritual." As late as 1954, in his presentation of fundamental morality, O. Lottin could write:

> The moral value of a life is measured not primarily by the yardstick of external return, but by that of the earnestness of the dispositions of the soul. Subjectively, in the order of realization, the perfection of external activity is measured by the perfection of the internal act, inasmuch as the latter is the efficient cause of the former.[14]

"This theology," as José Comblin rightly asserts, "is a direct derivative of the conceptual world of Hellenism."[15] Thanks to this interiorizing posture, Clement won his bourgeois audience in the year 200, just as so many preachers down through subsequent history have won their audiences by repeating the same tranquilizing argument. In his *Stromata* (V, 66, 1), Clement vigorously attacks the mistrustfulness exhibited by "simple minds" with regard to any openness on the part of Christianity toward the enlightened thought of Hellenistic philosophy.[16]

As has already been shown, Clement has marginalized the theology of marginality, and with it the interpretation of charity as a community of goods among Christians. With him commences the process of the loss of the Christian memory concerning the community of goods among all Christians without discrimination.

CHAPTER XV

A New Relationship
between Women and Men

THE MONASTIC AND CONVENTUAL MODEL

The European countryside is dotted with convents and monasteries. This fact alone would suffice to show the importance of the monastic and conventual model, not only in the church but also in society as a whole. The monastic model has extended its hegemony over our way of understanding Christianity to the point that it is difficult for us to imagine the pre-fourth-century church — the church before this model began to spread throughout the entire Christian social body. A brief examination of some of the steps in this revolution will lead to a better perception of the contrast with what it overthrew.

St. Anthony, the "father of monks," who inaugurated his experiment in Egypt around 305, is the symbol of monasticism for all time: the desert, silence, a renunciation of society the better to transform it, the struggle with the body and its desires in order to satisfy the desire for God, prayer, the eyes of the human creature fixed on God. Pachomius is the warrior who battled the demons who dwell within us and in society, the "powers of this world." Basil is the organizer of the common life for communities of monks and nuns, and the founder of the conventual model, based on a dichotomy between "within" and "without" the monastery walls. St. Benedict was the first to conceptualize the whole of Christianity as a monastic religion, positing the monk as the Christian ideal and seeking to mold the whole of society according to the model lived by monks and nuns. St. Gregory the Great organized a veritable campaign to monasticize Western Christianity. In the course of history, this entire movement, initiated by Saints Anthony, Pachomius, Basil, Benedict, and Gregory, culminated, in its Western vector, in the super-monastery of Cluny, in Burgundy (near Macon), which in the year 1000 had 1,450 dependent monasteries with a total of 10,000 monks and an abbot who had become the most powerful person in the Western world. The Cluniac model of the Christian life exerted a decisive influence on the history of Western Christendom, by way of the reform wrought in the pinnacle of the church, in Rome, by Clunaic monasticism in the person of the mighty Pope Gregory VII (1073–85). Just as Cluny was a state within the state, so Rome transformed the church, by way of the Gregorian reform toward the end of the eleventh century, into an ecclesiastical state.

THE FAMILY MODEL IN THE PRIMITIVE CHURCH

Such extensive historical conditioning can cause us to forget that Christianity in the first three centuries was the living experience of groups of families, and that the "state of perfection" was the conjugal state. There was no dichotomy between a monastic state lived by celibates and a married state reserved to the laity. Not that there was no room for celibacy in primitive Christianity. Far from it. But celibacy was not lived as a state of perfection. It was lived as a charismatic Christian witness sustaining the faith of the faithful, as the Third Vision of the *Shepherd* of Hermas recalls; or, as in the Ninth Comparison, ministry was the base, supporting the charism of the virgins, martyrs and prophets, and this charism in turn supported the faith of Christian families. Christianity mounted a dogged resistance to the notion that celibacy was more in conformity with Christian perfection than was marriage. In a passage of rare perspicacity, Clement of Alexandria explains:

Some say that marriage is fornication, and the invention of the devil. They claim that, by remaining unmarried, they are imitating the Lord. They are ignorant of the reason for [Jesus' celibacy]. In the first place, Christ does have a spouse: his church. Second, he was not an ordinary man, with a need for a helpmeet according to the flesh. And he had no need of children [to continue his work], as he continues in being eternally as the only-begotten Son of God. [Clement of Alexandria, *Stromata,* III, 1–46, 49]

Daniélou comments: "Virginity is holy when it seeks its source in the love of God. But it ceases to be a good thing when it proceeds from a contempt for marriage."[1] Even St. Paul's image of a presbyter is that of the father of a family who merits the trust of the community because he knows how to govern his household:

As I instructed you, a presbyter must be irreproachable, married only once, the father of children who are believers and are known not to be wild and insubordinate. . . . He should . . . be hospitable and a lover of goodness; steady, just, holy, and self-controlled. [Titus 1:5–8]

The Canons: On Marriage and Ministry

We find the very same image in the famous thirty-third canon of the so-called Council of Elvira in the year 300 — an image maintained all through the early centuries amidst controversy and confusion that has not entirely died out even today. Let us pause to examine this canon, as it furnishes quite a clear elucidation of the entire question of the marriage of ministers in the church in the first three centuries.

History has preserved intact a collection of eighty-one canons or decrees, dating from the year 300, of the local church of Elvira in Andalusia in southern Spain. As there was a Spanish council at the beginning of the fourth century representing thirty-three local churches, historians have attributed this collection of canons to that council and called it the "Council of Elvira." Actually there is no evidence that the Elvira decrees are truly those of the Spanish council. Be this as it may, however, the document in question is of great historical importance. It is the first to present church decisions in the form of canons, the first to furnish such ample attestation to the presence and character of ecclesial life in Spain, and the first to present a large number of very carefully developed canons, all without any apparent historiographical context. It is understandable, then, that this document should hold such great interest for our knowledge of church tradition in the era of the juridical autonomy of the local churches, which extends to the seventh century, the era when great collections of canons finally began to appear and with them the tendency to a centralization of canon law.[2] In the Elvira collection we have the first canonical collection in the West, antedating that of Arles in Gaul (A.D. 314) and its twenty-one canons.

At that time, in the East as well as in the West, great variety prevailed in church law, depending on time, place, the needs of the faithful, and a greater or lesser rigor where ministerial discipline was concerned. Each church kept its own archives, with its laws and other determinations. At the same time, a comparative study of the councils of the fourth century — basically those of Elvira in the year 300, Arles in 314, Ancyra in Galatia in the same year (twenty-five canons), Neocaesarea in Cappadocia between 314 and 325 (fifteen canons), Nicaea in 325 (the famous first ecumenical council, with twenty canons), Laodicaea in Phrygia between 343 and 381 (sixty canons), Gangra in Paphlagonia in the middle of the fourth century (twenty canons) — clearly shows that the churches made no attempt to deal with their disciplinary problems apart from their communion with other churches, at times very distant from themselves, and we have an indication of this in the thirty-third canon of Elvira:

> We decide generally to forbid bishops, presbyters, and deacons, and all established in the ministry, from abstaining from their wives and not generating children. Let those who do so be expelled from the ministry.[3]

In the light of the later development of the ministry in Latin Christendom, this text is passing strange, of course, and it is understandable that later commentators would make an effort to "correct" the formulation and simply to reverse its meaning. But M. Meigne is very much to the point when he recalls that the canon is not so strange when placed in its context and compared with other texts, especially with a collection of eighty-five *sententiae* preserved in Greek and enjoying great authority with the churches of the fourth century under the title of the *Apostolic Canons*. The origin of these canons is unknown.[4] Canon 6 reads as follows:

> The bishop, presbyter, or deacon shall not expel his wife under pretext of piety (*eulabeia*). If he does so, let him be removed. If he persists in his intent, let him be deposed.[5]

Or canon 51 of the same *Apostolic Canons*:

> If a bishop, presbyter, deacon, or anyone else inscribed in the priestly catalogue abstains from marriage, meat, and wine, not out of asceticism but out of disgust, mindless that all is good and that God made man male and female, thus blasphemously indicting creation itself: let him either amend or be deposed and expelled from the church. [We decree] the same for a layman.[6]

Canon 33 of Elvira is simply part of a long tradition of struggle against an encratism and false asceticism that menaced the life of the communities. St. Paul himself had spoken of

> . . . Deceitful spirits and things taught by demons through plausible liars—men with seared consciences who forbid marriage and require abstinence from foods which God created to be received with thanksgiving by believers who know the truth. Everything God created is good. . . .
> [1 Tim. 4:1–4]

In East and West alike, the communities had to be on their guard against spiritualizing gnostics and later the fourth-century Manichees, who looked upon marriage, like the use of wine and meat, as expressions of an evil creation. Canon 33 of Elvira is an attestation of this concern. Christianity has always insisted on the basic goodness of creation and on the identity between the God who creates and the God who saves. The right to marry, denied by the heretics, may be abandoned in a free asceticism that is respectful of creation, but never in a false, presumptuous asceticism that despises the goodness and beauty of the Creator's work. Meigne, once more, writes:

> The thirty-third decree had a different aim from that later attributed to it. This celebrated canon belongs to a Christian tradition unbroken since the apostolic age, and testifies to the doctrinal unity between East and West.[7]

Unhappily, the Elvira canon did not succeed in its attempt to resolve the question for good and all. In the 360s, in Spain, an ascetical movement developed along the same encrastistic lines. Bishop Priscillian took charge of it in 380, and it was five times condemned over the course of twenty years: at Saragossa (380), Trèves (380), Bordeaux (384), Turin (398), and Toledo (400). Priscillian himself was sentenced to death at Trèves. Yet the movement thundered on and eventually gained broad hegemony within the Christian social body of the West.[8]

But Elvira's Canon 33 was not alone in its testimony to the struggle with a false asceticism. We have indications that the same questions arose in various of the Eastern churches. The council held at Gangra, for example — the metropolis of Paphlagonia in Asia Minor — in mid-fourth century, condemned the followers of a bishop of Sebaste, in Armenia, named Eustatius, who introduced into Asia Minor and Armenia a particularly fanatical monasticism that condemned marriage and the wearing of ordinary clothes, refused to participate in the Eucharist when it was celebrated by married priests, and launched a particularly vicious assault on the wealthy.[9] The canons of this council are impressive even today in their forceful assertion of a traditional Christianity against the novelties of a disoriented monasticism. An epilogue to the Gangra canons reads:

> Wealth accompanied by justice and good works we do not despise, as we magnify the liberality of the brothers who,

following the traditions, do good to the poor through the intermediary of the church.[10]

The Council of Ancyra, in Bithynia, celebrated in 314, indicates in its tenth canon both a movement in the direction of a freely assumed ministerial celibacy, and a respect for the order of nature:

> If the deacons, at the moment of their ordination, declare that they wish to marry rather than live in celibacy, and if they indeed marry, they may continue in their functions, since the bishop has so permitted; but if at the moment of their election they remain silent and accept the celibate life, and nevertheless marry later, upon marrying they lose the diaconate.[11]

This same norm was later adopted by the church of the Byzantine tradition. The Council of Neocaesarea in Cappadocia, held between 314 and 325, laid down the following prudent norm regarding admittance to the ministry:

> Let no one be ordained to the presbyterate before the age of thirty years, even one entirely worthy. Let him wait. For the Lord Jesus Christ himself was baptized and began to teach only at the age of thirty years. [Canon 11][12]

The Council of Nicaea, in 325, attacked a deep-rooted evil to whose existence Justin had attested long before. A young man would have himself castrated by a physician in order to be able to live Christianity in "perfection" (Justin, *Apol.,* I, 29). Eusebius of Caesarea reports that Origen himself was one of those who had had this done (*Hist. Eccl.,* 6, 8). It was an aberration connected with encratism, then, and it enjoyed a long life in Christianity: St. John Chrysostom (*PG* 58:667), St. Jerome (*PL* 28:221–95), and St. Augustine (*PL* 40:409) all mention the practice.[13]

Various councils reiterated the prohibition against admittance to the ministry of eunuchs and those who had been voluntarily castrated.[14] The Council of Nicaea publicly condemned the case of a Christian called Leontius, a Phrygian by birth and a cleric of Antioch, who lived with the *virgo subintroducta* Eustolia in a "spiritual marriage." Lest he ever feel constrained to leave her or she him, Leontius mutilated himself, and his case was singled out as a special application of the general prohibition of the first canon of the council: "The self-mutilated shall be excluded from the clergy."[15] Along the same lines, canon 19 of the Council of Ancyra declares: "We forbid virgins to live as sisters with men" — which in turn is consonant with Elvira's canon 27 and Nicene canon 3. The practice of the "spiritual marriage" gave occasion for numerous scandals, and one hears of a veritable "plague of agapetes." (*Agapetē*, "beloved sister," was the term used for a virgin who lived with a male ascetic, probably with a pejorative connotation.) St. John Chrysostom devoted one of his compositions to the problems arising from this cohabitation (*PG* 47:495).

The question of the "spiritual marriage" aroused controversy when Paul of Samosata was bishop of Antioch in Syria (260–72). Paul was a vigorous champion of Syrian Christianity against the encroachments of Hellenism. But Syrian Christianity had always been characterized by its asceticism, as expressed in a rigorous catechumenate in preparation for baptism, prolonged fasts, and the seriousness with which penance and reconciliation were undertaken. And one of the traditions of Syrian Christianity was the spiritual marriage.[16] The practice was highly valued in the Syrian tradition, then, but was regarded as suspect by the Hellenistic tradition. By all indications, this co-habitation between a Christian man and a woman was serious and devout, and anything but a frivolous dalliance. It was praised even by the pagan physician Galenus.[17] It deserves closer investigation than that to which it has thus far been subjected, as it seems to have been a practice common to many churches over a long period of history. At all events, Bishop Paul of Samosata was condemned by two successive councils, in 264 and 268, and the practice of the spiritual marriage met with ostracism on the part of Christian officialdom. We certainly cannot deny that this practice verged on encratism and smacks of a rejection of sexuality. No wonder that Manichaeism, which developed from the fourth century onward (Mani lived between 216 and 277), would be regarded, in the words of Jean Daniélou, as

> . . . a development of original Syrian Christianity, whose tendencies led to the most extreme consequences: a cosmic dualism culminating in a total condemnation of the material world; and a moral encratism that proscribed marriage and the use of certain foods.[18]

The enormous influence of Manichaeism, and through Manichaeism of encratism, on the later development of Christianity is a subject worthy of the attention of anyone wishing to gain a clearer view of the historical development of Christianity, Eastern and Western alike.

A New Relationship

But let us return to what Christianity brought that was new to married life. The documents transmit nothing sensational here, as family life rarely gains the attention of Christian writers. They are concerned to defend doctrine, posit theses, and develop theories. Family life is made up of a thousand little things, deeds done or left undone in the quest of peace, harmony, gentleness, temperance, humility, faith, and hope. Though these matters escape the attention of philosophers, they appear in writers such as Paul, Peter, Clement of Rome, Ignatius of Antioch, and Polycarp. Two texts especially develop the theme of Christian family life more broadly: the *Letter to Diognetus*,[19] already mentioned, and the *Apologia* of the second-century philosopher Aristides of Athens.[20] The following is a passage from the latter that I feel to be of special importance for the subject under consideration:

> [Christians] do not commit adultery, or practice fornication, or bear false witness, or refuse to return a loan. Nor do they appropriate what does not belong to them. They honor their fathers and their mothers, do good to their neighbor, and, when in the position of judge, judge with fairness and equity. . . . What they do not desire others to

do unto them, neither do they do themselves. . . . They beg those who afflict them to be friends with them. They do good to their enemies. Their wives are pure as virgins, their daughters modest. Their men abstain from any illegitimate union or impurity, in the hope of the reward they are to receive in the other world. Their slaves, if they have them, male or female, they persuade to become Christians, by reason of the love they bear them, and when they are converted call them brothers and sisters just as if they were free. . . . They live in humility and mildness, and tell no lies. They love one another, nor do they despise the widows among them. They protect orphans from exploiters. If they have goods, they share them generously. If they spy a stranger, they invite him into their homes, and rejoice as much at his visit as if he had been a blood brother. For they are accustomed to call one another brothers, not according to the body, but according to the spirit, in God. If a poor person passes from this world, someone learning of this takes charge of his burial, to the extent of his resources. If they learn of someone imprisoned or oppressed for the name of their Christ, they are solicitous for his welfare, and they deliver him if they can. When a poor or needy person appears among them and they lack adequate resources to assist him, they fast for two or three days, in order to lay up the wherewithal for his maintenance. . . . Every morning, every hour, they praise and glorify God for the benefits that they have received, thanking him for their food and drink. . . . Such is the constitution of the law of the Christians, and such their conduct.[21]

The Christian memory is the depository of an important inversion in the relationship between men and women. This inversion is an important element in the practice of the novelty of Christianity. In the various cultures, it is ever men who hold the dignity and wield the power. The gospel, however, subverts their primacy and presents women as the heralds of the novelty of Christ, the ones who inspire and encourage their community. It is Christian women who support the faith of their brothers. This was the role of Mary, mother of Jesus, in the events of

Pentecost. This was the role of Mary Magdalen, of the prophetesses of Montanism, and of countless other women down through the course of Christian history. A miniature in the Syrian Rabula Codex (folio 13), preserved in Florence, represents woman as holding the absolutely central place in the church event. It is she who reveals Jesus to believers, she who teaches and inculcates hope, she who is the center of all the radiation of the evangelizing movement. The apocryphal literature includes a female cycle, which was gradually expunged from the body of writings officially regarded as worthy of Christian trust, but which has nevertheless exerted great influence on the Christian imagination to our very day.

There was a Gospel of Mary (in Greek, *Genesis Marias*), which recounted the story of Joachim and Ann, the infancy and childhood of Mary and her presentation in the temple, her betrothal to the "widower" Joseph, and the annunciation of the birth of Jesus.[22] Homemakers, housemaids, laundresses, and slave women found an example for their lowly, anonymous lives in the story of this most renowned among women. Despite all official sanctions, the Gospel of Mary has been enormously popular throughout the history of Christianity, and many a Marian legend owes its origin to this apocryphal gospel.

Another apocryphal writing, known as the Passing of Mary, describes Mary's death and arrival in heaven.[23] There are likewise a number of apocalypses of Mary.[24]

The most interesting composition in this cycle is the second-century Gospel According to Mary Magdalen.[25] A recent study by A. Jelsma has pointed up the originality and importance of this "gospel" whose protagonist is a woman.[26] In it, in virtue of her special place at Jesus' side, Mary Magdalen evangelizes men. Her authority with the disciples is great. Still it is hard for men to accept a woman's precedence over themselves in the love of the Lord. Peter especially has difficulty accepting female leadership in the communities and asks: "Can the Savior have spoken secretly with a woman without consulting us? Must we listen to her? Can she be more than we?" Here Levi intervenes to defend Mary: "If the Savior has esteemed her, who are you to reject her? Surely the Savior knew her very well, and it is for this reason that he loved her more than us."[27] We are at the nub of the question. Does a woman have the right to introduce into the circle of the disciples elements of the Christian message of which the men of that circle are ignorant? Must men be converted in the sense, too, of having to learn to listen to women in order to receive the gospel? Will this not be too much of a humiliation for men?

Another unexpected element in the Gospel According to Mary Magdalen emerges at the moment of Jesus' ascension into heaven. According to Acts 1:11, it was two angels who then encouraged the disciples: "Men of Galilee, why are you downcast?" In the Gospel According to Mary Magdalen, it is Mary Magdalen who encourages the community to continue the journey without Jesus in their midst: "Weep not! Be not sad and without resolve, for his grace will be with you and to protect you. . . ."[28] In her Gospel, Mary Magdalen's great authority is owing to visions and dreams—her mysticism, then. Mysticism is the search for value in the feminine word of dialogue as opposed to the authoritarian word. Mysticism is the contrary of the confusion of Babel, or the languages of power in which no one understands anyone else because no one listens to anyone else. The visionary word of Mary Magdalen at the commencement of the history of the church is the inauguration of the current of Christian mysticism, that dialectical antithesis to the authoritarian currents down through the entire history of the church. Michel de Certeau, in his suggestive study on sixteenth- and seventeenth-century mysticism, defines mysticism—most felicitously, I think—as the quest for a language of dialogue, for an "I-Thou" language, in a world jammed with authoritarian discourse, and at the same time an apprenticeship in the art of listening to the "other" in a world that seeks only to speak, convince, and indoctrinate.[29] De Certeau writes:

> Unlike theology, mysticism makes no attempt to constitute a particular set of articulated enunciations based on the criteria of a truth and furnished by the threefold source of scripture, magisterium, and tradition . . . but seeks to speak the common language spoken by all, not the technical language of the disciplines.[30]

Hence the popular nature of mysticism. The great enemy of mystical language is the language of power, which strives to maintain society in the status quo. The language of power is a mendacious language, in the Christian view, for it ceases to orientate its hearers toward the horizon of faith in the coming Reign of God.

Applying de Certeau's observations to the Gospel According to Mary Magdalen, we perceive that the feminine presence in the predominantly and even exclusively masculine apostolic world can only be a "mystical" presence. That is, it constitutes an ongoing invitation to abandon the power game, not only among men but between men and women. Mysticism functions within the Christian social body as a subversive element, then, just as Mary Magdalen's "visions" overthrow Peter's "certitudes" in the descriptions with which we are favored in this "gospel."

Finally, Mary Magdalen is a "mystic" only because the masculine world is, at least potentially, authoritarian. She disturbs the position of Peter who, at least according to the text, arrogates to himself first place among all evangelizers. In this view of things, we can see why the Gospel According to Mary Magdalen is necessarily "apocryphal," or "concealed": it contains a mystical teaching "hidden from the wise and prudent but revealed to the simple." By mysticism infants teach adults, as Jesus taught the doctors of the Law in the temple of Jerusalem. By the same mysticism, "idiots" instruct the wise, as St. Francis of Assisi taught Guido, the bishop of his city, by abandoning the sensible life of the dutiful son of a rich businessman. Mysticism enables the poor to teach the rich and inspires the great preacher Tauler to exclaim, in a sermon of 1498: "Christ has taught me in the space of a scant hour more than you—you and all the doctors of this world—can teach me from now till doomsday."[31]

Christian marriage is part of this mystical current. At bottom, Christian marriage is a vocation to dialogue and a rejection of authoritarianism. An eleventh-century miniature from a manuscript of the Apocalypse, belonging to the French monastery of St. Severinus, shows Adam and Eve standing naked with the tiny tree of good and evil between them. So it is with the couple. They are naked. For them there is no recourse to the power game. The ancient church opened up its treasury of prayers, sacraments, liturgies, blessings, celebrations, and festivals all for the purpose of the mystical "edification" (in the original sense of "emolument, upbuilding") of the couple and the family. The

Byzantine tradition still has numerous elements of this primeval practice. Jesus shows the way, with his constant attention to family life and his elevation of that life to the status of an image of the Reign of God. Jesus watched women sweep their houses, saw one searching for a lost coin — a small, everyday coin — and observed them salting food or leavening dough. He begged his daily bread from them. He went to a spring in search of water — fresh, flowing, "living" water. He became concerned for a sick child. He watched men, too, planting, clearing their land, hoping for an abundant harvest or fearing a poor one, watching the "signs of the times" — the weather — and performing their everyday tasks. The Lord's Prayer is a family prayer: "Give us this day our daily bread." And: "Forgive us our trespasses as we forgive those who trespass against us." And in the same spirit: "Where two or three are gathered in my name, there am I in the midst of them" (Matt. 18:20). After all, Clement of Alexandria reminds us, these "two or three" are the Christian family. Family life is the daily bread from which community action takes its nourishment.

The original model of church was the family model. But as already observed, this original model changed a great deal with the propagation of the monastic model and a consequent emphasis on the practice of celibacy in the living experience of the church and Christianity. The relationship between man and woman was gradually sublimated, or spiritualized, in the church. It came to stand as a symbol for God's love for humanity, or Christ's love for the church. A mosaic in the church of Santa Maria de Trastevere in Rome, dating from the years 1140–48, represents Mary, the Mother of God, as the majestic spouse of Christ, enthroned beside her husband and Lord. But from her throne on high, in splendid raiment and wearing a crown, Mary gestures toward the book of sacred scriptures. Clearly, then, in this mosaic she symbolizes the church, for the church, and not Mary, is the spouse of Christ. Marriage is sublimated and spiritualized in this mosaic. It has come to signify ideas developed by the theologians. It no longer reflects the living reality of everyday family life.

CHAPTER XVI

Martyrdom

In the prolonged, if intermittent, conflict between the authorities of the Roman Empire and the Christian communities, between A.D. 64 and 313, many Christians suffered martyrdom. The impact of this phenomenon on the historical memory of the Christian people of subsequent centuries was enormous. Viewing the history of the church from the standpoint of the people, we can only call the veneration of the martyrs one of the greatest movements in that entire history. That movement began immediately after the general persecution known as that of Diocletian (304–13), deeply marking popular religion in the fourth century. The whole fervor of popular piety centered on the martyrs. People longed to be buried near the resting place of a martyr (burial *ad sanctos*, near the saints). Even more, they sought to venerate the "relics," or mortal remains, of a martyr, or at least something the holy martyr had touched or used during life. So great was the popular eagerness to win the "intercession" of the holy martyrs through the veneration of their relics that the Emperor Theodosius himself (378–95) had to forbid the dissection of the bodies of the saints and traffic in their relics. The veneration of relics — the passion to acquire some memento that would bind a Christian community to the holy martyrs — has marked the Christian life of the people to our very day.

Thereby an image has been created among the Christian people of the first three centuries as the "age of persecutions," with the "peace of the church" following the Edict of Constantine. This popular image brings with it impressive symbols like that of the great Roman Colosseum where "the Christians" were thrown to the beasts (*"ad bestias,"* Tertullian's phrase), or like the catacombs, where Christians are supposed to have taken refuge in times of persecution. Today we know that this image was created in the seventeenth century, in the heat of a literary battle between those who sought to maximize the impact of the Roman persecutions on the historical formation of Christianity and writers who relativized, even minimized, the importance of the dialectic of persecution-and-martyrdom in the development of Christianity.[1]

One thing is certain: behind the tendency to exalt the "age of persecutions" an ideology lurks. That ideology says: the "others" (pagans, Jews, Turks, Communists, and enemies generally), in persecuting the church, are persecuting God. If we are to escape the pitfalls of this ideology, we should do well to recall that Jesus Christ himself was a martyr, and that the persecution he anticipated was to be a persecution against justice, and not simply one against the institution: "Lucky those persecuted for justice' sake; theirs is the Reign of God" (Matt. 5:10). Just as Christian practice made a distinction between true and false miracle, true and false prophecy, or true and false religion, so it distinguished between true and false martyrdom. St. Augustine expressed that distinction in a felicitous theological formula: "Martyrem non facit poena, sed causa"—"What makes a martyr is not the suffering, but the cause" in which the martyr suffers.[2] Elsewhere Jesus warns of the contradictions inherent in persecution: "The hour will come in which the one who kills you will think he is doing something pleasing to God" (John 16:2). The false religion of those who seek to defend religious stability by killing the prophets and the defenders of justice enters into conflict with the religion of the genuine martyrs.

> Blest are you when they insult you and persecute you
> and utter every kind of slander against you because of me.
> Be glad and rejoice, for your reward is great in heaven;
> they persecuted the prophets before you in the very same
> way. [Matt. 5:11–12]

Here, then, are the genuine martyrs. Here are the Christians who bear witness to Jesus Christ by their life, and whose death, violent though it be, is the confirmation of a life in the service of the new values that came into the world with the coming of Christianity. We readily understand, then, that the majority of the martyrs, the witnesses of the Christian faith, should have been anonymous — women and men whose names are known to God alone and whom the church commemorates on the Feast of All Saints. It is these anonymous martyrs, whose memory is recorded only in the Christian cemeteries, the so-called catacombs, who revealed the Christian novelty to a pagan world through their lives before revealing it through their death.

It is not in sensational documents, then, that we shall learn the truth about the martyrs, but in the humble accounts that describe the daily life of Christians, as in the *Letter to Diognetus* or the *Apologia* of Aristides,[3] already cited, or again in the *Petition in Behalf of the Christians* of the philosopher Athenagoras.[4] These three documents, all dating from the latter half of the second century and the beginning of the third, reveal the most precious element in the Christian witness of "martyrdom" (in the original sense of the word). Here is a passage from Athenagoras' *Petition*:

> You will find among us many simple folk, artisans, elderly women . . . who, incapable though they be of arguing the utility of their religion in word, show in their deeds the quality of the choice that they have made. Here are folk who lack any desire for fine words. They simply perform good actions. They do not strike those who strike them, they do not take to court those who despoil them, they give to all who ask, and they love their neighbor as themselves. Now, unless we believed in a God superior to the human race, could we lead so pure a life? Surely not. It is in the persuasion that we shall have to give an account of our present life to the God who created both us and the world that we make our option for a moderate and charitable life, disdained though it be by others. . . . Those who say, "Let us eat and drink, for tomorrow we die" (1 Cor. 15:32) are taken for pious, and look on death as a deep sleep. We,

on the contrary, hold the present life to be of short duration, and little worth. We are moved by the desire to know, first, the true God and the Word who is within him; then what communion obtains between the Father and the Son; then what the Spirit is; then what the unity of such magnificent realities among themselves, together with the distinction among those thus united—the Spirit, the Son, and the Father. We know that the life for which we hope will be inexpressible in words, provided only we can attain to it pure of all injustice and with affection and love for our friends.[5]

THE VALUES OF THE EARLY CHRISTIANS

If we are to have an adequate understanding of this sober text, we must compare its content with the values lived by Christians of the time. What were these values? What was the ideal of a perfect life at the time when Athenagoras wrote those lines (180)? To answer this question we must remember that the popular religion of the age was marked by the Greek spirit (more specifically by the legacy of the thought of Plato), whether in Stoicism or in Epicureanism. Middle Platonism had popularized Plato's intuitions throughout the Hellenized world, by way of a de-politicized, interiorized religiousness.

Stoicism, for example, offered an "escape" from the prevailing pessimism. Instead of political liberty, which had become impracticable after the defeat of democracy of the Greek type, Stoicism preached an interior freedom, a liberty of which nothing could deprive a person, "neither death nor poverty, neither men nor the anger of the gods" (Seneca). This interior liberty, in Stoic thinking, was superior to political liberty, which was "only" external. Side by side with Stoicism went the Epicureanism to which our text directly alludes, and which reacted to the general pessimism of the day with its *Carpe diem*—"Pluck the day," get all you can out of this fleeting life, for tomorrow we die. The Epicureans ignored crisis, suffering, and death, asserting that the present life was the highest value, and that concern for the morrow must be banished from religious minds. Besides Stoicism and Epicureanism, people sought still another kind of religious experience in the "mystery religions," which introduced their adepts into the "higher spheres" of perception, protected them against "demonic powers," offered them blessings and religious raptures, and bestowed on them the grace of "salvation" (in Greek, *sōtēria*).

These three currents, then—Stoicism, Epicureanism, and the mystery religions—constituted the basic, typical religiousness that prevailed in the Roman Empire. It was an essentially a-politicized, spiritualized, and, especially, theorized religiousness. Not surprisingly, then, Christianity had a powerful impact on the society that was the seedbed of these religious currents. Christianity was practical, realistic, sober. It was also bent on the transformation of society, despite the distance of its social matrix from the spheres of political power.[6]

The contrast between the values of a Hellenized piety and those of the new Christian religiousness was especially striking when it came to respect for life. The value of an individual life was not very great in the mind of the age. Abortion, for example, was a common practice, despite legal prohibitions. The *paterfamilias* (the father of the family and lord of all who dwelt in the home, free and slave) could dispose of a newborn with impunity, and this abuse was so prevalent and accepted that even in the Christian empire, as late as the fourth century, it had to be tolerated in law. Besides this there were the games in the circus, cruel and bloody, which demonstrated, in their treatment of beings regarded as inferior, such as infants, women, slaves, prisoners, deserters, and Christians, the degree to which the Romans had lost their respect for life. Here the Christian novelty leaps into relief. We need only examine the *Apostolic Constitutions*, which compile the oldest ecclesiastical ordinations.[7]

You shall not destroy your child by abortion, nor immolate the newborn, for every being formed in its mother's womb has received a soul from God and will be revenged if unjustly destroyed. [*Apostolic Constitutions*, 8, 3]

Justin is no less assertive:

We reckon the practice of exposure of infants a crime, as it almost always means abandoning children to prostitution, girls and boys alike. Children today are easy prey to immorality. . . . But there is another reason why we do not expose our infants. We fear lest no one take them in, and they die, so that we should be guilty of homicide. [*Apol.,* I, 26, 29]

The apologist Athenagoras rejects the allegation that Christians are cannibals and murderers:

If we cannot bear the sight of a capital execution, how can we be accused of murder or cannibalism? Who else among our contemporaries absent themselves from the contests of the gladiators and the beasts, or fail to honor those who schedule these events? As for us, rather, we account a casual assistance at the killing of persons as [a complicity] of nearly the dimensions of killing [those persons] oneself, and it is for this reason that we abstain from attending such spectacles. How could we, who are unwilling so much as to behold killing lest we soil ourselves with the filth of the act [through our mere presence], ourselves kill? How can we, who accuse abortionists of murder and remind them that they shall have to render an account [of those lives] to God, be capable of killing? Between the conviction that a woman carries in her womb a living being — and hence the object of divine providence — and the summary murder of an infant who has thus already begun its life, there is no reconciliation.[8]

Christianity has maintained this same strong position on respect for life all through its history. We have a clear instance of this in the fifth canon of Elvira (A.D. 300) proscribing another abuse that must have been common at the time, that of scourging a maidservant so viciously that she would actually die. "If a woman becomes so angry with her servant that she has her flogged to the point of giving up the ghost (*animam effundat*) within three days, . . ." she must do seven years' canonical penance if she has killed her with "intent" and five years otherwise.[9] Canons 62 and 67 of the same Elvira collection, testifying to the aversion felt by Christians for the theaters and "pantomimes," are to be interpreted along the same lines of Christian respect for life. The same is to be observed in canon 4 of the Council of Arles (314), which censures chariot drivers in the circus races and participants in violent games in general: "Let them be separated from communion."[10]

The difference in attitude between Christians and pagans regarding respect for life culminated in the question of military service. Until the end of the second century Christianity categorically condemned this service, for reasons of both false morality (because it is murder, brutality, and pridefulness) and false worship (because a soldier must swear an oath to the emblems of the state and offer sacrifice). The *Apostolic Tradition* (A.D. 218) determined that the catechumen who intended to become a soldier must be refused baptism. (Those who were already professional soldiers, however, were admitted to baptism.) Tertullian and Origen both insisted that a Christian's "spiritual militancy" was not very compatible with a terrestrial one.[11] As early as the 170s Celsus had made a direct, impassioned appeal to Christians at the close of his *True Discourse*: "Cease to flee your civic duties and military service!"[12] We have many indications, then, that up until the end of the second century Christianity's position with regard to military service, which at the time was not obligatory for all, was clear and definite: a Christian does not practice a service that consists in killing or preparing to kill.

Even a century after Celsus, in 270, another pagan author, a certain Porphyry (232?-303), practically repeated Celsus' accusations in a work entitled *Against the Christians* (in Greek, *Kata ton Christianon*).[13] In the opinion of Adolf von Harnack, this work was the most important of all of the literary attacks by Greco-Roman paganism on Christianity. Only a few insignificant fragments have been preserved, however, since Constantine and his successors prohibited the publication and use of the treatise as far too dangerous to be allowed to exist. Even the twenty-five-book apologia of Eusebius of Caesarea in response to Porphyry has all but disappeared. We know Porphyry's positions through the writings of his other Christian adversaries.

Porphyry accused the Christians of basically the same things as had Celsus a hundred years before. Christians refuse to collaborate in building society. Indeed, they actually destabilize institutions. They demoralize the army, they are the enemies of the established order, they are revolutionaries and consequently barbarians. The ancient Romans were capable of conceptualizing only one form of polity: the Roman. This explains the virulence of Porphyry's attacks on the Christians. He characterized Christianity as the work of impostors, a concatenation of old-wives' tales. Jesus himself was a failed leader who turned to ignorant women and children because he had been unable to launch his project in any other way. Porphyry was struck with admiration at Christianity's rapid and deep expansion. But he found the reason for this in the supposed fact that the movement had managed to penetrate only the popular strata. This, he asserted, was why Christianity was to be found only among the "ignorant."

The criticisms of Celsus and Porphyry, then, show that the question of military service was only the sorest point in a whole series of questions that set Christians and pagans at odds in practical life.[14] Now we understand the classic indictment of Christians for their "hatred of the human race" (*"odium generis humani"* — Tacitus),[15] their "isolation from other persons" (Celsus),[16] and their behavior as "public enemies" (*"publici hostes,"* the accusation recorded by Tertullian).[17] From allegation to persecution was only a little step.

THE BLOOD OF THE MARTYRS

And so we return to the subject of violent persecution and martyrdom in blood. For some Christians, the martyrdom of everyday life indeed culminated in martyrdom by the shedding of their blood. Christian memory venerated in St. Stephen the first martyr after Jesus himself, and the Acts of the Apostles devote a great deal of space to the account of his martyrdom (Acts 6:8–8:3). Of the martyrs of apostolic times, Saints Peter and Paul, whom an age-old tradition joins in martyrdom, are the objects of a special veneration. From the second century, the best remembered martyrs are St. Ignatius of Antioch, St. Polycarp, St. Justin and his companions, and the Holy Martyrs of Lyon (177–78). From the third century, Christian devotion has a predilection for Saints Perpetua and Felicity, the many who fell under the persecution of Decius (250), and the equally numerous martyrs of the greatest and most general of the persecutions, that of Diocletian (304–13). Scholars are anything but unanimous in their conclusions as to the actual duration of the respective persecutions, their extent, and especially the number of their victims.[18] Ancient authors spoke of 200,000 martyrs. Hertling reduced this number to 100,000, and a recent study by Henri Grégoire asserts that 10,000 "would doubtless be much too high a figure."[19] Here as in other areas of Christian historiography there are good monographs available to help those desiring to know more.

All of the persecutions, but especially the one under Decius (250), placed the Christian on the horns of a dilemma. What was to be done with the "fallen," the *lapsi*? Have understanding for their frailty and forgive them? Or repudiate them forever? Take them back into the communities? The question was debated with fiery intensity throughout all the second half of the third century, and was still having repercussions on councils in the fourth century. The course decided upon was one of leniency and acceptance with regard to the *lapsi* (canon 8 of the Council of Nicaea), heretics (canons 7–9 of the Council of Laodicaea), and even pagans (canon 39 of the Elvira collection). The liberal solution adopted only after long discussion between the leaders of the church of Africa, led by Bishop (or "Pope") Cyprian, and those of Rome, headed by Bishop Stephen, snatched Christianity from the perilous path that would have led it to become a closed religion like Judaism or various other religions of the age.[20] Unless it be tempered by a generous dose of the spirit of forgiveness and understanding for human frailty, Christianity can become a religion of fanatics, a merciless, intolerant sect capable of leading persons into the worst ideological deformations and authoritarianism.

Here, as with other aspects of the Christian message, the memory of Jesus and his practice of always forgiving, "not seven times but seventy times seven times," must be normative. Jesus' most moving parables were those of forgiveness and compassion for sinners, like the parables of the lost sheep, the lost coin, or the prodigal son. Furthermore: Jesus was a friend of sinners and made a point of ignoring their past. He refused to harbor any sentiment of resentment in their regard. After all, it was with them, and not with those who judged themselves to be superior and perfect, that Jesus sought to realize his project, the Reign of God. The moment any discussion of repentance and forgiveness arises, Christians should be mindful of Jesus' remarkable attitude toward sinners and should remember that the church is built on forgiveness alone. To be sure, there were hard, intransigent authors in the first three centuries, like Tertullian. But there were also authors who breathe a spirit of understanding, like Hermas, or later, Clement of Alexandria.

THE RESURRECTION OF THE FLESH

It remains to analyze the deepest element in the Christian witness or "martyrdom": faith in the resurrection of the flesh. Aristides of Athens, in describing Christians' manner of living and being, calls attention to the following attitude, which surely must have puzzled their contemporaries:

> When any just one among them passes from this world, they rejoice, and give thanks to God, as they accompany the corpse as if from one home to another. And just as they praise God when a child is born, so they glorify God if it dies in infancy, as it has passed through this world without sin. But seeing someone die in evil and sin, they weep bitterly, and groan for him, supposing he has gone to his punishment.[21]

Justin gives the reason for this behavior, so unlike that of his contemporaries:

> Whom have you known to be called king among his people whose hands and feet had been pierced, dying in this mystery—I refer to the crucifixion—other than Jesus alone?[22]

Veneration for a torture victim who became a king after his death is surely a Christian novelty that found acceptance in pagan milieus only after a long, difficult penetration of ideas. The Greco-Roman religion of antiquity swung back and forth on the question of human destiny after death, hesitating between a vague spiritism with long wanderings of the souls of the departed before finding "eternal rest" (or the "deep sleep" of which Athenagoras speaks) and the Platonic doctrine of the immortality of the soul.[23] Between these two conceptualizations, the one more popular, the other more philosophical, Christian faith in the resurrection of the flesh had to walk a tightrope, and we have to say that it did not always keep its balance. At times it fell into an animism that removed it from earthly realities and political tasks. At other times it veered into a Platonizing spiritualism that despised the body and material reality in general, with the same outcome: alienation from political tasks. In any case, the notion of the immortality of the soul in the Platonic sense is not original with Christianity and was slow to penetrate the Christian social body, as P.-A. Février shows in his monograph on Christian images of death in the early centuries.[24] Christian faith was originally faith in the resurrection of the flesh—that precious treasure preserved in the memory of the Christian people, codified in the Apostles' Creed, and rehearsed in the prayer of the church in the Eucharist to our very day.

The Christians of the first three centuries did not defend their faith in the resurrection of the flesh by way of a theoretical discourse or philosopical ratiocination. They defended it by concrete deeds, as in their rejection of abortion and the exposure of infants, or their refusal to attend the games held in the circus, in which the human body was delivered up to violence and brutality, or their conscientious objection to military service and other public duty involving danger of death to oneself or others, or their rejection of divorce and adultery, which they regarded as offenses to the dignity of the body. When the anonymous author of the *Letter to Diognetus* stated that Christians "marry as does everyone, and have children, but do not abandon their newborn infants" (5, 1–6), he made a beautiful profession of faith in the resurrection of the flesh. Even babies' bodies must be respected, for they too are called to eternity. The same holds for Tertullian's realistic observations:

> We live with you [pagans], we have the same food, the
> same clothing, the same way of life. We are neither
> Brahmins or gymnosophists from India. We frequent your
> forum, your market, your baths, your hotels, your homes.
> . . . [But] I do not go to your baths at dawn at the
> Saturnalia, lest my bath take me a night and a day. I bathe
> at the hour that suits me. [Tertullian, *Apolog.*, 41:1-3]

Early Christianity's Attitude toward the Body

The guiding principle of Christian morality is that of respect for
a body called to resurrection. Christians despised not bathing
but the Saturnalia, which were prejudicial to one's health. Why
does Clement of Alexandria reject a "fondness for adornment
and deceitful artifices"?

> What am I to say of a fondness for adornment, of
> variegated vesture, of the vanity of colors, of the luxury
> of pearls, of jewels and gold, of hair waved or curled or
> gathered, of made-up eyes, of dyed hair, and of all such
> deceitful artifices? [*Paid.*, II, 10, 104, 1][25]

The whole of Clement's *Pedagogue* breathes a climate of
optimistic spirituality—of a natural, simple love for the body
and its beauty, without artifices that demean that body. Clement
has the same attitude toward food and drink. He pauses long
over the question of wine and comes to the conclusion that wine
is good when used to the advantage of the body and of natural
pleasure, but evil when used for intoxication and the excesses of
the banquet table. The body, for these writers, is the temple of
God and called to resurrection. Consequently its health and
welfare, its enhancement, and its potentialities ought to be
respected. To touch our bodies is to touch God himself. The
Octavius of Minucius Felix[26] contains a sentence that sums all of
this up in a few words: "There is not a single member of the
human body that does not have its beauty or its usefulness."[27]

And Clement of Alexandria completes that thought: "The man created by God is an end in himself."[28] This is the Christian witness that provided the wherewithal for an in-depth dialogue with Judaism and paganism alike: the human person is an end and not a means. God has placed all things at the service of human beings. They are the rulers of creation. Christianity's fundamental humanism enabled the Christian imagination to take up Jewish as well as pagan themes in all tranquillity, transforming them only in their ultimate import. We have an example of this in Christianity's assimilation of Jewish angelology, as attested by a passage from the *Shepherd* of Hermas:

"There are two angels with every human person, one just and one evil."

"But how can I distinguish their activity if both live within me, Lord?"

"Give ear, and seek to understand. The good angel is gentle, delicate, modest, and calm. He speaks of justice, chastity, temperance, sanctity, holy actions, noble virtues. . . . The bad angel is full of bitterness, stupidity, and rage. . . . Listen: when you feel hatred, when you feel envy . . . know that he is within you. This is the activity of the two angels." [Precept 6, 2–10]

Christian Imagination

The Christian imagination operates on two levels, then—the visible and the invisible. The visible plane is expressed from the standpoint of the perception of reality, while the invisible level signifies the faith that animates the Christian life. Christian iconography provides us with numerous expressions of this two-tiered imagination. In the church at Daphni, near Athens, we find an eleventh-century mosaic representing Jesus Christ at the moment of his baptism by John. Here the visible is joined to the invisible: St. John the Baptist on one side, two "just" angels on the other; Jesus immersed in the water but with a dove over his head (signifying the Holy Spirit), the hand of God, and the heavenly firmament. The co-existence in the same work of art of images representing visible and invisible realities meant for Christians the co-existence and co-operation of an eye turned to external reality and an eye turned to the realities of faith. We find the same dynamics in the very ancient Christian custom of facing East when at prayer. Jews prayed facing Jerusalem, and Christians "updated" the practice by praying with their faces turned toward the East. This Christian innovation vis-à-vis Judaism was anything but casual. It represented the very early assimilation of Christ to the sun, especially the rising sun, the eastern sun, according to the still definitive 1925 study by F. J. Dölger.[29] The rising sun becomes the Sun of justice, the Sun of salvation (the *Sol salutis* of the Christian hymns). Jesus is greeted as "the rising Sun who shines on those lying in darkness and in the shadow of death" as early as Zechariah's Canticle (Luke 1:79); and Tertullian, summing up a whole tradition in one clipped phrase, says: "The East is the prefiguration of Christ" ("*Orientem, Christi figuram*," *Adv. Val.*, 3, 1).

This relationship of figurative identity between Christ and the sun was even further consolidated when the Emperor Aurelian, at the close of the second century, wished to revive the worship of *Sol Invictus*, the Invincible Sun. Pagans celebrated the Birthday of the Invincible Sun each year on December 25, the date of the winter solstice according to the Julian calendar of that time, when, in the Northern Hemisphere at least, the sun begins to climb the sky once again to bring warm weather and green fields to a cold world. Christians converted this festival into the Feast of the Nativity of Christ, the Sun of the Universe. Romance languages still call Christmas simply, "Birthday."[30]

The National Library of France houses an eleventh-century engraving of Christ as the Sun in the circle of the zodiac.[31] In this engraving, each sign of the zodiac is inscribed with its own name and the name of the part of the human body it governs. The zodiac, then, and consequently one's horoscope, find their point of convergence in Christ, the human being at the center of the universe. The message is clear. The human being is absolutely central in the world and in history, as even the stars whirl about this pinnacle of God's creation. The engraving expresses a Christian tradition that goes back to earliest Christian times.

CHRISTIANITY AND PAGANISM

These final observations, on the dialogue between primitive Christianity and paganism, lead me to an apologia for paganism. It seems to me that primitive Christianity's position vis-à-vis paganism constitutes one of the most important lessons in the history of the church of the first three centuries. Earliest Christianity by no means represented a condemnation of paganism. On the contrary, it sprang up in the Roman Empire as a new interpretation of paganism. Apologetes like Justin, Athenagoras, Aristides of Athens, Tertullian, Irenaeus, and even the writers of the Alexandrian school, Clement and Origen, were tireless in their insistence that Christianity was consonant with paganism's deepest aspirations. And indeed it has always been consonant with these aspirations.

Without paganism, Christianity loses its vitality to become a dry, sterile "Judaism." Paganism raises the great problems of humanity—health, life, justice, land, peace, happiness. Paganism is as necessary to Christianity as is the soil of a garden to the growing things that strike root in it. Jesus was extremely sensitive to the fact that Judaism was moving too far from paganism, and consequently becoming a closed religion of lifeless rules and Pharisaisms, a religion of meaningless observances. Paganism brings vitality to Christianity, offering it the opportunity to testify to its faith. Christianity has genuinely flourished over the course of time when it has rediscovered its responsibility to the paganism in whose midst it lives—when Christians have shouldered the responsibility of showing pagans by their manner of life the new values that Jesus brings to humanity.

I have tried in these pages to present some of these new Christian values, values lived rather than formulated: miracles, holding of goods in common, a new relationship between women and men, the new concept of male adultery, conscientious objection to military service, the option for the marginalized, the rejection of abortion and exposure, a refusal to attend the games in the circus and the theaters where the

dignity of the human body was not respected, the rule according
to which "the greater shall serve the smaller," the notion and
practice of mission, the base church community, the development of a theology of the election of the marginalized, martyrdom, forgiveness, the resurrection of the flesh. Far from
constituting an occasion for Christians to close themselves up in
a circle of perfect persons, the new values being lived by
Christians provided them precisely with the dynamic capacity to
open themselves up to the paganism around them.

By way of this experience, Christian communities acquired a
remarkable flexibility and capacity for adaptation to new circumstances. We can verify this in the missionary attitude of St.
Paul, as recorded in Acts 4:15–17, when the apostle has to
abandon the theme of the God of Abraham, Isaac, and Jacob to
take up that of the god of rain and harvest, thence to move on
to the God of universal liberation and not just the God of Israel.

The apologists and the other writers of the first three centuries refused to regard the church as an absolute beginning. The
church was a continuation and universalization of earlier forces.
Before there was a church of Christ there was the church called
that "from Abel, from Abraham, from Moses" ("*Ecclesia ab
Abel, ab Abraham, a Moyse*"), in which Abel is the prototype of
all victims of injustice, Abraham the prototype of all those who
leave their stability to go in quest of faith, and Moses the
prototype of all the liberators. Jesus came to complete, or
"recapitulate," as Irenaeus of Lyon would say, the path that had
led as far as himself — or better, the several such paths. Jesus
came to radicalize the "old Law" and universalize what was
already present in the history of Israel. St. Paul himself stated:
"The law of Moses leads to Christ" (Rom. 10:4), and added:
"Now there is no longer any distinction between Jew and Greek"
(Rom. 10:12). And Ignatius of Antioch repeated: "Christ is the
doorway of God, the entryway of Abraham, Isaac, and Jacob,
the prophets, the apostles, and the church" (*Letter to the
Philippians*, 9, 1). This being the case, why would not Christ be
"God's doorway" and entryway for the martyrs of the native
peoples of Latin America, the enslaved peoples of Africa, or the
other humiliated peoples of the Third World? In his *First Letter
to the Corinthians*, Clement of Rome asserted that "Moses was

God's miracle-worker" (1 Clem. 51:5). Cannot this expression be applied to other persons, as well, who wrought miracles for their people in the sense of assisting them to flee the "land of Egypt," pass through the "Red Sea," and cross the "desert"? In the *Letter* of Pseudo-Barnabas we read that the church is the "new people" (*ton laon ton kainon*) whose sign is that "the greater serves the lesser" (5, 7 and 13, 5). Are there not various "new peoples" in the Lord who actualize this sign of divine election? In other words, with the passage of Jesus Christ among us the question of openness to paganism becomes a basic one, since Jesus came precisely to open salvation to all persons without discrimination: "In Christ there is neither Jew nor Greek, man nor woman, free nor slave."

The question of paganism became vividly present in the sixteenth and seventeenth centuries, although in altogether different terms. By way of a long political process, Christianity had been transformed into a Christendom allied with colonial powers that were embarking on a project of economic and political expansion in America, Africa, and even Asia. It was precisely this alliance that prevented the church of the sixteenth and seventeenth centuries from repeating the experience of the communities of the first three centuries in the sense of an in-depth dialogue with paganism on the continents to which colonialism had spread. After all, it was from the paganism of the colonial lands that the themes of justice, fellowship, charity, and respect for the life of the small and humiliated emerged, and the church was incapable of opening up to these themes, being itself committed to the colonial project that was causing precisely an absence of justice, fellowship, charity, respect for life, and so on.

There was a further attempt to reverse the process in the efforts of the Italian Jesuit Matteo Ricci, the missionary to China who sought to sensitize the Vatican to the question of Chinese paganism. Ricci went so far as to say that Chinese Confucianism was not, properly speaking, a religion but a philosophy, and he did that in an attempt to demonstrate that, far from being Christianity's rival, Confucianism was the vehicle of an opportunity for openness on the part of the Christian witness. All was in vain. The upshot of Ricci's experiment was a foreign, unassimilated religiousness that, at least in its official instances, found it all but impossible to articulate religious content in any other language than that of power.

The same Christianity that, by way of the effort of innumerable anonymous Christians, had assimilated European paganism, refused a dialogue with the paganisms it confronted, beginning in the sixteenth century, in America, Africa, and Asia. And the question that was posed in the historical period of Christianity's alliance with the powers of European expansion remains the same today.

Glossary

Unless an exception is indicated, the technical terms below are in (or from) *Koine* Greek, the language of most of the documents of primitive Christianity and the *lingua franca* of the Roman Empire in the first three Christian centuries. First a literal translation of the term in question is given (in parentheses), and then a definition or brief explanation.

ALEXANDRIAN SCHOOL—The name given to a theological tendency, originating in Alexandria, to apply the allegorical method in reading of the memorial texts of the Christian tradition.

ALMS (Compassion)—Historically, a new "reading" of Christian charity whereby common ownership of goods was no longer regarded as essential to the concept of charity.

APOCALYPSE (Revelation)—A literary genre appearing in Judaism during the centuries immediately before Christ. Based on revelations concerning the end of the world, the apocalypses exerted a key influence on primitive Christianity.

APOCRYPHAL (Hidden)—Books were "hidden" when it was feared they might be destroyed if found. The Christian apocrypha include gospels, acts of apostles, and apocalypses, all representing the common people's understanding of the rise of Christianity.

CANONICAL (According to the rule)—Beginning in the second century, in order to combat distortions of the Christian memory, the communities began to be concerned with establishing a "rule" or "list" of the books of the New Testament.

CATACOMB (Along the hillside)—The name given to a valley of the city of Rome, now the site of the cemetery of St. Callixtus. This name came to be used for Christian cemeteries generally, and only from the seventeenth century did the "myth" of a Roman "underground" (literally) appear, a place where Christians were supposed to have hidden.

CATHARI (Pure) — A derogatory expression used by the "orthodox" for those who sought to recover the "pure" memory of Christianity.

CATHOLIC (Whole, integral) — In antiquity, this term did not yet denote membership in a specific sociological totality.

CHARISM (Grace) — God's call, addressed to each one, whereby an individual is both invited to perform a specific service in the community and rendered apt for this service.

CHRISTENDOM (Equivalent to the Latin *Christianitas*) — A politico-cultural system based on an alliance between the ecclesiastical estate and the established powers of a political society. The first hegemonic Christendom was the Byzantine (A.D. 325–1453), centered on the city of Constantinople.

COLLEGE (Lat., association) — An association for mutual assistance, having legal status, established by the slum-dwellers of any large metropolis of the Roman Empire.

COPTIC (Egyptian) — The ancient popular Egyptian culture was marginalized by Hellenism and driven out of the great centers of the Roman Empire. A Christian monasticism sprang up among the Coptic peasants of the interior of Egypt in the latter part of the third century.

DIAKONIA (Service) — The basic organizational concept of primitive Christianity.

DIASPORA (Dispersal) — The scattering of the Jewish community throughout the Mediterranean Basin and the appearance there, especially in the slums of the great cities of the Roman Empire, of synagogues as the nuclei of the new communities.

DIDASCALIA (Lat., teaching) — The forerunner of modern catechesis. Each Christian community had its teachers who "did *didascalias.*"

EGYPTIAN MODEL — A political model without representation at or of the base, implemented throughout the Roman Empire by the Emperors Diocletian (A.D. 284–305) and Constantine (313–37).

ENCRATISM (Sexual continence) — The doctrine that sexual activity is incompatible with a full Christian life. See "Spiritual marriage."

EUSEBIAN TRADITION — The historiographical tradition of Christianity initiated by Eusebius of Caesarea and based on an ecclesiastical positivism.

GNOSIS (Knowledge) — Here, a highly erudite knowledge accompanied by a contempt for, or at least the marginalization of, popular wisdom.

HERESY (Choice) — A derogatory name applied by "orthodoxy" to any heterodoxy.

LAPSI (Lat., fallen) — Those who had showed weakness in the face of persecution, especially during the persecution under Decius (A.D. 250). The question of what attitude to take toward the "fallen" agitated the communities in the second half of the third century. The practice of forgiveness prevailed.

MAGIC (Divination) — A salvation practice redounding to the maintenance of established structures or the prestige of the practitioner.

MARCIONISM — A missionary movement initiated by Marcion in Asia Minor around A.D. 144, markedly Pauline and rejecting the Old Testament. It survived the assaults of orthodoxy until the sixth century.

MARTYRDOM (Testimony) — "What makes a martyr is not the suffering, but the cause" (St. Augustine). We seek to emphasize the concrete, practical, realistic nature of Christian martyrdom, which is witness borne to Christ in the everyday experiences of the community life, and which in exceptional cases can lead to the "martyrdom of blood."

MIRACLE (Lat., wonder) — A salvation practice redounding in particular to the benefit of the poor and marginalized. Gradually the word has acquired the illuministic meaning of a suspension of the laws of nature.

MONTANISM — A prophetic, encratistic, and Johannine missionary movement arising in Phrygia in Asia Minor around 156.

MYSTERY (Initiation) — Various Middle Eastern mystery religions were at times confused with Christianity by its contemporaries.

ORTHODOX ("Pertaining to the straight doctrine") — Those who follow, or that which is in accord with, the official dictates of faith rather than the views or practices of *Cathari* or heretics.

PARISH (Life without citizenship) — The first Christians lived a "parish" life (1 Pet. 1:17), far from their native lands and without civil rights.

PHILOSOPHER (Lover of wisdom) — In the age of Christianity's infancy, itinerant sages, very popular with the masses, who spoke to audiences in the squares or streets to inculcate a life of the renunciation of pleasure and the pursuit of wisdom.

PROSELYTISM (Regard for newcomers) — The system whereby the synagogues of the diaspora spread the faith.

PROTO-CATHOLICISM (Embryonic Catholicism) — The term used by Conzelmann and others to designate the first stirrings of what would later become Catholicism.

SPIRITUAL MARRIAGE — The co-habitation of a female and a male ascetic. The former was referred to in Greek as the *agāpetē* (Lat., *virgo subintroducta*). See "Encratism."

SYNAGOGUE (Gathering) — The organizational model articulated by the unofficial Judaism of the diaspora after the Babylonian Captivity, consisting of a genuine base community, with autonomy and a certain experience of democracy.

TORAH (Heb., law) — The Pentateuch, the five books of the Mosaic Law, the foundation of the synagogical tradition.

Notes

INTRODUCTION

Chapter I: Christianity and Memory

1. H. Butterfield, *The Origins of History* (London, 1984).
2. "Ut in signum memoriae meae benedictionis et mci testamenti semper diligant se ad invicem."
3. Altaner-Stuiber, *Patrologie*, 8th ed. (Freiburg, 1978), pp. 52–3. (Abbreviated hereafter as Altaner-Stuiber.) Eng. trans. of earlier ed.: *Patrology* (New York, 1961).
4. Ibid., pp. 109–10.
5. Ibid., pp. 65–70; M. Greschat, ed., *Alte Kirche* (Stuttgart, 1984), vol. 1, p. 64.
6. Altaner-Stuiber, pp. 110–17.
7. Simone Weil, *A condição Operária e Outros Estudos sobre a Dominação* (Rio de Janeiro, 1979), p. 347. Trans. of *La Condition Ouvrière* (Paris, 1951).

Chapter II: Eusebius of Caesarea and Church History

1. Altaner-Stuiber, pp. 217–24; Greschat, vol. 1, pp. 224–35.
2. J. Daniélou and H. Marrou, *Nova História da Igreja*, vol. 1 (Petrópolis, Brazil, 1966), p. 33. (Abbreviated hereafter as Daniélou-Marrou.) Eng.: *The Christian Centuries, a New History of the Catholic Church*, vol. 1, *The First Six Hundred Years* (New York, 1964).
3. Ibid., p. 52.
4. Ibid., p. 118.
5. Ibid., p. 123.
6. Altaner-Stuiber, pp. 185–88.
7. Daniélou-Marrou, p. 70.
8. Ibid., p. 206.

269

9. H. Jedin, *Manual de Historia de la Iglesia*, vol. 1 (Barcelona, 1966), p. 52. Trans. of *Handbuch der Kirchengeschichte* (Freiburg, 1964). Eng.: *Handbook of Church History*, vol. 1, *From the Apostolic Community to Constantine* (London and New York, 1965).

10. Estudos Biblicos (Petrópolis, Brazil, 1984), no. 4, passim.

11. G. Alberigo, " 'Réforme' en tant que critère de l'histoire de l'Église," *Revue d'Histoire Ecclésiastique* 76 (1981), pp. 72–81.

12. Daniélou-Marrou, p. 155.

13. Ibid., pp. 120, 155.

14. Ibid., p. 155.

15. The prodigious *Dictionnaire de Théologie Catholique*, published in more than thirty volumes, deals with animism in three columns (vol. 15, col. 3099, and vol. 6, cols. 559–60), condemning the deviations of a European animistic thinker. The German *Die Religionen in Geschichte und Gegenwart*, six volumes, likewise devotes three columns to animism (vol. 1, cols. 389–91), to condemn the teachings of anthropologist E. B. Tylor (1870s). *Lexikon für Theologie und Kirche*, ten volumes, gives animism two columns (vol. 1, cols. 565–66), likewise in reference to Tylor. Fries' *Dicionário de Teologia*, published in Brazil (São Paulo), five volumes, does not even broach the subject.

16. M. Halbwachs, *Les cadres sociaux de la mémoire* (Paris, 1925).

17. Cited by E. Bosi, *Memória e Sociedade* (São Paulo, 1979), p. 21.

18. L. Boff, *Igreja: Carisma e Poder* (Petrópolis, 1981), p. 85. Eng. trans.: *Church: Charism and Power* (New York and London, 1985).

19. *Humboldt Review* 7 (1963), pp. 99–102.

20. A. Lorscheider, "The Re-defined Role of the Bishop in a Poor, Religious People," *Concilium* 176 (1984), pp. 47–9.

Chapter III: Toward a Christian Geography of History

1. Y. Lacoste, *La geógraphie, ça sert, d'abord, à faire la guerre* (Paris, 1976), Along the same lines: N. Abreu Telles, *Cartografia Brasilis, ou: Esta História Está Mal Contada* (São Paulo, 1984).

2. U. Tucci, "Atlas," in *Enciclopédia Einaudi*, vol. 1 (Lisbon, 1984), cols. 130–57.

3. See S. Buarque de Holanda, *Visão do Paraíso* (Rio de Janeiro, 1959).

4. The map is reproduced in E. Rosenstock-Huessy, *Die europäischen Revolutionen und der Charakter der Nationen* (Stuttgart, 1951), pp. 118–19, 565. See also the maps in the same work on pp. 266 and 570, 120 and 565.

5. M. Clévenot, *Les hommes de la fraternité*, vol. 2 (Paris, 1981), p. 37, has some interesting material on the origin of the expression "college" in the tradition of the church.

6. See, among many studies on the "Romanization" of the end of the eleventh century, H. Cowdrey, *The Cluniacs and the Gregorian Reform* (London, 1970).

7. An excellent study of eschatology is that of J. Le Goff, "Escatologia," in *Enciclopédia Einaudi*, vol. 1 (Lisbon, 1984), cols. 425–57.

8. J. Pixley, "The People of God in Biblical Tradition," *Concilium* 176 (1984), pp. 17–23.

PART ONE

Chapter IV: The First Christian Self-Awareness

1. J. H. Elliott, *A Home for the Homeless: A Sociological Exegesis of 1 Peter, Its Significance and Strategy* (London and New York, 1982). (Summary in *Revue Théologique de Louvain* 14 [1983], pp. 230–33.)

2. For the theological dimensions of this change of perspective see E. Schillebeeckx, *Christus und die Christen* (Freiburg, 1977), pp. 274–5, 542. Eng. trans.: *Christ: The Experience of Jesus as Lord* (New York, 1980).

3. A. Droogers, "Symbols of Marginality in the Biographies of Religious and Secular Innovators," *Numen* (1980), pp. 105–21.

4. F. Houtart, *Religião e Modos de Produção Pré-Capitalistas* (São Paulo, 1982), pp. 225–33. Trans. of: *Religion et modes de production précapitalistes* (Brussels, 1980).

5. K. Tagawa, "Galilée et Jérusalem," *Revue d'Histoire et de Philosophie Religieuses* 57 (1977), pp. 439–70.

6. J. M. Pires, *Do Centro para a Margem* (Petrópolis, 1980).

7. On the meaning of the word "catacombs" and its history, see F. A. Figueiredo, *Curso de Teologia Patrística*, vol. 1 (Petrópolis, 1983), pp. 105–8.

8. Altaner-Stuiber, *Patrologie*, 8th ed. (Freiburg, 1978), p. 59. Eng. trans. of earlier ed.: *Patrology* (New York, 1961).

9. Ibid., pp. 59–60. I cite the edition by J. J. Pauvert, *Celse, Discours vrai contre les chrétiens* (Utrecht, 1965), and use the numbering in that edition.

10. L. Prunel, "Les Pauvres et l'Église," in *Dictionnaire Apologétique de la Foi Catholique* (Paris, 1911), col. 1664.

Chapter V: The Theology of the Marginalized as "Chosen"

1. Houtart, *Religião e Modos de Produção,* pp. 226–27.
2. C. J. Hefele, *Histoire des Conciles,* in numerous editions: the first German edition, in 9 vols. (1855–90); the second German edition, in 6 vols. (1873–82); the first French edition, in 12 vols. (1869–78); the first English edition, in 5 vols. (1871–96).
3. This image can be seen in E. Rosenstock-Huessy, *Die europäischen Revolutionen und der Charakter der Nationen* (Stuttgart, 1951), p. 147.
4. J. Daniélou and H. Marrou, *Nova História da Igreja,* vol. 1 (Petrópolis, Brazil, 1966), p. 55. Eng.: *The Christian Centuries, a New History of the Catholic Church,* vol. 1, *The First Six Hundred Years* (New York, 1964).
5. For rabbinical Christianity, see ibid., pp. 33–4.
6. T. Mommsen, *Das Römische Imperium der Cäsaren* (Berlin, 1941), p. 406.
7. J. Pixley, "Pueblo de Dios: Mayorías populares en la Biblia" (mimeographed).
8. Daniélou-Marrou, p. 51.
9. Altaner-Stuiber, pp. 65–71.
10. Ibid, pp. 110–17.
11. Ibid., pp. 148–63.
12. C. Folch Gomes, *Antologia dos Santos Padres* (São Paulo, 1979), contains lengthy passages from Justin's *Dialogue.*
13. Ibid., p. 69.
14. Ibid., pp. 70–1.
15. Ibid., p. 75.
16. Ibid., p. 78.
17. Figueiredo, *Curso,* p. 121.
18. Ibid., p. 117.
19. A. Hamman, *Os Padres da Igreja* (São Paulo, 1980), p. 32.
20. Ibid.
21. Daniélou-Marrou, p. 110.
22. Ibid., p. 111.
23. M. Greschat, ed., *Alte Kirche* (Stuttgart, 1984), vol. 1, pp. 82–96.
24. Folch Gomes, *Antologia,* p. 135.
25. Ibid., p. 116.
26. Figueiredo, *Curso,* provides a good introduction to Irenaeus' writings, and Folch Gomes, *Antologia,* translates selections from the *Adversus Haereses.*

27. Folch Gomes, *Antologia*, p. 116.
28. Ibid., p. 124.
29. Ibid., p. 135.
30. Ibid., p. 119.
31. Ibid., p. 116.
32. The history of the "divorce" between erudite theology and popular faith is related in the old but still unsurpassed article by J. Lebreton discussed in part 2, below.
33. Mommsen, *Das Römische Imperium*, p. 491.
34. Ibid., p. 492.
35. A. Donini, *História do Cristianismo das Origens a Justiniano* (Lisbon, 1980), p. 158.
36. Figueiredo, *Curso*, p. 51. Figueiredo also gives a sketch of Tertullian's life and writings, ibid., pp. 49–56.
37. Cited by Folch Gomes, *Antologia*, p. 165.
38. Cited in ibid., pp. 162–3.
39. See the excellent article by the noted patrologist H. von Campenhausen in M. Greschat, *Alte Kirche*, vol. 1, pp. 97–120. The last citations come from this article.
40. Ibid., p. 107.
41. Altaner-Stuiber, p. 152.
42. *De Exhortatione Castitatis*, 7, 3 (cited in Altaner-Stuiber, p. 162).
43. The notion is developed by von Campenhausen in Greschat, *Alte Kirche*, vol. 1, p. 108.
44. Cited by J. Lebreton, "Le désaccord de la foi populaire et de la théologie savante," *Revue d'Histoire Ecclésiastique* 19 (1924), pp. 481–506, 20 (1925), pp. 5–37.

PART TWO

Chapter VI: A Great Popular Movement

1. N. Brox, *Kirchengeschichte des Altertums* (Düsseldorf, 1983), pp. 28–30.
2. Tertullian, *Adversus Judaeos*, 7, 4.
3. See Migne, *PG* 34, 1106–7.
4. J. Moingt, "Services et lieux d'Église," *Espirit* (Sept. 1979), pp. 365–7.
5. M. Clévenot, *Les hommes de la fraternité,* vol. 2 (Paris, 1981), p. 145, contrasts Jesus with founders of religions, such as Mani, the Buddha, and Zarathustra.

6. Eusebius of Caesarea, *Ecclesiastical History,* III, 38, 1.
7. E. Schillebeeckx, *God is ieder ogenblik nieuw* (Baarn, 1982), p. 43. Eng. trans.: *God Is New Each Moment* (New York, 1983).
8. Altaner-Stuiber, *Patrologie,* 8th ed. (Freiburg, 1978), pp. 52–3. Eng. trans. of an earlier ed.: *Patrology* (New York, 1961).
9. Ibid., p. 77.
10. C. Folch Gomes, *Antologia dos Santos Padres* (São Paulo, 1979), pp. 110–11.
11. See chap. 4, n. 4, above.
12. A. Donini, *História do Christianismo das Origens a Justiniano* (Lisbon, 1980), p. 151.
13. M. Greschat, ed., *Alte Kirche,* vol. 1 (Stuttgart, 1984), p. 86.
14. Irenaeus of Lyon, *Adversus Haereses,* IV, 30, 3.
15. Schillebeeckx, *God is ieder,* p. 107.
16. A. Mandouze, "Les persécutions à l'origine de l'Église," in *Histoire vécue du peuple chrétien,* ed. J. Delumeau, vol. 1 (Toulouse, 1979), pp. 47–74.
17. See J. Le Goff, "Escatologia," in *Enciclopédia Einaudi,* vol. 1 (Lisbon, 1984), pp. 425–7.
18. Ibid., p. 446.

Chapter VII: Mission Cycles of the First Two Centuries

1. J. Daniélou and H. Marrou, *Nova História da Igreja,* vol. 1 (Petrópolis, 1966), p. 63. Eng.: *The Christian Centuries, a New History of the Catholic Church,* vol. 1, *The First Six Hundred Years* (New York, 1964).
2. M. Clévenot, *Les hommes de la fraternité,* vol. 1 (Paris, 1981), pp. 88–94.
3. E. Schillebeeckx, *Christus und die Christen* (Freiburg, 1977), pp. 169–71. Eng. trans.: *Christ: The Experience of Jesus as Lord* (New York, 1980).
4. Daniélou-Marrou, p. 46.
5. Ibid., p. 104.
6. Ibid., p. 72; Altaner-Stuiber, pp. 117–44.
7. Daniélou-Marrou, p. 73.
8. Altaner-Stuiber, pp. 45–6; C. Folch Gomes, *Antologia,* pp. 17–28.
9. Altaner-Stuiber, pp. 47–9; Folch Gomes, *Antologia,* pp. 33–45.
10. Folch Gomes translates: "Savior and guardian (*episkopos*) of all spirits" (*Antologia,* p. 25).

11. Folch Gomes, *Antologia,* pp. 21–2.
12. E. Schillebeeckx, *God is ieder,* p. 114.
13. Folch Gomes, *Antologia,* pp. 33–4.
14. *Santo Inácio de Antioquia, As Cartas* (Lisbon, 1960), p. 146.
15. Ibid., p. 162.
16. Folch Gomes, *Antologia,* p. 44.
17. *Santo Inácio,* p. 199.
18. Ibid., p. 205.
19. Ibid., p. 214.
20. Folch Gomes, *Antologia,* p. 42.
21. Ibid.
22. Ibid., p. 44.
23. T. Mommsen, *Das Römische Imperium der Cäsaren* (Berlin, 1941), p. 252.
24. Ibid., p. 231.
25. Ibid., p. 250.
26. F. A. Figuciredo, *Curso de Teologiu Patrística,* vol. 1 (Petrópolis, 1983), p. 95.
27. Ibid.
28. Daniélou-Marrou, p. 126.
29. Ibid., p. 125.
30. Ibid.
31. Schillebeeckx, *God is ieder,* p. 107.
32. For the position of Rome in the primitive church, see M. Wajtowytsch, *Papsttum und Konzile von der Anfängen bis zu Leo I (440–61): Studien zur Entstehung der Überordnung des Papstes über Konzile* (Stuttgart, 1981)—in *Revue d'Histoire Ecclésiastique* (1982), pp. 464–6; G. Schwaiger, ed., *Konzil und Papst* (Munich, 1975), esp. the articles by J. Speigl and P. Stockmeier. As for the celebrated text of Irenaeus in *Adv. Haer.*, III, 3, 2, "*Ab his qui sunt undique. . . .*" see *Revue d' Histoire Ecclésiastique* (1975), p. 70.
33. For Marcion and Marcionism, see P. Johnson, *A History of Christianity* (London, 1982), pp. 45–6; A. Donini, *História do Cristianismo,* pp. 140–42; Altaner-Stuiber, pp. 106–7; K. Beyschlag, "Marcion von Sinope," in M. Greschat, ed., *Alte Kirche,* vol. 1, pp. 69–81; Daniélou-Marrou, passim. For Montanism, see Altaner-Stuiber, pp. 107–8; Donini, *História do Cristianismo,* pp. 145–7; Daniélou-Marrou, passim.
34. Cited in P. Johnson, *A History of Christianity,* pp. 45–6.
35. See J. Delumeau, *La peur en Occident* (Paris, 1978), as well as other works by the same author.

36. K. Beyschlag, "Marcion von Sinope," p. 79.
37. Schillebeeckx, *God is ieder,* pp. 89–90.
38. Daniélou-Marrou, p. 75.
39. Ibid., p. 116.
40. Ibid., p. 168.
41. Ibid., p. 157.
42. A. Donini, *História do Cristianismo,* p. 148.
43. Daniélou-Marrou, p. 136.
44. Altaner-Stuiber, pp. 107–8.
45. Daniélou-Marrou, p. 46.
46. Mommsen, *Das Römische Imperium,* p. 342.
47. Ibid.
48. Ibid., p. 344.
49. Daniélou-Marrou, p. 203.
50. Ibid., p. 104.
51. A. de Halleux, "Saint Ephrem le Syrien," *Revue Théologique de Louvain* (1983), pp. 328–55.
52. Daniélou-Marrou, p. 292.
53. De Halleux, "Saint Ephrem," p. 344.
54. Ibid., p. 353.
55. Ibid., p. 355.
56. Ibid., p. 348.
57. De Halleux, "Ephräm der Syer," in M. Greschat, ed., *Alte Kirche,* vol. 1, pp. 284–301, with an extensive bibliography on pp. 300–301.
58. Donini, *História do Cristianismo,* p. 157.
59. Daniélou-Marrou, pp. 165–71.
60. Ibid., p. 166.
61. Ibid., p. 206.
62. For Donatism, see M. Bénabou, *La Résistance africaine à la romanisation* (Paris, 1976); J. P. Brisson, *Autonomie et christianisme dans l'Afrique romaine* (Paris, 1958); W. H. C. Frend, *The Donatist Church* (Oxford, 1952); E. Tengström, *Donatisten und Katholiken* (Göteborg, 1964).
63. For the Vandals in Africa, see C. Courtois, *Les Vandales et L'Afrique* (Paris, 1955).
64. Mommsen, *Das Römische Imperium,* p. 444.
65. Daniélou-Marrou, p. 295.
66. Altaner-Stuiber, p. 141.
67. Ibid., p. 124.
68. Ibid., p. 125.

69. Schillebeeckx, *Christus und die Christen,* pp. 485–6, 536–7.
70. Ibid., pp. 486–8.
71. Ibid., p. 536.
72. Ibid.
73. A. M. Heidt, in the encyclopedia *Catholica* (Hilversum, 1968), vol., 1, pp. 718–33.
74. W. Y. Adams, *Nubia* (Princeton, N.J., 1977).

Chapter VIII: Marginalization of the Theology of Marginality

1. Cited by Mommsen, *Römische Imperium,* p. 426.
2. J. Bergman, "Beitrag zur Interpretatio Graeca: Ägyptische Götter in griechischer Übertragung," in *Syncretism* (Upsala, 1969), pp. 207–27.
3. M. Rostovtzeff, *Historia social y económica del Imperio Romano* (Madrid, 1937), vol. 2, p. 78. Eng. trans.: *The Social and Economic History of the Roman Empire* (Oxford, 1957).
4. F. A. Figueiredo, *Curso de Teologia Patrística,* vol. 2, pp. 73–4.
5. For Clement of Alexandria, see Altaner-Stuiber, pp. 190–97; Figueiredo, *Teologia Patrística,* vol. 2, pp. 78–87; J. Lebreton, "Le désaccord de la foi populaire et de la théologie savante," *Revue d'Histoire Ecclésiastique* 19 (1924), pp. 481–506; 20 (1925), pp. 5–37; A. M. Ritter, "Klemens von Alexandrien," in M. Greschat, *Alte Kirche,* vol. 1, pp. 121–33. I follow Lebreton's article in the main.
6. J. Lebreton, "Désaccord de la foi populaire," p. 492.
7. Ibid.
8. M. Clévenot, *Les hommes de la fraternité,* vol. 2, pp. 114–21.
9. Ibid.
10. J. Lebreton, "Désaccord de la foi populaire," p. 499.
11. Ibid., p. 501.
12. Figueiredo, *Curso,* vol. 2, p. 74.
13. A. M. Ritter, "Klemens von Alexandrien," p. 129.
14. Ibid., p. 132.
15. For Origen, see Altaner-Stuiber, pp. 197–208; H. Chadwick, "Origines," in Greschat, *Alte Kirche,* vol. 1, pp. 134–57; J. Lebreton, "Désaccord de la foi populaire"; Figueiredo, *Curso,* vol. 2, pp. 88–112.
16. P. Johnson, *A History of Christianity,* p. 59.
17. J. Lebreton, "Désaccord de la foi populaire," p. 503.
18. Ibid., p. 506.
19. Ibid., p. 5.

20. Cited in C. Folch Gomes, *Antologia dos Santos Padres*, p. 154.

21. J. Lebreton, "Désaccord de la foi populaire," p. 34.

PART THREE

Chapter IX: The Synagogical Model

1. H. Conzelmann, *Geschichte des Urchristentums* (Göttingen, 1969), pp. 31–2.

2. T. Mommsen, *Das Römische Imperium der Cäsaren* (Berlin, 1941), p. 387.

3. Ibid., p. 388.

4. K. Müller, "Die jüdische Synagoge: das ältere Modell einer funktionierenden Basisgemeinde," in E. Klinger and R. Zerfass, eds., *Die Basisgemeinden* (Würzburg, 1984), pp. 141–50.

5. Jean Daniélou and Henri Marrou, *Nova História da Igreja*, vol. 1 (Petrópolis, Brazil, 1966), pp. 41–2. Eng.: *The Christian Centuries, a New History of the Catholic Church*, vol. 1, *The First Six Hundred Years* (New York, 1964).

6. See M. Clévenot, *Les hommes de la fraternité*, vol. 2 (Paris, 1981), pp. 101–6.

7. See B. Bagatti, *A Igreja da Circuncisão* (Petrópolis, 1975).

8. K. Baus, *Manual de Historia de la Iglesia*, vol. 1 (Barcelona, 1966), pp. 489–92.

9. Ibid., p. 491.

10. N. Brox, *Kirchengeschichte des Altertums* (Düsseldorf, 1983), p. 88, recounts a case in which the community excommunicated its bishop (Cyprian, *Letters,* 67, 3).

11. K. Baus, *Manual de Historia*, p. 499.

12. Henri Marrou, *Décadence romaine ou antiquité tardive?* (Paris, 1977).

13. K. Hughes, *The Church in Early Irish Society* (Dublin, 1966).

14. The question is discussed in P. Richard, *Morte das Cristandades e Nascimento da Igreja* (São Paulo, 1982). Eng.; *Death of Christendoms, Birth of the Church* (Maryknoll, N.Y., 1987).

15. For Novatian, see Altaner-Stuiber, *Patrologie,* 8th ed. (Freiburg, 1978), pp. 170–72. Eng. trans. of an earlier ed.: *Patrology* (New York, 1961); C. Folch Gomes, *Antologia dos Santos Padres* (São Paulo, Brazil, 1979), pp. 197–201; Daniélou-Marrou, pp. 209–10.

16. Altaner-Stuiber, p. 171.

Chapter X: Some Documents from the Base Communities

1. For the First Letter of Clement of Rome, see C. Folch Gomes, *Antologia*, pp. 17–28 (text in Portuguese); F. A. Figueiredo, *Curso de Teologia Patrística*, vol. 1 (Petrópolis, 1983), pp. 43–50; Altaner-Stuiber, pp. 45–6; F. X. Funk, *Patres Apostolici*, vol. 1 (Tübingen, 1901), pp. 98–183 (text in Greek and Latin).

2. For the letters of St. Ignatius of Antioch, see the works cited in chap. 7, above; Altaner-Stuiber, pp. 47–9; C. Folch Gomes, *Antologia*, p. 33–45 (with passages in Portuguese); the complete edition in Portugese translation published by Edições Paulistas, Lisbon, 1960; F. X. Funk, *Patres Apostolici*, pp. 211–95 (text in Greek and Latin); F. A. Figueiredo, *Curso*, vol. 1, pp. 51–5.

3. For the two letters of St. Polycarp of Smyrna, see Altaner-Stuiber, pp. 50–2; C. Folch Gomes, *Antologia*, pp. 46–55 (text in Portuguese); F. X. Funk, *Patres Apostolici*, pp. 296–312 (text in Greek and Latin).

4. For the letter of Pseudo-Barnabas, see Altaner-Stuiber, pp. 53–4; Funk, *Patres Apostolici*, pp. 38–97 (text in Greek and Latin).

5. For the apocryphal literature, see Altaner-Stuiber, pp. 117–44; F. Bovon, *Les actes apocryphes des apôtres: Christianisme et monde païen* (Geneva, 1981)—reviewed in *Revue d'Histoire Ecclésiastique* (1982), pp. 462–64. W. Speyer, *Büchervernichtigung und Zensur des Geistes bei Heiden, Juden und Christen* (Stuttgart, 1981)—reviewed in *Revue d'Histoire Ecclésiastique* (1983), pp. 473–4; E. Junod and J.-D. Kaestli, *L'histoire des actes apocryphes des apôtres du 3e au 9e siècle* (Geneva, 1982)—reviewed in *Revue d'Historie Ecclésiastique* (1984), pp. 101–3.

6. Cited in *Revue d'Histoire Ecclésiastique* (1984), p. 102.

7. The studies by Bovon, Speyer, and Junod and Kaestli, cited in n. 5, are manifestations of this renewed interest.

8. E. Bosi, *Cultura de Massa e Cultura Popular* (Petrópolis, 1977).

9. For the *Didache*, see Altaner-Stuiber, pp. 79–82; F. A. Figueiredo, *Curso* vol. 1, pp. 30–6; C. Folch Gomes, *Antologia*, pp. 29–32 (text in Portuguese); F. X. Funk, *Patres Apostolici*, pp. 2–37 (text in Greek and Latin); *Didaké* (Lisbon, 1960) (text in Portuguese).

10. For the *Didascalia Apostolica*, see Altaner-Stuiber, pp. 84–5; F. A. Figueiredo, *Curso* vol. 2, p. 39; K. Bihlmeyer and H. Tuechle, *História da Igreja* (São Paulo, 1964), vol. 1, 108, 135, 193. Eng.; *Church History* (Westminster, Md., 1958); K. Baus, *Manual de Historia de la Iglesia*, pp. 489–92.

11. For the *Apostolic Constitutions*, see Altaner-Stuiber, pp. 255–56; K. Bihlmeyer and H. Tuechle, *História da Igreja*, p. 393.

12. For Wycliff, see D. Knowles, *Nova História da Igreja*, vol. 2 (Petrópolis, 1974), pp. 483–84. This theme is being taken up again in our own century by Hans Küng.

13. K. Baus, *Manual de Historia de la Iglesia*, p. 499.

14. K. Bihlmeyer and H. Tuechle, *História da Igreja*, p. 108; K. Baus, *Manual de Historia de la Iglesia*, p. 500.

15. For Hippolytus' *Apostolic Tradition*, see Altaner-Stuiber, pp. 82–4; N. Brox, *Kirchengeschichte des Altertums*, pp. 96–7; Daniélou-Marrou, pp. 158–59; M. Clévenot, *Les hommes de la fraternité*, pp. 129–37; A. Faivre, *Naissance d'une hiérarchie* (Paris, 1977), an exhaustive study on the origin of hierarchical organization in the church.

16. For the history of ministerial celibacy, see R. Gryson, *Les origines du célibat ecclésiastique* (Gembloux, 1970) — commentary in *Revue d'Histoire Ecclésiastique* (1970), pp. 320–33; (1983), pp. 90–3. Gryson asserts categorically: "The law of celibacy is not of apostolic origin. Nor is it, strictly speaking, of ancient origin. It was only rather late in the course of the Middle Ages that the Church of the West definitively renounced the ordination of married men" (cited in *Revue d'Histoire Ecclésiastique* [1983], p. 92).

17. A Faivre, *Naissance d'une hiérarchie*, p. 54.

18. Ibid., pp. 415–16.

19. Ibid., p. 51.

20. Altaner-Stuiber, p. 82.

21. For the *Shepherd* of Hermas, see Altaner-Stuiber, pp. 55–8; C. Folch Gomes, *Antologia*, pp. 56–61 (with passages in Portuguese); F. A. Figueiredo, *Curso*, vol. 2, pp. 32–3; N. Brox, *Kirchengeschichte des Altertums*, p. 125; K. Baus, *Manual de Historia de la Iglesia*, p. 465; F. X. Funk, *Patres Apostolici*, pp. 414–639 (text in Greek and Latin); and especially, A. Rousselle *Porneia* (São Paulo, 1984).

22. Folch Gomes, *Antologia*, pp. 56–61.

23. Cited in A. Rousselle, *Porneia*, pp. 121–2.

24. Ibid., p. 122.

Chapter XI: The Christian Life in the Base Church Communities

1. Folch Gomes, *Antologia*, p. 47.

2. M. Clévenot, *Les hommes de la fraternité*, pp. 147–52.

3. See chap. 6, above. For the *Letter to Diognetus*, see Altaner-Stuiber, pp. 77–8; Folch Gomes, *Antologia*, 109–14 (text in Portuguese).

4. St. Basil (*PG* 31:324–5).

5. St. John Chrysostom (*PG* 62:562–4). See also J. Leuridan and G. Múgica, *Por que a Igreja Critica os Ricos?* (São Paulo, 1982).

6. Eusebius of Caesarea, *Ecclesiastical History*, V, 1.

7. J. Pépin, "Survivances mythiques dans le Christianisme ancien," in *Dictionnaire des mythologies* (Paris), vol. 2, p. 474.

8. R. Alves, *O Suspiro dos Oprimidos* (São Paulo, 1984), p. 95.

Chapter XII: Service in the Base Church Communities

1. S. Armando Soares, "Entre vocês tem de ser diferente," in *Dom Helder: Pastor e Profeta* (São Paulo, 1983), p. 69.

2. For the historical origin of the word "catacomb," see F. A. Figueiredo, *Curso,* vol. 1, pp. 105–7.

3. Armando Soares, "Entre vocês tem de ser diferente," p. 72.

4. *Corpus Scriptorum Christianorum*, Series Latina, 1:343.

5. *PL* 16:204.

6. Thomas Aquinas, *Summa Theologiae,* I Pars, q. 92, a 1, ad 2; q. 93, a. 4, ad 1.

7. Ibid., q. 99, a. 2; II Pars, q. 149, a. 4; q. 165, a. 2.

8. N. Brox, *Kirchengeschichte des Altertums,* p. 93.

9. Ibid., p. 92.

10. Altaner-Stuiber, pp. 52–3.

11. Cited in Folch Gomes, *Antologia,* p. 135.

12. Cited in Figueiredo, *Teologia Patrística,* vol. 1, p. 66.

13. Clement of Rome mentions presbyters in 1:3, 3:3, 21:6, 44:5, 47:6, 54:4, 57:1.

14. Cited in F. X. Funk, *Patres Apostolici,* pp. 354–5.

15. Ibid., p. 351.

16. Ibid., p. 359.

17. Ignatius mentions presbyters in his *Letter to the Ephesians*, 2, 2; 4, 1; 20, 1; *Letter to the Magnesians,* 2; 3, 1; 7, 1; 13, 1; *Letter to the Thralians,* 2, 2; 7, 2; 12, 2; 13, 2; *Letter to the Philadelphians,* 4; 5, 1; 7, 7; *Letter to the Smyrneans*, 8, 1; 12, 2; *Letter to Polycarp,* 6, 1.

18. Cited in Folch Gomes, *Antologia*, p. 34.

19. Cited in Funk, *Patres Apostolici*, p. 247.

20. Cited in Folch Gomes, *Antologia,* p. 48. Polycarp mentions presbyters in 5, 3; 6, 1; 11, 1.

21. *Shepherd* of Hermas, Vision 2, 4, 2–3; 3, 1, 8.

22. Irenaeus of Lyon, *Adversus Haereses*, II, 22, 5; IV, 27–28, 30, 1; IV, 32, 1; V, 5, 1; V, 30, 1; V, 33, 3; V, 36, 1.

23. E. Schillebeeckx, *God is ieder ogenblik nieuw* (Baarn, 1982), pp. 42–3.

24. J. Holzner, *Paulus* (Freiburg, 1937).

25. H. Conzelmann, *Geschichte des Urchristentums*, pp. 127–8.

26. Hans Küng, "The Charismatic Structure of the Church," *Concilium* 4 (1965), pp. 23–33 (U. K.).

27. See *Shepherd* of Hermas, Vision 3, 5, 1 (Funk, *Patres Apostolici*, p. 441); Comparison 9, 25, 2 (Funk, p. 621).

28. I draw my inspiration for the present considerations from Michel de Certeau, "O cristianismo na cultura contemporânea ou a ruptura instauradora," mimeographed translation of his article in *Espirit* (1971).

29. R. Gryson, "L'autorité des docteurs dans l'Église ancienne et médiévale," *Revue Théologique de Louvain* 13 (1982), pp. 63–73.

30. Altaner-Stuiber, p. 198.

31. In the original Latin: "Ut praeter sacerdotes nullus audeat praedicare, sive monachus, sive laicus, cuiuslibet scientiae nomine glorietur."

32. H. Conzelmann, *Geschichte des Urchristentums*, p. 9.

33. N. Brox, *Kirchengeschichte des Altertums*, p. 94.

34. Folch Gomes, *Antologia*, p. 43; Funk, *Patres Apostolici*, pp. 282–3.

35. A. de Halleux, "L'Église catholique dans la lettre ignacienne aux Smyrniotes," *Revue Théologique de Louvain* 13 (1982), pp. 23–4.

PART FOUR

Chapter XIII: The Practice of Salvation

1. F. J. Dölger "Der Heiland?" in *Antike und Christentum*, by various authors, vol. 6 (Münster, 1950), pp. 241–72; K. H. Rengstorf, *Die Anfänge der Auseinandersetzung zwischen Christusglaube und Asklepiosfrömmigkeit* (Münster, 1953).

2. H. E. Remus, *Pagan-Christian Conflict over Miracle in the Second Century*, Ph.D. dissertation (Univ. of Pennsylvania, 1981).

3. K. Baus, in H. Jedin, *Manual de Historia de la Iglesia*, vol. 1 (Barcelona, 1966), p. 162. Eng.: *History of the Church*, vol. 1, *From the Apostolic Community to Constantine* (London and New York, 1965–81).

4. Henry Chadwick, *Early Christian Thought and the Classical Tradition: Studies in Justin, Clement and Origen* (Oxford, 1966).

5. A. Suhl, ed., *Der Wunderbegriff im Neuen Testament*, Wege der Forschung, no. 295 (Darmstadt, 1980).

6. F. C. Rolim, "Religião do pobre e seu anúncio," *Revista Eclesiástica Brasileira* (1981), pp. 745–6. See also M. Groetelaars, *Milagre e Religiosidade Popular* (Petrópolis, 1981).

7. F. C. Rolim, "Religião do pobre e seu anúncio," p. 762.

8. Ibid.

9. B. A. Willems, "De verlossing als menselijke werkelijkheid," *Tijdschrift voor Theologie* (1965), pp. 28–48.

10. K. Baus, in Jedin, *Manual de Historia*, vol. 1, pp. 152, 154, 158, 162.

11. L. Prunel, "Les pauvres et l'Église," in *Dictionnaire apologétique de la foi catholique* (Paris, 1911), cols. 1655–1735.

12. W. A. Jayne, *The Healing Gods of Ancient Civilizations* (New Haven, 1925).

13. The case is reported in H. E. Remus, *Pagan-Christian Conflict*, pp. 241–2, and is cited by Eusebius of Caesarea, *Ecclesiastical History*, V, 13, 2; Tertullian, *De Praescriptione Haereticorum*, 6 and 30; idem., *Adversus Marcionem*, III, 11, 2.

14. J. M. van Gangh, "Miracles des rabbins et miracles de Jésus," *Revue Théologique de Louvain* 15 (1985), pp. 28–53.

15. E. Trocmé, *Jésus de Nazareth vu par les témoins de sa vie* (Neuchâtel, 1970).

16. J. Pépin, "Christianisme et mythologie: jugements chrétiens sur les analogies du paganisme et du christianisme," in *Dictionnaire des Mythologies* (Paris, 1981), vol. 1, pp. 161–71.

17. For Simon Magus, see Clement of Alexandria, *Stromata*, 2, 11; Origen, *Contra Celsum*, I, 57, 39–42; Hippolytus of Rome, *Ref.* 6, 19, 4, 6, and 6, 20, 2.

18. See *Theologisches Wörterbuch zum Neuen Testament*, vol. 8, cols. 115–16; vol. 7, cols. 202, 205.

19. G. Bardy, "Origène et la magie," *Recherches de Science Religieuse* 18 (1928), pp. 126–42.

20. A. Nolan, *Jésus avant le christianisme* (Paris, 1979), p. 46. Eng.: *Jesus before Christianity* (Maryknoll, N.Y., 1978).

Chapter XIV: A Communion in Goods

1. Altaner-Stuiber, *Patrologie*, 8th ed. (Freiburg, 1978), pp. 172–81. Eng. trans. of an earlier ed.: *Patrology* (New York, 1961).

2. Ibid., p. 176.

3. Cyprian of Carthage, *De Opere et Eleemosynis*, 9–12.
4. L. Prunel, "Les pauvres et l'Église," cols. 1657–9.
5. R. Staats, "Deposita pietatis: Die Alte Kirche und ihr Geld," in *Zeitschrift für Theologie und Kirche*, 1979, pp. 1–29, esp. pp. 4–5.
6. Ibid., p. 9.
7. For the value of the sesterce in terms of the dollar, see ibid., p. 8, n. 16.
8. Ibid., pp. 8–9.
9. C. Folch Gomes, *Antologia dos Santos Padres* (São Paulo, 1979), p. 47.
10. R. Staats, "Deposita pietatis," p. 7.
11. Altaner-Stuiber, p. 194.
12. C. Folch Gomes, *Antologia dos Santos Padres,* pp. 141–6; M. Clévenot, *Les hommes de la fraternité*, vol. 2 (Paris, 1981), pp. 114–21.
13. For the relationship between Christianity and poverty, see Julio de Santa Ana, *A Igreja e o Dessafio dos Pobres* (Petrópolis, 1980); J. Leuridan, *Por que a Igreja Critica os Ricos?* (São Paulo, 1982).
14. O. Lottin, *Morale fondamentale* (Tournai, 1954), p. 262.
15. José Comblin, *O Tempo da Açâo* (Petrópolis, 1982), p. 151, n. 27.
16. Altaner-Stuiber, p. 193.

Chapter XV: A New Relationship between Women and Men

1. Cited in J. Daniélou and H. Marrou, *Nova História da Igreja*, vol. 1 (Petrópolis, 1966), p. 139. Eng.: *The Christian Centuries, a New History of the Catholic Church*, vol. 1, *The First Six Hundred Years* (New York, 1964).
2. In this material we rely on M. Meigne, "Concile ou Collection d'Elvire?" *Revue d'Histoire Ecclésiastique* (1975), no. 2, pp. 361–87. See also C.-J. Hefele, *Histoire des conciles* (Paris, 1907), vol. 1/1, pp. 238–9. Hefele comments on canon 33: "The redaction is faulty. The canon seems to ordain what it means to forbid." For this question see also M. Clévenot, *Les hommes de la fraternité*, vol. 2 (Paris, 1981), pp. 200–201.
3. M. Meigne, "Concile ou Collection d'Elvire?" p. 383; C.-J. Hefele, *Histoire des conciles*, vol. 1/1, pp. 238–9; M. Clévenot, *Les hommes de la fraternité*, vol. 2 (Paris, 1981), p. 201.
4. C. Mirbt and K. Aland, *Quellen zur Geschichte des Papsttums und des römischen Katholizismus* (Tübingen, 1967), vol. 1, pp. 147–53,

has the *Apostolic Canons* in Greek. For a Latin translation, see C.-J. Hefele, *Histoire des conciles*, vol. 1/2, pp. 1203-4.

5. C. Mirbt and K. Aland, *Quellen zur Geschichte des Papsttums*, vol. 1, p. 147.

6. Ibid., vol. 1, p. 150.

7. M. Meigne, "Concile ou Collection d'Elvire?" p. 387.

8. Ibid., p. 385.

9. C.-J. Hefele, *Histoire des conciles*, vol. 1/2, pp. 1029-30.

10. Ibid., vol. 1/2, p. 1043.

11. Ibid., vol. 1/1, p. 313.

12. Ibid., vol. 1/1, p. 326.

13. Here is St. Augustine's opinion: "Seipsos non in corpore sed in ipsa concupiscentiae radice castrantes." ("Castrating themselves not in their bodies but in the very root of their concupiscence.")

14. C.-J. Hefele, *Histoire des conciles*, vol. 1/1, p. 532, treats the subject at length and provides a bibliography.

15. Ibid., vol. 1/1, pp. 531-2.

16. K. Bihlmeyer and H. Tuechle, *História da Igreja* (São Paulo, 1964), vol. 1, p. 140.

17. Ibid., vol. 1, p. 139.

18. Daniélou-Marrou, p. 205. However, see R. Murray's reflections in *Reveu d'Histoire Eccléstique* (1976), p. 124, to the effect that the Syrian tradition defended the dignity of the human body against the anti-materialistic theories of Marcion, the gnostics, and the Manichaeans. Murray relies on Syrian iconography to support his position. The subject deserves an examination in depth.

19. See chap. 11, above.

20. Altaner-Stuiber, pp. 64-5; C. Folch Gomes, *Antologia*, pp. 62-4.

21. C. Folch Gomes, *Antologia*, p. 64.

22. Altaner-Stuiber, pp. 125-6.

23. Ibid., p. 139.

24. Ibid., p. 144.

25. Ibid., pp. 130-31.

26. A. Jelsma, "Als Maria Magdalena aan het woord komt," *Tijdschrift voor Theologie* (1975), pp. 394-409.

27. Ibid., p. 399.

28. Ibid., p. 398.

29. Michel de Certeau, *La fable mystique, 16e-17e siècle* (Paris, 1982).

30. Ibid, pp. 223-4.

31. Ibid., p. 322.

Chapter XVI: Martyrdom

1. F. A. Figueiredo, *Curso de Teologia Patrística,* vol. 1 (Petrópolis, Brazil, 1983), pp. 105–7. See also A. Mandouze, "Les persécutions à l'origine de l'Église," in *Histoire vécue du peuple chrétien,* ed. J. Delumeau (Toulouse, 1979), vol. 1, pp. 49–74, with the basic bibliography.

2. A Mandouze, "Les persécutions à l'origine de l'Église," vol. 1, p. 54.

3. For Aristides of Athens, see C. Folch Gomes, *Antologia,* pp. 62–4; Altaner-Stuiber, p. 64.

4. For Athenagoras, see C. Folch Gomes, *Antologia,* pp. 98–101; Altaner-Stuiber, pp. 74–5. For the *Letter to Diognetus,* see Folch Gomes, *Antologia,* pp. 109–14; Altaner-Stuiber, p. 77.

5. Cited in Folch Gomes, *Antologia,* pp. 99–100.

6. A. Rousselle, *Porneia: De la maitrise du corps à la privation sensorielle* (Paris, 1983) – Brazilian edition, São Paulo, 1984.

7. C. Mirbt and K. Aland, *Quellen zur Geschichte des Papsttums,* vol. 1, pp. 153–7.

8. Cited in C. Folch Gomes, *Antologia,* p. 101.

9. Cited in C.-J. Hefele, *Histoire des conciles,* vol 1/2, p. 225.

10. Ibid., vol. 1/2, pp. 261, 283.

11. Daniélou-Marrou, p. 192.

12. See the Introduction to this book. See also Altaner-Stuiber, pp. 59–60.

13. Altaner-Stuiber, pp. 60, 221, 332.

14. N. Brox, *Kirchengeschichte des Altertums,* p. 46.

15. Tacitus, *Annals,* XV, 44, 4.

16. Origen, *Contra Celsum,* 8, 2.

17. Tertullian, *Apologeticum,* 2, 4; 35, 1.

18. See A. Mandouze, "Les persécutions à l'origine de l'Église," vol. 1, p. 61.

19. Cited in ibid.

20. L. Meulenberg, "A discussão aberta na Igreja Antiga," *Revista Eclesiástica Brasileira* (1985), pp. 16–31.

21. C. Folch Gomes, *Antologia,* p. 64.

22. Ibid., p. 78.

23. For Athenagoras, see ibid., p. 100.

24. P.-A. Février, "La mort chrétienne: images et vécu collectif," in *Histoire vécu du peuple chrétien,* ed. J. Delumeau (Toulouse, 1979), vol. 1, pp. 75–103.

25. Altaner-Stuiber, p. 192.

26. Ibid., pp. 146–7.

27. Cited by P.-A. Février, "La mort chrétienne: images et vécu collectif," vol. 1, p. 79.

28. Ibid.

29. F. J. Dölger, *Sol Salutis: Gebet und Gesang im christlichen Altertum* (Münster, 1925).

30. J. Pépin, "Survivances mythiques dans le christianisme ancien," in *Dictionnaire des mythologies* (Paris, 1981), vol 2, p. 474.

31. National Library of France, MS. 7028, fol. 154.

Bibliography

1. PRIMARY SOURCES

For an orientation in the documentation on the first three centuries of Christianity I have used especially the Altaner-Stuiber patrology manual, in its eighth edition (1978). F. A. Figueiredo, *Curso de Teologia Patrística,* vols. 1 and 2 (Petrópolis, 1983–84), has also been of great utility to me.

I have read the ancient texts themselves in the little collection *Patrística,* published by the Paulists of Lisbon in the 1960s. This collection contains the *Didache* and the letters of Ignatius of Antioch, Polycarp, and Clement of Rome, as well as the fragments of Papias and some of the *Acts of the Martyrs.* I have made much use of the *Antologia dos Santos Padres,* compiled by C. Folch Gomes (Paulinas, 1980), which contains passages, occasionally rather lengthy ones, from Clement of Rome, the *Didache,* Ignatius of Antioch, Polycarp, Hermas, Aristides of Athens, Justin, Athenagoras, the Martyrs of Lyon, Theophilus of Antioch, the *Letter to Diognetus,* Irenaeus, Clement of Alexandria, Origen, Tertullian, Hippolytus, Methodius of Olympus, Cyprian, and Novatian. Less useful to me was another anthology, *Os Padres da Igreja,* compiled by A. Hamman (Paulinas, 1980), as it contains only brief passages from Ignatius of Antioch, Justin, Irenaeus, Tertullian, Cyprian, Clement of Alexandria, and Origen. The series *Os Padres da Igreja,* currently being published by Editora Vozes, so far has only one text from the period studied in this book: that of Tertullian on baptism.

For texts not available in Portuguese, I have had recourse to editions in the Latin or the Greek, such as F. X. Funk, *Patres Apostolici*, vol. 1 (Tübingen, 1901), which contains the integral text of the *Didache*, Clement of Rome, Pseudo-Barnabas, Ignatius of Antioch, Polycarp, Papias, the *Letter to Diognetus*, and the *Shepherd* of Hermas. I have referred as well to the edition published under the direction of Mirbt-Aland, important because it contains the *Canons of the Apostles* (pp. 147–53) — which in turn are important for a knowledge of the life of the communities — as well as the *Apostolic Constitutions* (pp. 153–7) and the complete collection of the canons of Elvira (pp. 106–8). For the canons of the councils of the first half of the fourth century I used the old, but still definitive, edition of C.-J. Hefele, *Histoire des conciles*, vol. 1 (Paris, 1907).

A final detail: The text of Celsus cited in this essay is from the edition by J.-J. Pauvert, *Discours vrai contre les chrétiens* (Utrecht, 1965).

SECONDARY SOURCES

Aalst, A. J. van der. "Het oosterse Christusbeeld in de syrische kerken." *Tijdschrift voor Theologie* (1975), pp. 141–56.

Alberigo, G. " 'Réforme' en tant que critère de l'histoire de l'Église." *Revue d'histoire ecclésiastique* (1981), pp. 72–81.

Baert, E. "Het thema van de zalige Godsaanschouwing in de griekse Patristiek tot Origenes." *Tijdschrift voor Theologie* (1961), pp. 289–308.

Bagatti, B. *A Igreja da Circuncisão*. Petrópolis: 1975.

Bardy, G. "Origène et la Magie." *Recherches de science religieuse* (1928), pp. 126–42.

Bénabou, M. *La résistance africaine à la romanisation*. Paris: 1976.

Boff, L. *Igreja: Carisma e Poder*. Petrópolis: 1981. Eng. trans.: *Church, Charism, and Power: Liberation Theology and the Institutional Church*. New York: 1985.

Botte, B. "Collegial Character of the Priesthood and the Episcopate." *Concilium* 4 (1965), pp. 177–83 (U.S.), 88–90 (U.K.).

Brox, N. *Kirchengeschichte des Altertums*. Düsseldorf: 1983.

Butterfield, H. *The Origins of History*. London: 1984.

Certeau, M. de. *La fable mystique*. Paris: 1982.

Chadwick, H. *Early Christian Thought and the Classical Tradition: Studies in Justin, Clement and Origen*. Oxford: 1966.

Clévenot, M. *Les hommes de la fraternité*. 2 vols. Paris: 1981–82.

Comblin, J. *O Tempo da Ação*. Petrópolis: 1982.

Conzelmann, H. *Geschichte des Urchristentums.* Göttingen: 1969.

Cornélis, E. "Origenes als theoloog: recente interpretaties." *Tijdschrift voor Theologie* (1964), pp. 416–21.

Crouzel, H. "Divorce et remariage dans l'Église primitive." *Nouvelle revue théologique* (1975), pp. 891–917.

Daniélou, J., and H.-I. Marrou. *Nova História da Igreja.* Petrópolis: 1966. Vol. 1, pp. 25–234. Eng. trans.: *The Christian Centuries, a New History of the Catholic Church.* Vol. 1: *The First Six Hundred Years,* pp. 1–220. New York: 1964.

Davids, A. "Het begrip gerechtigheid in de Oude Kerk." *Tijdschrift voor Theologie* (1977), pp. 145–69.

De Halleux, A. " 'L'Église catholique' dans la lettre ignacienne aux Smyrniotes." *Ephemerides Theologicae Lovanienses* (1982), pp. 5–24.

_____. "Saint Ephrem le Syrien." *Revue théologique de Louvain* (1983), pp. 328–55.

Dölger, F. J. *Antike und Christentum.* Munich: 1950. Vol. 6, pp. 241–72.

_____. *Sol Salutis. Gebet und Gesang im Christlichen Altertum.* Munich: 1925.

Donini, A. *História do Cristianismo das Origens a Justiniano.* Lisbon: 1980.

Duchesne, L. *Origines du culte chrétien.* Paris: 1920.

Elliott, J. H. *A Home for the Homeless: A Sociological Exegesis of 1 Peter, Its Significance and Strategy* (London and New York, 1982).

Faivre, A. *Naissance d'une hiérarchie. Les premières étapes du cursus clérical.* Paris: 1977.

Février, P.-A. In *histoire vécue du peuple chrétien.* Toulouse: 1979. Vol. 1, pp. 75–103.

Fischer, J. A. "Das sogenannte Apostelkonzil," in *Konzil und Papst,* ed. G. Schwaiger, Munich: 1975, pp. 1–18.

Frank, K. S. "Vita Apostolica und Dominus Apostolicus: zur altkirchlichen Apostelnachfolge," in *Konzil und Papst,* ed. G. Schwaiger. Munich: 1975, pp. 19–42.

Gréa, D. A. *De l'Eglise et de sa divine constitution.* Paris: 1885.

Greschat, M. *Alte Kirche.* Stuttgart: 1984.

Gryson, R. "L'autorité des docteurs dans l'Église ancienne et médiévale." *Revue théologique de Louvain* (1982), pp. 63–73.

_____. *Les origines du célibat ecclésiastique du premier au septième siècle.* Gembloux: 1970.

Heidt, A. M. *Catholica.* 2 vols. Hilversum: 1968.

Holzner, J. *Paulus*. Freiburg: 1937.

Houtart, F. *Religião e Modos de Produção Pré-Capitalistas*. São Paulo: 1982. Trans. of *Religion et modes de production précapitalistes*. Brussels: 1980.

Jedin, H., ed. *Manual de Historia de la Iglesia*. Barcelona: 1966. Vol. 1: *De la Iglesia primitiva a los comienzos de la gran Iglesia*, by Karl Baus, pp. 109–631. Trans. of vol. 1 of *Handbuch der Kirchengeschichte*. Freiburg: 1964. Eng. trans.: *History of the Church*, 10 vols. London and New York: 1965–81. Vol. 1: *From the Apostolic Community to Constantine*.

Jelsma, A. "Als Maria Magdalena aan het woord komt." *Tijdschrift voor Theologie* (1975), pp. 394–408.

Johnson, P. *A History of Christianity*. London: 1982.

Kamstra, J. H. "Een moeielijke keuze: de godsdienst van de gewone man." *Tijdschrift voor Theologie* (1980), pp. 253–78.

Küng, H. "The Charismatic Structure of the Church." *Concilium* 4 (1965), pp. 41–61 (U.S.), pp. 23–33 (U.K.).

Lebreton, J. "Le désaccord de la foi populaire et de la théologie savante dans l'Église chrétienne du 3ième siècle." *Revue d'histoire ecclésiastique* (1924), pp. 481–506, and (1925), pp. 5–37.

Le Goff, J. "História." *Enciclopédia Einaudi*. Lisbon: 1984. Vol. 1, cols. 158–259. See also in the same work his "Memória." Vol. 2, pp. 11–50.

————. *Hérésies et sociétés*. Paris: 1961.

Loew, J., and M. Meslin. *Histoire de l'Église par elle-même*. Paris: 1978.

Lorscheider, A. "A Redefinição da figura do Bispo no meio popular pobre e religioso." *Concilium* (1984), pp. 754–7. Eng. trans.: "The Re-defined Role of the Bishop in a Poor, Religious People." *Concilium* 176 (1984), pp. 47–9.

Lortz, J. *Geschichte der Kirche*. Munich: 1955. Eng. trans.: *History of the Church*. Milwaukee: 1956.

Mandouze, A. *Histoire vécue du peuple chrétien*. Toulouse: 1979. Vol. 1, pp. 49–74.

Marrou, H.-I. *Décadence romaine ou antiquité tardive?* Paris: 1977.

Meigne, M. "Concile ou Collection d'Elvire?" *Revue d'histoire ecclésiastique* (1975), pp. 361–87.

Meulenberg, L. "A discussão aberta na Igreja Antiga." *Revista Eclesiástica Brasileira* (1985), pp. 16–31.

Múgica, G. *Por que a Igreja Critica os Ricos?* São Paulo: 1983.

Müller, K. "Die jüdische Synagoge, das ältere Modell einer funktionierenden Basisgemeinde," in *Die Basisgemeinden*, ed. E. Klinger and R. Zerfass. Würzburg: 1984, pp. 141–50.

Nehlig, Y. *Le rôle des femmes dans l'Église du premier au troisième siècle*. Bibl. de la Faculté de Théologie de Monpellier: 1981.

Nolan, A. *Jesus before Christianity*. Maryknoll, N.Y.: 1978.

Pépin, J. "Christianisme et mythologie." *Dictionnaire des mythologies*. Paris: 1981. Vol. 1, pp. 161–71. See also in the same work, "Survivances mythiques dans le Christianisme ancien." Vol. 2, pp. 469–75.

Pierrard, P. *Histoire de l'Église catholique*. Paris: 1978.

Pixley, J. "The People of God in Biblical Tradition." *Concilium* 176 (1984), pp. 17–23.

Prunel, L. "Les Pauvres et l'Église." *Dictionnaire Apologétique de la Foi Catholique*. Paris: 1911. Cols. 1655–1735.

Quinlan, J. "Engelen en Duivels." *Tijdschrift voor Theologie* (1967), pp. 43–62.

Quispel, G. "De Heilige Geest volgens de Oude Kerk," in *De Spiritu Sancto*. Utrecht: 1964, pp. 76–88.

Remus, H. E. *Pagan-Christian Conflict over Miracle in the Second Century*. Ph.D. Dissertation, University of Pennsylvania, 1981.

Rengstorf, K. H. *Die Anfänge der Auseinandersetzung zwischen Christusglaube und Asklepiosfrömmigkeit*. Munich: 1953.

Richard, P. *Morte das Cristandades e Nascimento da Igreja*. São Paulo: 1982. Eng. trans.: *Death of Christendoms, Birth of the Church* (Maryknoll, N.Y. 1987).

Rouet, A. *A Missa na História*. São Paulo: 1981.

Schillebeeckx, E. *God is ieder ogenblik nieuw*. Baarn: 1982. Eng. trans.: *God Is New Each Moment*. New York: 1983.

Seznec, J. *La survivance des dieux antiques*. London, 1940.

Soares, S. A. " 'Entre vocês tem de ser diferente': notas sobre participação na Igreja," in *Perspectivas Teológico-Pastorais*. Recife: 1984, pp. 57–83.

Speigel, J. "Von der Hauskirche zur Stadtkirche und zurück?" in *Die Basisgemeinden*, ed. E. Klinger and R. Zerfass. Würzburg: 1984, pp. 151–7.

Spidlik, T. "Fous pour le Christ." *Dictionnaire de la spiritualité*. Paris: 1970. Vol. 5, cols. 752–61.

Staats, R. "Deposita Pietatis: die alte Kirche und ihr Geld," in *Zeitschrift für Theologie und Kirche*. Tübingen: 1979, pp. 1–35.

Suhl, A. *Der Wunderbegriff im Neuen Testament*. Darmstadt: 1980.

Thérel, M.-L. *Le symboles de "l'Ecclesia" dans la création iconographique de l'art chrétien du 4ième au 7ième siècle*. Rome: 1973.

Trocmé, E. *Jesus de Nazareth vu par les témoins de sa vie*. Neuchâtel: 1970.

Van Gangh, J. M. "Miracles des Rabbins et miracles de Jésus." *Revue théologique de Louvain* (1984), pp. 28–53.

Vanhoye, A. "Sacerdoce commun et sacerdoce ministériel." *Nouvelle revue théologique* (1975), pp. 193–207.

Van Iersel, B. "The Book of the People of God." *Concilium* 10 (1965), pp. 25–38 (U.S.), pp. 15–22 (U.K.).

Wajtowytsch, M. *Papsttum und Konzile von der Anfängen bis zu Leo I (440–461): Studien zur Entstehung der Überordnung des Papstes über Konzile.* Stuttgart: 1981.

Willems, B. A. "De verlossing als menselijke werkelijkheid in Ireneus." *Tijdschrift voor Theologie* (1965), pp. 28–47.

Index

Abortion, 251, 257
Adultery, 257
Adversus Marcionem ("Against Marcion") (Tertullian), 65-66, 99-101, 103
African Christianity, 62, 64, 72
African cycle, 112-20; Ethiopian, 114-20
Against the Christians (Kata ton Christianon), 253-54
Against the Heresies (Adversus Haereses) (Irenaeus), 58-61
Agrippinus, Bishop, 113
Aizanas (Ezana), King, 116-17
Alexander of Abonoteichos, 211-12
Alexander the Great, 123
Alexandria, 39-40, 72, 122, 125-31
All Saints, Feast of, 249
Altaner-Stuiber patrology, 177
Alves, Rubem, 173
Ambrose, St., 179
Ancyra, Council of, 239, 240
Anselm, St., 5, 208
Anthony, St., 233
Antioch, 72, 91, 106-8
Antiochian Cycle, 89-90
Apocryphal, use of term, 153-54
Apocryphal literature, 153-56
Apollonius of Tyane, 211

Apologeticum (Tertullian), 65
Apologia (Aristides of Athens), 241, 249
Apostles, 186-91
Apostolic, use of term, 156
Apostolic Canons, 237
Apostolic Constitutions, 156, 162, 188, 251
Apostolic succession, 161
Apostolic tradition, codification of, 7
Apostolic Tradition (attributed to Hippolytus), 159-62, 188, 253
Aquinas, St. Thomas, 5, 73, 97, 179, 208
Arabs, 114
Arianism, 7-8
Aristides of Athens, 241-42, 256
Aristotle, 123
Arius, 7-8
Arles, Council of, 253
Armando, Sebastião, 176, 179
Asceticism, 109; Marcionite, 102; Montanist, 105; true vs. false, 237-38. *See also* Celibacy
Asclepius, 206-7, 209-12
Asia Minor, mission in, 72
Asian Cycle: first-century, 90-91; second-century, 96-106
Athenagoras, 249-50, 252, 257